# the fearless home buyer

## Elizabeth Razzi

D0373603

STC Paperbacks
Stewart, Tabori & Chang
New York

Editors: Marisa Bulzone and Dervla Kelly
Designer: Jay Anning/Thumb Print
Production Manager: Kim Tyner
Cover Design: Scott Idleman
Author Photo: Peter Ross

**Library of Congress Cataloging-in-Publication Data:**

Razzi, Elizabeth.
  The fearless home buyer / Elizabeth Razzi.
    p.  cm.
  Includes index.
  ISBN 1-58479-439-9
  1.  House buying—United States. 2.  Residential real estate—Purchasing—
United States. 3.  Mortgage loans—United States. I. Title.
  HD259.R39 2006
  643'.12'0973—dc22
                                            2005020549

Copyright © 2006 by Elizabeth Razzi

Published in 2006 by Stewart, Tabori & Chang
An imprint of Harry N. Abrams, Inc.

All rights reserved. No portion of this book may be reproduced, stored in a
retrieval system, or transmitted in any form or by any means, mechanical, electronic, photocopying, recording, or otherwise, without written permission from
the publisher.

The text of this book was composed in Electra

Printed and bound in the United States of America

10 9 8 7 6 5 4 3 2 1

# HNA ■■■■■
harry n. abrams, inc.
a subsidiary of La Martinière Groupe

115 West 18th Street
New York, NY 10011
*www.hnabooks.com*

*Dedicated to the memory of my parents,*
*Nancy and Ed Long*

# Acknowledgments

A funny thing happens after you spend years working as a reporter. You pick up an amazingly broad array of knowledge tidbits. Much of it you keep to yourself lest you turn into the neighborhood Cliff Claven, the know-it-all barstool buddy on the TV show *Cheers*. But some of those tidbits really deserve to be pulled together and turned into coherent advice. And that is my goal with this book, to pull together the bits I've picked up over the years from some very smart people—real estate agents and brokers, home builders, architects, engineers, economists, government officials, lobbyists, academics, consumer counselors, and, not least, from readers who have shared their questions and experiences. All together, the insights they have passed along add up to a good bit of wisdom that can help home buyers manage their complicated deal with a sure hand.

This is not intended to be an exhaustive education in the ways of real estate. Instead, the *Fearless* approach is intended to give readers the tools they really need—and not to bog them down in other people's horror stories or the intricate details of real estate laws and regulations. You're paying other people—the agents, brokers, lawyers, appraisers, and so-on—to have that expertise and to use it on your behalf. My goal is to make you a savvy consumer of their services and to know when someone has a hidden incentive to sell you on one decision or another. Most important, fearless home buyers will learn how to be their own best counsel; to know their own budgets, their goals, and their limits. This knowledge leads to control, and a buyer who remains in control of the deal faces very few sleepless nights.

I would like to thank a couple of pros who reviewed the advice in these pages. In particular, electrical contractor (and baseball coach extraordinaire) Michael Goldsmith offered his expertise on examining a home for warning signs of electrical trouble. And Guy Razzi, my husband and a structural engineer, provided the advice on how a layperson can eyeball a home for structural concerns that need further examination. Scott Mendel, my agent, and Marisa Bulzone, my editor, provided invaluable help in bringing it all together with a clear focus.

An extra share of credit, however, goes to my husband. Because of his real love for both architecture and construction, Guy has taught me how to look at buildings in a different way than I ever would have on my own. Buildings—and our homes, in particular— shelter us, protect us, and provide a vehicle for us to display our own style and personality. I hope this book helps you find the right home that will provide shelter, comfort, and style to you and your family. I welcome you to share your own insights and questions— and to find updates of information presented on these pages—at *www.fearlesshome.com*.

—ELIZABETH RAZZI

# Contents

**PART THREE**

# Closing The Deal

# Why Buy?

"There was no door and there were no windows. There was no floor except the ground and no roof except the canvas. But that house had good stout walls, and it would stay where it was. It was not like the wagon, that every morning went on to some other place."

Laura Ingalls Wilder, *Little House on the Prairie*

A SENSE OF PERMANENCE—one that lasts for at least several years—may be the best reason for buying a home instead of renting. *The home is yours.* You can paint the walls any color you wish, rip out shabby carpet, plant fruit trees, and eventually collect the harvest. When the home increases in value, you gain the added wealth. No landlord can slip a note under the door telling you the rent will go up, or that he needs to come in and check the smoke alarms, or even that he's sold out to a new owner who expects you to move when your lease is up. You're in control.

Owning a home is also one of the most fundamental building blocks in the process of accumulating wealth. There's more to wealth accumulation than the rising price of housing, which has been truly stunning in many parts of the country during recent years. There are also little savings that add up over the years—and that make your home unlike any other investment available through Wall Street brokers, financial advisers, or local banks.

First there is *leverage*. Just as a lever allows a person with a little bit of muscle to move a huge boulder, financial leverage allows an investor to take a little bit of money and turn it into an outsize amount. In this case, the lever is your mortgage. The smaller your down payment, the greater the leverage effect.

Say you have $30,000 available for a down payment and you want to buy a $300,000 home. With a mortgage that covers 90 percent of the purchase price, you can buy that home with just your 10 percent ($30,000) down payment. As the home's value appreciates over time, you keep all of the gain, even though you invested only 10 percent of the price. Say the value grows by 5 percent per year for five years (a modest estimate based on long-term trends in home prices). At the end of five years, that home would be worth $382,885, nearly 28 percent more than your purchase price. But your gain is actually much larger, thanks to leverage. Even though you put only $30,000 into the deal, you now have an asset worth $82,885 more than it was when you bought it. That's a 176 percent gain. Even when you factor in the interest that you paid over the years (which was tax deductible), you come out way ahead.

Another benefit, of course, is ownership itself. If you were to buy a home today, you could own it debt-free in fifteen, twenty, or thirty years, depending on the loan you use. Most people don't own a single home that long, but some folks do. Even if you end up buying two, three, or five homes during your life, you still could plan it so you enter retirement with a fully paid-for roof over your head. That will never happen if you rent.

Home equity is the single largest source of wealth for most Americans, according to the Federal Reserve Board. For many of us, the equity in our homes is greater than the amount of money we have invested in stocks, bonds, or bank accounts. In addition to the boost in home values that happens over time, the simple act of paying your mortgage month after month leaves most long-time owners with a significant nest egg. This is an asset they can borrow against (using a home-equity loan) or that they could tap by selling the home and moving somewhere less expensive. Eventually, that nest egg can be bequeathed to children.

## The Best Tax Breaks You'll Ever Find

The government wants you to own a home. According to the U.S. Census Bureau, just over 69 percent of American households own their home—a record share. One reason is that homeowners are more invested in their communities than are renters. Owners tend to push for better schools and services, and they squawk loudly against anyone who diminishes their neighborhood's quality of life by breaking the speed limit, littering, or vandalizing property. Owners are more likely to vote, and they are more likely to keep up their properties than are short-term renters. Renters faced with a declining neighborhood can pick up and move more easily than owners. Owners are more willing to stay and protect their investment.

To boost homeownership, the government showers owners with impressive tax breaks. In fact, until they become home owners and can claim the mortgage-interest deduction, itemizing deductions is usually not worthwhile for most people. Renters usually claim the standard deduction and may file only the short version of the IRS 1040 income tax form.

These are the tax deductions available to you as a homeowner:

- Interest on up to $1 million in mortgage debt used to buy, build, or renovate your home

- Any prepaid interest (called points) charged when you took out the mortgage

- Local property taxes

- Interest on a home-equity loan or line of credit of up to $100,000

When you sell the home, there are more tax breaks. A married couple can keep as much as $500,000 in profit (capital gain) from the sale of their main residence and pay no tax at all as long as they lived in the house for two of the five years before they sold it. (It doesn't have to be two consecutive years or the two years just before the sale.) Singles can keep up to $250,000. You can take advantage of this tax break repeatedly over the years, as long as you live in a house for two out of the five years before you sell it. (If a job relocation or change in health forces you to sell before you've lived in a home two years, you may be eligible to exclude part of your capital gain from tax.) If you plan things right, you could even get a tax-free gain from your vacation home—as long as you move in and make it your main home for at least two years before selling.

You might recall an old rule that said you needed to "roll over" your equity into another home. Those old tax laws were in effect so long they are probably still lingering in the back of the mind. But the concept of rolling over your home equity became history with the passage the Taxpayer Relief Act of 1997. Before 1997, if you wanted to avoid paying capital gains tax on your profit from the sale of your old house, tax laws required you to buy a house *at least* as expensive as the one you sold. Only once in a lifetime, after age fifty-five, were you allowed to downsize to a cheaper home and keep some of the sale profit (up to $125,000) tax-free. Under the current law, however, you are free to sell your big, expensive home in the suburbs of the big, expensive city, and replace it with a cheaper home in a small town and pocket the difference in price without worrying about the IRS. If you should be lucky enough to find an even cheaper place two years later, the IRS still won't tax your profits. Chapter One provides more details on those tax breaks and how you can take advantage of them as soon as you buy your home.

## Real Estate Is a Long-Term Investment

In some ways, buying a home is a stickier commitment than getting married—it can be harder to get out of the deal, at least. In most cases, you can't move to a new home until you find someone who wants to live in your old one. Certainly divorce can be a rough experience, but imagine what a nightmare it would be if you had to stick around until you found someone who was willing to move in with your ex? There would be far fewer divorces if they worked like real estate deals.

In recent years, there have been strong "seller's markets" in many parts of the country. In these areas, there have not been enough homes on the market to satisfy everyone who wanted one, and so sellers could hold out for high prices and, in many instances, breathtakingly unreasonable terms. There actually is a way to quantify whether a market favors buyers, sellers, or it is nicely balanced between the two extremes. Real estate brokers say that a balanced market has about six months' worth of inventory. That is, if you set aside all the houses on the market that day, it would take six months for the whole bunch to sell out. A balanced market benefits buyers *and* sellers. Buyers have choices, and there may be some room for negotiating prices. Sellers have confidence that they will be able to sell their homes in a reasonable length of time and at a decent price. When inventory falls below six months, it's a seller's market, and houses sell quickly and at high prices. Conversely, when inventory rises above six months, buyers get the upper hand. They have more choices, as homes sit on the market longer. Homes often sell for less than the asking price. You can gauge your own market by asking a real estate agent how much inventory is on the market, and compare it to that six-month standard. If your agent says he or she doesn't know (hardly a confidence-building sign) ask that agent to go and find out the inventory statistics from the broker's office or the local multiple listing service.

In balanced markets or in those favoring buyers, some sellers might have trouble getting rid of their homes. Why should you, a buyer, care about this? Because eventually, you will become a seller. Even if you're fighting to get a home in a seller's market today, prepare for the idea that down the road, when you want to sell, the tables could be turned. Buying an attractive home in a great neighborhood *today*—which will be easier to unload *then*—is a strategy that will serve you well. Cookie-cutter houses in Stepford neighborhoods don't fare well in buyer's markets. It's hard to hold out for a high price if there are three other homes just like yours on the market at the same time. It's even harder to hold out for a high price if developers are still building very similar homes not far away. Buyers often are willing to pay a little bit more for something that's brand new and to have the opportunity to choose their own flooring and cabinet finishes. Always keep in mind that real estate is a long-term investment. Homes are expensive to buy and sell, and markets can change over time. Buy a good home in a great neighborhood, without overpaying for the privilege, and you will lower your risk.

## Five Signs You Should Rent a Little While Longer

The worst reason to buy a home is because everyone else is doing it. Sometimes it is wiser to rent. Don't sweat it. Contrary to popular opinion, you *can* be a fully functioning, fiscally prudent adult without signing your name to a sales contract and mortgage! In fact, sometimes renting is truly the prudent thing to do.

Here are five good signs that you should rent a little while longer:

1. You can't imagine what type of work you'll be doing five years from now. You're not even sure *where* in the country opportunities might take you—and graduate school in another city may well be your first stop. Do yourself a favor and continue renting until life is more settled.

2. A new, romantic relationship looks like it might be getting serious. Give it a little while before you settle down in a home. This is emphatically *not* to say that a single person should not buy a home. There's no reason why singles shouldn't take advantage of all the opportunities that go along with ownership.

But if you're in a relationship that seems to be changing and developing, keep your options open by renting a while longer. If you should decide to commit to each other, the home you shop for together might be very different from the one either of you would buy on your own.

3. You don't feel safe in the kinds of neighborhoods where you can afford to buy right now. Often people are able to afford better neighborhoods while renting than they can when buying for the first time. If the neighborhoods open to you are unacceptable right now, you need to draw up Plan B. Hunker down with your budget and see if you can come up with a plan for saving (or for boosting your income) so you can afford to buy in a more desirable neighborhood in a year or two.

4. Buying now would wipe out your savings. You need to have some savings left over after closing day. Once you own, there's no landlord to call when things break. You might have to buy a new furnace in the middle of winter, or face a special assessment from the condo board or homeowners' association. You might even lose your job for a while. Everyone, whether owner or renter, needs to have an emergency fund, a stash of money sufficient to support you for three to six months if life plays one of its nastier little tricks.

5. You fear that if you don't buy something *now*, prices will keep rising and you'll never be able to buy. That's a pretty compelling argument in communities where prices have been increasing by 10 to 20 percent a year. But keep in mind that renters have lived in fear of that same scenario forever, even when prices rose

slowly. Don't get saddled with a bad home at an inflated price just because you were afraid of missing the boat. You won't miss it. When you have the money, something will be available, whether it's a condo apartment, a townhouse, or a modest single-family house with yard. Work on your finances, set a target for what you'd like to own, and buy only when you feel you're ready.

## Making the Move-up Decision: Is More Better?

In some ways, it's more difficult for someone who already owns a home to move up to something better than it is for a renter to buy a home for the first time. Sometimes, of course, the decision to move up is obvious—and unavoidable. A new job forces relocation. A growing family just won't fit in the old home. The kids are about to enter school, and you find the ones nearby unacceptable. You're getting older and can't stand the thought of cleaning rain gutters every spring and fall. These are compelling reasons to get a move on soon.

But often the decision is more ambiguous. You'd *like* a better home, but nothing compels you to look for one now. Procrastination rules. There are established neighborhood friendships and commuting and shopping routines that would have to change. What if the new home or neighborhood turns out not to be as nice as the old one? Not least, it's downright painful to trade in an old mortgage at a rock-bottom interest rate for a new mortgage at a higher rate.

Timing a move up can be tricky as well. Most people need to sell their old home to get the cash for a down payment on a new, more expensive home. First-timers, by contrast, only have to give notice to their landlords at the end of their lease (or maybe forfeit a bit of rent by breaking the lease early). You'll find more on the special needs of move-up buyers in Chapter Five.

But the gains of moving up to a better home can be compelling enough to overcome the inertia. Everyone in the family gets more room to spread out. The house can be tidier if there's enough storage space. The kids might attend better schools. In a larger home, you can enjoy things you never could accommodate before, perhaps a pool table, big-screen television, or more overnight visitors. Plus—it's okay to admit that it matters—a better home in a better neighborhood brings greater prestige.

## The Path Ahead of You

There are many tasks that need to be accomplished before moving day. Generally, they can be broken into the following steps, which you should try to perform pretty much in the same order as they are presented: Prepare a budget and assemble your financial information; line up your financing (which includes shopping for a lender and a specific type of mortgage loan); find the best real estate agent to help you; look for the best neighborhoods and homes; and, finally, manage the negotiations and paperwork that will bring this deal to a happy ending. This book carries you through these tasks in the sequence that you most likely will face them, but you may find it useful to flip back to material in the back-of-the-book appendices for definitions and extra resources, such as a list of helpful Web sites and a review of common closing costs that you can expect to pay before all is said and done.

As you travel through the home-buying process, you'll find that you need to do business with a surprisingly large cast of characters—real estate agents, mortgage lenders, appraisers, home inspectors, lawyers and even pest exterminators. That's one of the reasons the home-buying process is so complicated and so expensive. Each of these service providers stands to earn a commission or a fee from your home purchase, and combined, they exert a sometimes-subtle pressure on buyers to forge ahead with the deal, even when it begins to look less like an opportunity and more like a long-term burden. One of the goals of this book is to alert you to those subtle pressures and to equip you with the confidence that comes from truly understanding the process. Below, you'll find a cast of characters who commonly appear in the typical home-buying drama. Please turn to the Glossary at the back of the book for more definitions and translation of common acronyms.

## Cast of Characters

**Real estate agent:** Usually, the person you work most closely with is your real estate agent. An agent is someone who acts on behalf of someone else. A licensed real estate agent is working on behalf of a *broker*, who, in turn, is an agent of the buyer or seller who hired that broker. As a buyer, you cannot assume that a real estate agent is representing your interests unless you have signed an agreement saying that he or she will serve as your buyer's agent in this deal. Without such an explicit agreement, you always should assume the agent is working on behalf of the seller.

**Real estate broker:** Typically, a real estate agent works under the supervision of a licensed broker, and it is the broker with whom buyers and sellers have contracts for representation in the sale or purchase of real estate.

## Cast of Characters

**Buyer's broker or buyer's agent:** A real estate salesperson who has signed a written agreement to represent the buyer. Some of them make a living out of working only with buyers and call themselves *exclusive* buyer's brokers/agents. But many agents today will work with buyers or sellers, depending on the deal. An agent should not try to represent both parties in the same transaction, although some will try to perform as neutral go-betweens in such situations, if state law allows it and both buyer and seller are informed of the arrangement.

**Appraiser:** Someone licensed by the state to estimate the market value of homes based on recent, completed sales of comparable properties and taking into account a home's special assets and flaws. Before making a loan, lenders will insist on having an appraisal performed by one of their approved appraisers.

**Mortgage banker:** A business that originates, sells and services mortgage loans.

**Mortgage broker:** A person who deals with a number of different loan originators and can shop a borrower's loan application around for the best combination of interest rate and terms. The broker earns a fee for each mortgage he or she handles. Although good mortgage brokers will shop hard on behalf of borrowers, there is nothing to require a mortgage broker to represent the interests of the borrower. Some steer borrowers into loans that earn the most profit for the broker. Reputation is critical in choosing a mortgage broker.

**Loan officer:** The person who takes your application and ushers it through the loan-approval process.

**Escrow officer/closing officer:** In California, when a buyer and seller agree on terms of a sale, they enter into escrow, a time when all the demands of the buyer, seller, lender, and government need to be satisfied so the deal can become final. They hire a neutral third party, either a state-licensed escrow company or a title insurance company, or a bank, trust company, or attorney, to act as their escrow officer, who manages the flow of money and inspections and paperwork necessary to complete the deal. In other states, many of these same functions are performed by a title company or attorney, who acts as the closing officer.

**Title company:** A title company will perform a title search, an examination of the land-ownership records on file with the local government to verify that the seller is the rightful owner of the property, and that there are no outstanding claims against it, such as tax liens or undisclosed mortgages. The title company then will offer an insurance policy that will pay legal fees (or damages) if someone comes forward with a claim against the title after closing. Lenders require that buyers buy a title-insurance policy that would pay them if a dispute comes up; borrowers can (and should) pay extra to extend that coverage to themselves as well.

In this and all the other chapters in this book, you will find that the key points outlined in the chapter are summarized as "Razzi's Rules to Live By." They're little reminders of the strategies and principles that will help you maintain sure footing as you maneuver through the twists and turns of the typical homebuying process. You will find a complete list of Razzi's Rules in Appendix One.

# Razzi's Rules to Live By

### 🏠 Six months' inventory is key.

That's the dividing line that separates a balanced market from those favoring buyers or sellers. If it would take about six months to sell every home that's currently for sale, that's a balanced market. If it would take less time, the conditions favor sellers, creating a seller's market. If it would take more time, conditions favor buyers, which means it's a buyer's market. Ask your agent what kind of market you're in.

### 🏠 Take advantage of leverage.

A mortgage allows you to take a down payment of 20 percent or less and parlay that to earn much bigger profits based on the full value of the home. Such leverage allows a small investment to grow into large net worth.

### 🏠 The government wants you to own.

The government offers wonderful tax breaks to encourage ownership—so take Uncle Sam up on them!

# getting ready to make your move

# CHAPTER ONE

# Getting Ready to Make Your Move

"Durn that road . . . A-laying there, right up to my door, where every bad luck that comes and goes is bound to find it. I told Addie it want any luck living on a road when it come by here, and she said, for the world like a woman, 'Get up and move, then.'"

WILLIAM FAULKNER, *As I Lay Dying*

B UYING A HOUSE IS A BOLD ACT OF OPTIMISM. You're putting a high-dollar bet on the future! However, while home buying ought to be a fun, exciting experience, it's easy to succumb to the fears that travel hand in hand with the joys. Practically everyone worries, to some extent, that they might be buying at the top of the market and that they will get stuck in an overpriced house if values decline. At the same time, there's the worry that if you don't jump *today*, you'll never be able to afford a home. The string of fears goes on and on. You worry that you might settle for a house that's not nice enough or that needs unending repairs. You worry that you might hate your new neighbors; lose your job; or get taken advantage of by one of the brokers, lenders, inspectors or other pros eager to get you to make a decision and pay whatever they say—and to do it quickly, so they can move on to another client. Everybody faces these same concerns.

Be ready for the fears—and be ready to chase them off. The first step to vanquishing worry is to get a really good grip on how much money you have and how much of that money you're comfortable devoting to the roof over your head. No lender or real estate agent can figure this out for you; only you can know exactly how much you truly are willing to spend. Your total will include not only the payment for principal and interest, but also taxes, insurance, homeowners' association dues, utility bills, repairs, and furnishings. If you're a long-time homeowner, keep in mind that moving to a grander place will boost those expenses significantly.

## Figuring Your Budget

The best place to start figuring out your comfort level is to go over your checkbook registers (or online bank statements) for the past year. You need to be unflinching in your review of where your money has gone for the past twelve months. Don't leave your spouse or partner out of the discussion, even if he or she would be delighted to leave you with the dirty details. Both of you should know where the money is going so you can choose where to make sacrifices and thus afford the home you really want. This way, you'll help avoid many worried, sleepless nights long into the future.

Don't try to hide any frivolous spending, and don't punish each other for financial sins of the past. Everyone spends some money on tickets to bad movies and junky exercise gear and other odd *stuff* that looks wildly irrational long after the bills are paid. No matter how odd, you need to put it all on paper. A budget without room for at least some of that stuff—whether it's compact discs, expensive coffee, or computer gear—is like a crash diet of lentils and broth; you're not going to stick with it for long. Do your best to faithfully estimate your average monthly expenditures—all of them.

Don't explain away the big-buck exceptions to your budget, either. The rebuilt car engine won't need another overhaul anytime soon, and it's unlikely that another dying water heater will pick your pocket next year, but you can count on something equally urgent taking its place. Add up a year's worth of big bills. Divide the total by twelve to find the average cost per month, and let that serve as your estimate for future emergency expenses. You'll get an even better number for emergency spending if you go back several years and average how much you spent on other one-time expenses.

The following list contains some items you should be sure to include in your review. You will probably think of more, depending on your situation.

## Budget Items

### Basics

Current mortgage/rent _____

Utilities (electricity, water, etc.) _____

Phone (including cell phone) _____

Groceries _____

Gas/commuting _____

Clothing _____

Child support/alimony _____

Work lunches _____

Pet care (vet, grooming, food) _____

Weekly pocket money _____

## Monthly Bills

Insurance (home, life, car, health) _____

Medical/dental (copayments, prescriptions, orthodontist) _____

Loan payment (car, student, etc.) _____

Child care _____

Entertainment, entertaining, eating out _____

Internet access, cable, satellite TV _____

Home services (cleaning, lawn/garden, pool, etc.) _____

Investment (retirement, educations, etc.) _____

Dry cleaning _____

Sundries _____

## Yearly/Occasional Expenses

Property taxes, home repair/maintenance,

    homeowners' association fees _____

Car registration, repair/maintenance _____

Tuition (school/college, summer camps, sports, etc.) _____

Vacation _____

Computer (hardware, software) _____

Charitable contributions, gifts _____

Dues, subscriptions _____

## Your Balance Sheet: Assets and Debts

Also do a thorough listing—a "balance sheet" of your assets and debts. You will need to have much of this information available when you make your loan application, anyway, so you might as well dig out these records now. Draw a line down the middle of legal pad. The left side becomes your asset column, the right column lists your debts. The asset column should include savings and checking accounts, certificates of deposit, investments (stocks, bonds, mutual funds), 401(k) and other retirement accounts, and your best estimate of the equity in your current home. While you probably have other assets that could be included in a comprehensive net-worth report, it's not necessary to go into that level of detail. Are you really planning to sell the old saxophone or the stamp collection you inherited from granddad to raise money for your down payment? If so, go ahead and list the probable cash value, otherwise, just keep your list simple and note anything that you could cash in or borrow against to come up with money for a down payment. (Chapter Two discusses the assets you can tap for your down payment funds.)

The debt column should include all debts that will take longer than a year to pay off (according to the lender's established payment schedule). Credit card balances, a home equity loan, or money owed to a relative who eventually expects repayment would go in the debt column. (If you have an outstanding home equity loan, keep in mind that these are usually paid off with the proceeds of a home sale, shrinking the pot available for the down payment on a new home.)

Now, equipped with a true picture of where your money is going each month and of how much money you actually have, you can come up with a realistic estimate of just how much you are willing to devote toward the purchase of a home. Unless you have an unusual influx of money, such as an inheritance, the cash for a more expensive home is going to come out of this budget, either from reduced spending, reduced savings, or liquidated investments—or a combination of all three. The choices are all yours.

## Your Budget Versus the Lender's Budget

Lenders have fairly strict guidelines regarding the levels of household income and debt that are appropriate for a loan of a particular size. Real estate industry slang for your total monthly house payment is PITI, which stands for principal, interest, taxes, and insurance. If your down payment is less than 20 percent, you will also be required to pay private mortgage insurance, the cost of which is added to the monthly payment. (Lenders force low-down payment borrowers to pay for private mortgage insurance, to cover *their* risk if the borrower doesn't pay the mortgage.)

Most lenders want to see that your monthly payment, including the PITI, private mortgage insurance, and any condo/co-op or homeowners association fee you're required to pay does not exceed 28 percent of your gross (before-tax) income. They also want to see that those housing expenses *plus* your monthly debts (including the required payments on child support, alimony, car loans, student loans, and credit cards) don't exceed 36 percent of your gross monthly income. Some "sub-prime" lenders—those who specialize in lending money to borrowers with credit problems—will approve mortgages if your debt exceeds those levels. However, you'll pay dearly in the form of a high interest rate and more points—a form of interest that you pay up front—at the mortgage closing. Unless you have special circumstances (say, you have a lot of stock or bond assets that you *could* draw upon, but would rather not at this time), you should think long and hard about exposing yourself to more risk than a lender thinks is prudent. There's nothing wrong with renting while you shape up your finances.

Fact is, the loan officer is in the business of selling loans, and that guy would just love to load you up with all the credit you can carry. It's good business for him to sell you the *largest* mortgage for which you could qualify. It's no extra work for him, and he stands to make more money from the deal. If you're putting down more than a 20 percent down payment, often the loan officer will offer to set you up with a home equity line of credit, along with your mortgage. This is the loan industry's version of "Do you want fries with that?"

The trouble is that the loan officer doesn't share your priorities in life. For instance, consider a few of the spending categories that you might think are set in stone but that the loan officer doesn't even consider when qualifying you for a mortgage. Day care and tuition costs are two very good examples. Those payments don't count among your debts, because the lending world figures you might switch to a less-expensive alternative if money got so tight you were in danger of not paying the mortgage—and losing your home. Along with taxes, food, clothing, and utilities, commitments like these are all expected to be paid out of the two-thirds of your gross income that remains after you've made your monthly mortgage payment.

The only way to truly arrive at what is affordable for *you* is to work with your own budget. You might be willing to do without premium cable but unwilling to sacrifice the kids' summer camp. Or you might decide this is the summer for the kids to discover

Camp Iwannastayhome because that will help the whole family move to a better neighborhood.

Here's an experiment for you to try. Let's say your budget review shows you could comfortably spend $400 a month more than you spend now on rent or mortgage. Starting today, before you even start shopping for your own personal version of Graceland, force yourself to live on the new budget that will come along with owning such a home.

In fact, you might as well adopt this new, leaner budget permanently. After all, if you really can afford that extra $400 a month, the money has to be there month in and month out. If you discover that you miss the dinners out or the concert tickets too much to give them up for a few years, until your growing income restores more ease to your budget, then it's better to learn that now, before you commit to that big mortgage. If you trim your budget and discover you really can put away an additional $400 per month in savings, the exercise will help build up the cash available for your down payment—and relieve any middle-of-the-night doubts about whether you really *can* afford to spend so much.

## Tax Breaks Help Right Away

The good news is that the tax breaks associated with your new home could help you make your budget numbers work. For most Americans, the best and biggest source of tax breaks is the roof over their heads. There are some limitations (which I will soon explain) affecting those with high incomes, but most people can deduct all their mortgage interest from the income that's subject to federal and state taxes. You also can deduct local property taxes. And, as long as they lived in the home at least two of the five years before selling it, a married couple

33

can keep up to $500,000 in capital gains tax-free. Singles can keep $250,000 free from tax. The government *wants* Americans to be homeowners; politicians brag about the record rate of homeownership, and so they give us tax breaks to help the process along.

The mortgage-interest tax deduction can sometimes make the monthly cost of owning a home cheaper than the monthly cost of renting. It's especially beneficial just when you need it most—during the early years of the mortgage, when you're adjusting to the new expense. During the first year of the mortgage, 88 percent of your principal and interest payment goes toward interest—the part that is deductible on your federal and state returns. (Remember that you pay taxes and insurance on top of principal and interest, which will make your monthly payment higher.) Actually, interest accounts for at least 75 percent of your principal and interest payment through the first ten years of a 30-year, fixed-rate mortgage.

You don't have to wait until you've filed your tax return to start benefiting from the tax deduction. Go to your employer's personnel department and ask to file a new IRS Form W-4 to reduce the tax withheld from your paycheck. On the deductions and adjustments worksheet, you have an opportunity to estimate your adjustments to income. This is where you would plug in your estimate of deductible mortgage interest and property tax to bring your withholding more closely in line with what you will actually owe the IRS. That boost in your paycheck will help you handle the higher monthly payment.

There are some limitations on the home-mortgage interest deduction for higher-income households. If your adjusted gross income (AGI) is more than $139,500 ($69,750 if you are married and filing separately), some of your itemized deductions will be limited, including mortgage interest and taxes. If your adjusted gross income is high enough to trigger the limit, the IRS will limit all of your itemized deductions to the *smaller* of two numbers: either 3 percent of the amount by which your AGI exceeds the $139,500/$69,750 threshold, or 80 percent of the itemized deductions that count toward the limit. Also, if your income or deductions are great enough to trigger the alternative minimum tax, known as the AMT, that will limit the deductibility of your property taxes. Mortgage interest remains deductible under the AMT, except for some home-equity loans *not* used to buy, build or improve your home, but many other tax breaks disappear in the strange world of the AMT. The government came up with the AMT as an attempt to make sure that people with high incomes could not take advantage of so many loopholes and tax deductions that they end up paying little or no income tax. Under the AMT, the government disallows many of the tax deductions that are allowed under the ordinary income-tax system. Of particular concern to homeowners is that you stand to lose the deduction for local property taxes.

Although the AMT was created to rein-in high-income people adept at avoiding taxes, its thresholds were never indexed for inflation. Unfortunately, as each year passes, more taxpayers earning average incomes are finding that they've entered the world of the AMT and owe extra tax. You can find yourself subject to the AMT if you have a lot of personal exemptions, which you claim for yourself, your spouse and each of your children.

Another increasingly common trigger is claiming a big deduction for state and local taxes. In fact, the housing boom of recent years is one big culprit driving people into the AMT system. Booming home prices have driven up property taxes, sometimes high enough to trigger the AMT, which, in turn, takes away the deduction! For more information on the very complicated AMT, search for "Tax Topic 556" at *www.irs.gov*.

In the year you buy the home, you will qualify for a special tax break to account for the prepaid interest (or points) that you paid when you took out the loan. On top of ongoing interest, most mortgages also charge points, the name for interest that's payable up front when you close the deal. Each point equals 1 percent of the mortgage amount. For example, let's say you're taking out a 30-year fixed-rate mortgage for $200,000. It might carry an interest rate of 7 percent with two points. In this example, you would owe $4,000 in prepaid interest at closing (in other words, 2 percent of the mortgage amount). If you don't want to pay the points, you can choose to pay a higher interest rate instead. The trade-offs involved in that decision are discussed in Chapter Four. Points may also be called loan origination fees or discount points, but it's all the same animal—prepaid interest.

If there are a lot of homes on the market (and the real estate market thus happens to favor buyers), you may have good luck convincing a seller to pay some or all of those points. The good news is that regardless of whether the points are paid by you or by the seller, the IRS says it's always *the buyer* who gets to deduct points on his or her tax return. When you buy your primary residence, the IRS allows you to take the full deduction during the year you bought the home. On the other hand, if you're buying a vacation home, the IRS requires that you spread out the deduction over the life of the loan. In this example, you'd have to spread that $4,000 deduction out over thirty years, claiming only $133 each year. Similarly, points paid on a refinance must be spread out over the life of the loan.

There's one thing you should do to ensure you qualify for the deduction. Make sure the amount of money you bring to the table for various closing costs (including the down payment, points, and insurance payments) is equal to or greater than the dollar value of the points you want to deduct. The IRS says if you borrow the points, you cannot deduct them, so you need proof that you brought at least that much cash to the table.

## Expenses You Might Not Expect

First-time buyers, in particular, often are surprised at the seemingly unending string of needs that comes with owning a home. I remember dashing out to the home center at least weekly for quite a while after my husband and I moved into our first home, a brand-new townhouse in Virginia. Trash day! Of course we didn't own trash cans. Snow fall! We bought our first snow shovel. Lawn mower, rakes, window coverings, caulk guns, furnace filters—we had none of them when we moved out of our apartment. These surprise expenditures didn't even begin to account for all the things we *wanted* to buy—the furniture, artwork, flowers, shrubs, barbeque gear, and patio chairs that we could accumulate gradually. The National Association of Home Builders says that during the first twelve months after buying a newly built home, owners spend an average of $8,905 to furnish, decorate, and improve it. Buyers of existing homes spend $3,766 more during that first year than other homeowners who didn't move.

Even move-up buyers—who already own caulk guns and snow shovels—can be surprised at the degree to which their old belongings don't fit in their big new home. The snow shovel might have to be replaced by a snow-blower. Window coverings alone can cost several thousand of dollars for a home filled with windows. Any hired help you might need to manage a larger landscape, swimming-pool maintenance, or housecleaning should be factored into your new budget.

## What Will This Buy Me?

There is an old rule of thumb that says to find the amount you can afford to spend on a home, you simply multiply your gross yearly income by 2.5. Like most rules of thumb, this one's too crude to be of much use. It's also not a good idea to let an overeager real estate agent tell you what you can afford at this early stage of planning. Instead, you should take some time at your computer to fool around with what-if scenarios using online mortgage calculators. Knowing the after-tax monthly payment your budget can handle, you can use these calculators to arrive at a reasonable price range for your new home—and you won't frustrate yourself by making a classic mistake: shopping neighborhoods that you can't begin to afford. That's a quick route to dissatisfaction.

There are loads of financial calculators available free on the Internet. One of the best is offered by HSH Associates, a company that sells mortgage information rather than actual loans. Go to their Web site at *www.hsh.com*, where you can download a free suite of mortgage calculators. One of them will help you estimate what monthly payment you would qualify for, given your down payment, income, and debts. The HSH Web site is also a good place to keep tabs on current interest rates, which very directly influence how much you'll be able to afford.

## Should You Stretch to Get into a Home?

This, of course, is the question that keeps buyers awake at night—even if they've successfully bought homes several times before. Unfortunately, the answer is not at all clear cut.

There are several good arguments *for* stretching your budget as far as possible. In fact, most people have to stretch a bit to get what they want. One argument in favor of stretching is that, if you do it right, you may *lower* your risk of losing money. Buying a home—or any asset—does carry some risk. There is absolutely no guarantee that its value won't decline. During the early 1990s, homeowners in California, Texas, Massachusetts, and a few other states on the East Coast experienced this very painful phenomenon. The economy turned sour; people lost jobs and had difficulty paying their mortgages. Ordinarily, the best option in those circumstances is to sell the house and move somewhere cheaper, where, ideally, there might be better job prospects. But these homeowners were stuck. Home values had dropped by 10 percent or more, and many found that they couldn't get enough from a sale to pay off their mortgage. Many owners in that awful situation simply walked away from the mortgage. They defaulted on the loans and lost their homes—and acquired terrible credit histories in the process. Such dire market conditions don't happen often, but they're not out of the question, either.

That's a real-life example of the worst that can happen. Fortunately, even when prices decline, the vast majority of homeowners can afford to ride out such dips, holding on to their homes until the market gets stronger and values increase once again. Even in that horrible real-estate market crash that took hold on the East and West coasts in the early 1990s, long-term homeowners came out ahead. According to DataQuick Information Systems, a San Diego company that tracks real estate markets, the median home price across California (including condos and detached houses) peaked at $180,000 back in May 1991. Prices then slid for years, bottoming out at a median of $148,500 in January 1996. That was traumatizing for the homeowner unlucky enough to have bought at that 1991 peak; they had to watch their home value decline by 17.5 percent. Prices didn't recover to that 1991 level until March 1999. But once prices recovered the lost ground, they just kept rising. Between March 1999 and early 2004, the median price shot up to $336,000—or about 87 percent. An owner who managed to hold on through that housing bust was eventually made whole. Those who held on longer saw tremendous price increases. That's how time overrides risk.

What does that rollercoaster ride have to do with the decision to stretch? You can actually *shrink* the risk of buying a home if you buy a place that's big enough to accommodate your household's changing needs over at least five years. The extra bedroom can become a home office, a nursery for new babies—or even a place to put up a paying roommate, should times get tough. Similarly, you might not be forced into the real estate market at a bad time if your home is on a lot that's large enough to handle construction of a new room or two. You can build the extra space you need instead of buying a whole new house. Following this logic, a one-bedroom condo apartment is a safer investment than a studio. A two-bedroom is safer than a one-bedroom. A home with three bedrooms is safer than a home with two. Within reason, stretching to afford a more versatile home can be a sound decision.

It also can be sensible to stretch if you have a realistic expectation that your income will grow over the next five to ten years. It's expensive to buy and sell homes. You'll save if your first home suits your needs for five years or more—giving you a chance to benefit from normal (that is, single-digit) appreciation in market prices.

At the same time, it's risky to stretch during a booming real estate market, such as the one that many parts of the country experienced during the late 1990s and early 2000s. In particular, the same housing markets that experienced excruciating downturns in the early nineties—most of California, Massachusetts, the New York metropolitan area, and Washington, D.C.—have experienced raging seller's markets, in which there simply were not enough houses available for sale as there were buyers. Buyers found they had to offer *more* than the asking price, and even then they often lost out to another, higher bidder. The winners of those bidding wars—who may have paid tens of thousands of dollars above the asking price for a house—are definitely in a precarious position if those booming markets finally settle down.

The stretch is safer if the home is in an outstanding neighborhood, if the schools are good, the home is within a reasonable commuting distance to key business districts, and the home is big enough to suit your needs for at least five years. It's not unreasonable for you to plan on staying longer than five years, and ten years is an even safer span of time. According to the National Association of Realtors, the average seller has been in his or her home six years.

## Razzi's Rules to Live By

### 🏠 Budget without shame.

You and your spouse or partner should dive into a detailed budgeting exercise *together*. If you make it a no-blame, no-shame look at where your money really goes, you can identify where the money really will come from for your new home purchase.

### 🏠 Lenders don't care where your kids go to school.

Loan officers don't count as debts some big expenses that you might consider to be set in stone. They figure you might find a cheaper alternative if you needed the money for a mortgage payment. Keep this in mind when figuring out how much *you* can afford, not what the lender says you can qualify to borrow.

### 🏠 Time beats risk.

You only have to worry about slow housing markets or soft prices if you actually have to *sell* while the market is tough. Most owners ride out tough markets without any problem. A home that can accommodate changing needs over a decade or so is a very safe bet.

### 🏠 Test-drive your new budget.

If you think you can devote an extra $100 or $200 or whatever amount to the cost of living in a new home, make believe you've bought the home already. Adopt your new budget now and put the extra cash into the bank each month. Prove to yourself that you really can afford the move. You'll sleep better for it.

### 🏠 Adjust your tax withholding right away.

Go ahead—it's legal! Reduce the amount of money withheld from your paycheck for payroll taxes when you buy your new home. You don't have to wait until you file your taxes to benefit from the tax breaks.

# CHAPTER TWO

# Putting Together a Down Payment

"And he especially liked the house he had built there, largely because it represented his faith in a future that would include himself for at least a few more years."

CHARLES FRAZIER, *Cold Mountain*

T HE BIGGEST SINGLE CHECK YOU'LL EVER WRITE during your lifetime will almost certainly be for the down payment on a home. Even though there are many loan programs that allow you to buy with 5 percent, 3 percent, or even 0 percent down, the down payment decision will set the tone for your household budget for years to come.

## Finding and Figuring Your Down Payment

Thanks to soaring home prices in recent years, even those low down payments of 3 or 5 percent represent a big chunk of cash. Consider

this: The median price of an existing single-family home is more than $200,000. (In many booming urban areas, the median price is above $300,000.) Across the country, in other words, half the homes cost more than $200,000, while the other half cost less. So that little 5 percent down payment on a $200,000 home is a not-insignificant $10,000. That little 5 percent down payment jumps to $15,000 on a $300,000 home. You also should budget another $2,000 to $3,000 for closing costs. There are many obvious benefits to making low down payments; however, doing so inevitably increases the other costs of borrowing.

## The Ups and Downs of Down Payments

If you're a first-time buyer, you probably will have to stretch mightily to make the jump into a home of your own. But you shouldn't clean out your savings just to make the down payment on your first home. In fact, to avoid a savings wipeout, you would be better off making a smaller down payment and bearing those higher loan costs, if you must. Remember, after moving day, you will still need a safety net of savings—enough to cover at least three to six months of living expenses, including that new mortgage! You need to have some cash in reserve to handle the maintenance surprises that come with home ownership. After all, if the furnace quits during your first winter as a homeowner, you'll have no choice but to open your wallet for repairs. Also, lenders like to see that you have something in reserve after closing day.

## Money from the Sale of Your Old Home

If you're a move-up buyer who's gaining a sizable pot of cash from the sale of your old home, keep in mind that you don't necessarily have to spend that money all in one place. You may very well want (or need) to put every dollar into the down payment on your next home. In some situations, however, it may be wise to set aside some of the cash from the sale of your old home.

Many retirees like to downsize from the big, old house where they raised their family and buy a smaller, less expensive home for retirement. Sometimes they pay cash for the new home. It can be wonderfully liberating to live mortgage-free in retirement; it can even be critical step toward keeping your retirement budget manageable.

But, be sure to think this plan through. If you have enough cash flow to handle the monthly mortgage payment in retirement, you might be better off taking a chunk of that home-sale profit and putting it in an investment that will continue to grow during your early retirement years.

It's also wise to remember that a thirty-year mortgage might be easy to qualify for during the last years of your career, while the same mortgage might become very difficult to get when you no longer are drawing a steady paycheck. If you can handle the mortgage expenses each month, it may pay to keep some of your old home equity accessible in another sort of investment.

If you will be remodeling within a few years of moving in, you should also think about keeping some of your financial powder dry for that battle. Stash some of the money from your home sale in a money market fund or bank account or in a certificate of deposit until you need it for remodeling. You can thereby avoid taking out a home equity loan or line of credit—or even refinancing the whole mortgage—to finance the remodeling.

45

## Down Payment Gifts

Lenders allow you to use gifts of money from your parents, siblings, or employer as down payment on your mortgage. Some may still want to see that you have enough cash of your own to contribute at least 3 percent of the home's price toward the down payment. You can expect the loan officer to check up on the details of the gift, and you should hold on to the deposit slip that verifies that those funds were placed in your bank account. In fact, the lender will want to see a letter from the gift-givers spelling out that they do not expect to be repaid.

## Tapping Your Retirement Accounts Early

You may have to tap into your retirement savings to come up with money for a down payment. Smart buyers do this hesitantly—after all, these retirement accounts are designed to allow you to build up the cash you will need when your working days are over. Taking out money in your twenties, thirties, forties, or fifties means you not only give up that cash—you also give up the compound interest that cash would have earned for two to five *decades*.

Still, you might find yourself with no other choice. It's an easier choice if you only need to borrow the money for only a short time—say to help cover the down payment while your old home remains unsold—and can pay yourself back in a few months after that deal closes. You can tap your retirement funds to help put together a down payment, but you need to do it carefully to avoid triggering tax penalties.

### Borrowing Against a 401(k)

If you have a 401(k) retirement savings plan at work, you may be able to borrow against it. You will have to pay interest, but you pay that interest to yourself, adding it back into your 401(k) account as you repay the loan. Most companies that offer 401(k) plans, especially the larger ones, allow participants to borrow for a home purchase.

Typically, the rules allow you to borrow up to half of your vested account balance, to a maximum of $50,000. You repay the money through payroll deductions over a term as long as thirty years. The loan will carry a variable interest rate, typically the prime rate plus one percentage point. You don't owe income tax on the borrowed money, nor do you have to pay the 10 percent early-distribution penalty the IRS charges on cash taken out of 401(k) accounts before retirement.

However, there's one very big catch. If your employment by that company ceases for any reason, you must repay the loan immediately, sometimes in as little as sixty days. Otherwise, the money will be considered an early distribution and will trigger an income-tax bill—not to mention that nasty 10 percent penalty.

**Borrowing Against an IRA**

If you have an IRA, you can withdraw money outright without facing a tax penalty if you use the cash to buy, build, or rebuild your first home. (It doesn't *really* have to be your very first home. The IRS calls it your "first" home if neither you nor your spouse has owned a home during the previous two years.)

There are two varieties of IRAs. The traditional IRA allows you a tax deduction on the money you contribute, and then taxes the cash as you withdraw in retirement. The Roth IRA does not allow a tax deduction on the money you contribute, but you withdraw cash tax-free during retirement. With either type of IRA, you usually face a 10 percent penalty if you withdraw money before the age of fifty-nine and a half—*unless* you use the money to buy, build, or rehabilitate your first home. You can tap up to $10,000 in IRA funds for this purpose. You will owe regular federal income tax on the money, but not the 10 percent early-distribution penalty. You do not have to pay the money back.

There are a few additional rules for a Roth IRA. You don't have to pay income tax on withdrawals, because the taxes are already paid. (Remember, you don't get a tax deduction when you put money into a Roth—you get the tax break during retirement.) But the Roth has one drawback not present with traditional IRAs: You aren't allowed to tap the Roth IRA funds until at least five years have passed since the day you first set up the account and deposited money into it. As with the traditional IRA, you're limited to a $10,000 withdrawal for use on a first home.

## Government Assistance

You may be able to get some down payment assistance from the federal government, your local government, or local housing agencies. Usually this help is restricted to low- and moderate-income buyers, but not always. Local governments sometimes offer incentives to all buyers (or all first-time buyers) designed to attract homebuyers to run-down neighborhoods in hopes of revitalizing them, and some communities specifically target assistance toward teachers, nurses, firefighters or police officers who may be forced out of town by rising prices.

Grants of up to $10,000 are available to low-income first-time buyers through the U.S. Department of Housing and Urban Development. The American Dream Down Payment Initiative provides grants that can be used for down payments or closing costs, as well as for rehabbing a house, condo, or manufactured home. The grants are restricted to buyers who earn no more than 80 percent of the area's median income and who have not owned a home for the previous three years. Web sites and other information on the program are listed in Appendix Three.

A good real estate agent who specializes in working with buyers will know about local home-buying programs for which you might qualify. But don't hesitate to do some homework yourself. Look for phone numbers of community development and housing development authorities in your local phone book. You can also find links to local housing development organizations through the U.S. Department of Housing and Urban Development's Web site, at *www.hud.gov.*

Always remember that when dealing with any government program, you mustn't assume you are *not* a first-time buyer. Check the definition. It may be that you've regained your virginity (so to speak) if you haven't owned a home for several years.

## Private Mortgage Insurance (PMI)

You definitely get a payoff for making a down payment of 20 percent or more. Lenders can give you a loan with a smaller down payment, but this increases their lending risk. With a lesser amount of your own cash in the deal, there is also less of a guarantee that, should times get tough, you won't walk away and leave the lender with an unpaid mortgage and the deed to your home. If your local economy really turns sour, the home might even be worth less than it was on the day you bought it. To lessen that risk, the lender usually will force you to pay for private mortgage insurance, or PMI.

You pay for this insurance, with the premium added to your monthly loan payment, but the lender is the beneficiary. If you were to default on your loan (banish the thought!), the lender would be paid cash. PMI is *not* tax deductible. PMI costs about 0.5 percent of your mortgage balance per year, or about $1,000 on a $200,000 loan.

## Eliminating Your PMI

You don't have to keep paying PMI forever. If property values in your area have been rising quickly, and you've made payments faithfully for at least two years, you may be able to convince your lender to drop the coverage requirement. Rising values may have boosted your equity enough that the insurance is no longer justified.

You see, as the years go by, your loan balance slowly shrinks while your property's value increases. Because most of your payment in the early years of a mortgage goes toward interest, your loan balance shrinks slowly during the first ten years of the loan. In later years, however, more of the monthly payment is used to pay off principal, and your loan balance declines much more rapidly. Most of the equity you build up in the early years is thanks to rising market prices, also called appreciation.

Let's say you make a 5 percent down payment (of $10,000) on a house with a value of $200,000. Your $190,000 mortgage therefore would cover 95 percent of your home's value. After a few years, your home's value rises, or appreciates, by 20 percent to $240,000. In addition to your $10,000 down payment (and the minimal amount of principal you've paid in those first few years), you get to count that extra $40,000 toward your equity, for a total of $50,000.

Your $190,000 mortgage now represents just under 80 percent of the home's new, higher value.

Now that your equity in the home is above that 20 percent threshold, the lender should let you off the PMI hook. They usually require that you have made payments on-time for at least two years, however, and you'll have to make the request in writing. You'll also have to pay for an appraisal (usually $250 to $300) to prove that home values have grown this much, but it's money well spent if you expect to live in the house long enough to recover the appraisal cost. (Take the appraisal cost and divide it by the monthly cost of PMI to find your break-even point—the number of months it will take to recover your expenses and start saving real money.) When property values are rising quickly (and especially when interest rates are low) many homeowners instead choose to refinance to a new loan so they can get out from under the PMI requirement. Their new loan takes full account of the home's current market value, which means their equity may have risen above the magic 20 percent level. Voilà! No more need for expensive PMI. And if the interest rate on your new mortgage is a tad lower than it was on the old loan, that's just a cherry on top of the sundae.

## Avoiding PMI

Many lenders offer low-down payment mortgages *without* a separate PMI requirement. These are a fine choice, but don't be fooled into thinking there's really no PMI. It's there; the lender has simply incorporated it into the interest rate. You'll pay a higher interest rate on these loans.

The benefit is that the interest is tax-deductible, whereas PMI is not. The drawback is that the only way to get out of this higher interest rate is to refinance. But if you're likely to refinance in a few years anyway—or to move out of the home altogether—who cares that the PMI is built into the interest rate for thirty years? You and that loan will have long since parted ways.

## Play Piggyback with Two Mortgages

Another very common way to get around the PMI requirement is to arrange for what are called piggyback mortgages. You need to have a good credit rating to get a lender's approval for one of these plans. Here's how they work. Say you have enough cash for a 10 percent down payment and closing costs. The lender can set you up with a two mortgages: a traditional mortgage that covers 80 percent of the purchase price, plus a second (piggyback) mortgage for the remaining 10 percent. Because the first mortgage is for only 80 percent of the purchase price, the PMI requirement is not triggered.

Your second mortgage functions like an ordinary home-equity loan. It will have a variable interest rate (typically 1 or 2 percentage points above the prime rate), and it will last for only ten, fifteen, or twenty years. Depending on the individual mortgage, this second mortgage might not be fully paid off at the end of that term, requiring you to pay it off in a lump sum (called a balloon payment)—or forcing you to take out a new home-equity loan to stretch out the debt. Of course, if you sell the home or refinance before that time, paying off that second mortgage wouldn't become a problem. The interest on that second mortgage is tax-deductible. Piggyback deals can even be set up so your first mortgage covers 80 percent of the purchase price while the second mortgage covers the remaining 20 percent—eliminating your cash down payment altogether.

# Alternative Mortgage Types

There are some situations in which you might want to explore specialty mortgages. For instance, if you have plenty of stock or bond assets but would prefer to keep your investments intact and growing you might choose a pledged-asset mortgage. Or home buyers with limited cash for a down payment might choose a loan insured by the Federal Housing Authority (FHA). Guarantees by the Veterans Administration also make zero-down payment loans easily available to current and former service members.

## Pledging Assets Instead of Making a Cash Down Payment

First-time home buyers aren't the only ones concerned about tying up a huge chunk of cash in a down payment. Many affluent buyers would rather keep their money in wealth-producing investments rather than park it in a down payment. Pledged-asset mortgages are a special type of loan that allow you to borrow 100 percent of the home price. Instead of making a down payment, you pledge your assets—stocks, bonds, mutual funds, or certificates of deposit—as collateral for the loan. You continue to own those assets and to reap the earnings they generate, and you avoid paying PMI. Even though you're borrowing most or all of the purchase price, the lender's risk is still reduced. If you were to quit paying the loan, the lender could seize not only your home but your pledged assets as well. Plans allow you to pledge assets for your own home purchase as well as for a home bought by your child, grandchild, or other close relative.

Depending on the plan, you may need to pledge a lot of assets to secure one of these mortgages. Here's how a plan offered by Merrill Lynch Credit Corp. works. First, you must finance your mortgage with Merrill Lynch *and* keep your assets in one of their brokerage accounts. You can finance 100 percent of the home price, but you must pledge assets equaling a hefty 30 percent of the loan amount.

But because market values fluctuate, Merrill Lynch wants you to have some padding in that account. When you set up the deal, the brokerage account you pledge against must equal 130 percent of the pledge amount. In other words, for a $300,000 home purchase, you would make a 0 percent down payment and pledge assets worth 30 percent of the home's value, or $90,000. But your Merrill Lynch account must have at least $117,000 in assets on day one. If the value of your investments should fall significantly, Merrill Lynch could require you to put more money into the account.

With a pledged asset mortgage, the numbers are big but the payoff is, too. Not only do you buy the $300,000 house, you get the biggest possible mortgage-interest tax deduction. You keep your investment portfolio intact and (one hopes) growing, *and*, because you never had to sell those investments, you haven't had to pay capital gains tax on them or a stockbroker's commission on the trade.

## FHA Mortgages

Through the Federal Housing Authority (FHA), the federal government has its own alternative to PMI, called the FHA-insured mortgage. The main FHA mortgage program is limited to buyers who will live in the home for several years, and it excludes investors. The buyer applies for the loan from a regular lender who is approved to work with FHA (as many are), and the government provides the mortgage insurance to cover the extra risk of a low-down payment loan. While FHA still requires borrowers to make at least a 3 percent down payment on their home, they will allow the full 3 percent to come from a gift given by family or other sources.

The FHA also allows your closing costs (typically another 2 to 3 percent of the home price) to be rolled into the mortgage amount, further shrinking the amount of cash needed at closing.

As an FHA borrower, however, you still have to pay the cost of the mortgage insurance. The FHA charges an up-front mortgage insurance premium equal to 1.5 percent of the mortgage amount, but allows that to be rolled into your mortgage amount along with other closing costs. The agency also charges an annual mortgage insurance fee of 0.5 percent of your mortgage amount. That fee is broken into monthly installments and paid through your monthly mortgage payment.

If you're a move-up buyer who used an FHA loan when you bought your old home, you might be eligible for a refund of part of the up-front premium that you paid when you closed on that loan. This *only* applies to FHA loans taken out before December 8, 2004. (A change in federal law took away refunds for FHA borrowers after that date.) But some sellers with older loans can still claim a refund, and that cash will help a bit with the closing costs you face on a new loan. You're eligible in two circumstances: if you took out the loan before January 1, 2001, and pay off the loan before its seven-year anniversary; or if you took out the loan between January 1, 2001, and December 8, 2004, and pay it off before its fifth anniversary.

Your mortgage company is supposed to notify the U.S. Department of Housing and Urban Development (HUD) when you pay off an FHA mortgage and might qualify for a refund, but mistakes happen. If you think you qualify and haven't received the refund within 120 days of paying off the loan, take matters into your own hands. Write to the U.S. Department of Housing and Urban Development, P.O. Box 23699, Washington, D.C., 20036-6399 or call the office at (800) 697-6967. Be sure to include your name, FHA case number (from your loan documents), the date that your mortgage was paid off, the address of the home you bought with that FHA loan, and your daytime phone number.

The FHA doesn't actually limit the price of the home you can buy, but it *does* limit the size of the mortgage you can take out, and that effectively limits the price of the home. The FHA raises its loan limits a bit each January. The limits are tied to local median prices. For 2005, the limit for most communities was $172,632. In certain high-cost areas, the FHA has approved a loan limit of up to $312,895. In a handful of areas where construction costs are exceptionally high, FHA sets even higher limits. For 2005, the loan limit could be as high as $469,344 in Alaska, Hawaii, Guam, and the Virgin Islands. Real estate agents and lenders can advise you of current loan limits for your area. You can look these up for yourself on the HUD Web site (*www.hud.gov.*)

## Veterans (VA) Mortgages

Active-duty military personnel, members of the Selected Reserves or National Guard, and veterans are eligible to take out no-down mortgages guaranteed by the U.S. Department of Veterans Affairs (VA). Even with no down payment, these mortgages do not require any mortgage insurance. The government recently boosted the dollar amount of loan guarantees, making the program more useful for borrowers who live in expensive housing markets.

The VA doesn't lend money or issue mortgage insurance. What it offers is a guarantee. Though the borrower makes no down payment, the VA pledges that if the borrower quits paying the loan, the VA will cover the lender's losses up to the guarantee amount.

For 2005, that guarantee amount could run from $36,000 to as high as $89,912, depending on local housing costs. That amount is indexed to rise along with home prices each year. Lenders generally allow mortgages for up to four times the guarantee amount without a down payment, as long as the borrower's income and credit rating are good enough to qualify for the loan. In higher-cost communities, therefore, VA borrowers may be able to borrow homes costing up to $359,648 with a 0 percent down payment.

You can find more information on VA loans, including eligibility rules, at *www.homeloans.va.gov*. You apply for VA mortgages through ordinary mortgage lenders, but not all lenders participate in the VA program. If you're having trouble finding a local lender offering VA loans, you can find a referral through the Department of Veterans Affairs at *www.va.com*.

## Where to Stash Your Down Payment Savings

Accessibility and safety are the keys to deciding on a place to keep your down payment money as you save for a new home. That is *not* money you should invest in stocks or in mutual funds that invest in stocks. The value of stocks—and of mutual funds that invest in them—fluctuates too much too quickly to be a safe place to hold your down payment kitty. During a time when stock prices are rising, it can be nearly irresistible to use these investments to help your down payment fund grow more quickly. But the risk is too great that a temporary slump in the stock market will wipe out a big chunk of your down payment—right when you need it. Leave stock and mutual-fund investments for your retirement savings and young children's college funds, where you have the luxury of time necessary to ride out market slumps.

The best place for your down payment savings is in a certificate of deposit (CD), a money-market account offered by your bank, or a money-market mutual fund offered by a Wall Street brokerage company. Banks have the advantage of having federal deposit insurance, which protects accounts up to $100,000.

When using CDs to accumulate your down payment savings, pay close attention to the term of the investment. Money invested in CDs is unavailable for terms of one month to five years—or even longer. You don't want to find yourself ready to make a down payment tomorrow when your money is locked up for another couple of years. You *could* take the money out earlier, before the CD matures, but you will have to pay an early-withdrawal penalty.

As your savings grow and the time for home-shopping nears, you'll want to make sure your CDs are shorter-lived. Circle those maturity dates on your calendar! You don't want a bank to roll your funds over into a new CD automatically if you will soon need the cash. By the time you start looking at homes, all of your down payment money should be in a money-market account. This way, you can access the cash for an earnest money deposit—and then again for the rest of your down payment—immediately, simply by writing a check.

## Razzi's Rules to Live By

### 🏠 You might be a first-time buyer, again.

Even if you have owned before, you still might qualify as a first-timer. Government programs typically define "first-time" as not having owned within the last two or three years.

## 🏠 Tap retirement funds gingerly.

Be aware of the tax penalties you might trigger—*and* remember that you're spending not only today's retirement dollar, but all the earnings that dollar would garner between today and retirement day.

## 🏠 Beware the stock market.

The stock market is no place to keep your down payment savings. Stock prices swing too wildly to be a safe place for money that you will need soon. Stick to money-market funds, bank money-market accounts, and short-term certificates of deposit while you build your down payment fund.

## 🏠 Get some help.

Look for local programs that help first-time buyers come up with a down payment. You just may be eligible for a little grant!

## 🏠 Think twice about paying in cash for a retirement home.

You might do better if some of that cash goes into an investment that continues to grow during the early years of what everyone hopes will be a long retirement.

# CHAPTER THREE

# Mortgages Explained

"They lent Gerald the money, and in the years that followed, the money came back to them with interest. Gradually the plantation widened out, as Gerald bought more acres lying near him, and in time, the white house became a reality instead of a dream."

MARGARET MITCHELL, *Gone With the Wind*

AHHH, MORTGAGES. The same things arranged neighbor-to-neighbor at the Bailey Bros. Building and Loan Association (in Frank Capra's *It's a Wonderful Life*) are now sold through nationwide lenders and even over the faceless Internet. We may have lost the homey touch of doing business with neighbors, but we've gained access to a huge array of amazingly sophisticated financial instruments that help us buy homes. You can find a loan that's practically tailored to your individual needs. Before you go shopping, it's worth a little time reviewing the lingo and learning more about the different types of mortgages on the market today.

Let's begin with a few definitions. What we call a mortgage is actually two different instruments. One is the loan, while the other is the actual mortgage. The loan part is fairly straightforward. The traditional deal is to borrow money at a specific interest rate and repay the loan in equal monthly chunks for thirty years. Technically, the mortgage is a separate document in which you pledge your home as security for that big loan. Basically, we, the buyers, offer up our homes as hostage to guarantee that we will repay the loan. Because we are the ones offering the home as hostage, we are called the mortgagors. The lender holds the hostage and thus is the mortgagee. You'll see those terms on mortgage loan documents; don't let the lingo confuse you.

## Old Reliable: The 30-Year Fixed-Rate Mortgage

The traditional 30-year fixed-rate mortgage offers unequaled peace of mind, and that's why it remains a favorite of home buyers. You know what your housing payment is going to be every month, regardless of whether the economy is going through boom or bust. And thirty years turns out to be a sweet spot among repayment schedules. A shorter period raises your payment significantly, and a longer period (many lenders are offering 40-year loans) boosts your interest expense further—and means you might *never* actually own the home free and clear.

### Shorter Loan Terms

However, many buyers choose to take on the bulkier monthly payment that comes with a 15- or 20-year loan term. There are some good reasons to do it if you can swing the payments. One good reason is to get a lower interest rate—roughly half a percentage point less than you'll get on a 30-year loan. But even bigger savings come from your ability to cut the loan's duration in half. The power of compound interest comes into play here. The longer a debt is outstanding, the higher the interest tab ratchets. If you cut a loan's term by half, you save a surprisingly large amount of interest. Combine the lower rate with the shorter term, and you'll really save a bundle in the interest tab over the life of a loan. For example, on a loan for $200,000, you would save $167,000 in interest over the life of the loan by taking a 15-year loan at 6.42 percent instead of a 30-year loan at 7 percent. But the long-term savings come at a significant short-term price, namely a mortgage payment that is $402 higher each month. Also, by retiring your mortgage 15 years early, you give up your mortgage-interest deduction sooner, as well.

The argument for a shorter mortgage is particularly compelling if you're already in your late forties and would like to get that mortgage out of the way before retirement day. But, depending on your overall financial picture, it may make more sense to choose the 30-year loan with its easier-to-manage payments. After all, you could discipline yourself to invest the monthly savings ($402 per month, in our example) and possibly earn an even greater return than the money you would have saved on interest.

## Paying Down Your Principal Faster

There is still an opportunity for you to carve huge chunks out of your long-term interest tab if you take out a 30-year mortgage. Most of them allow you to prepay the principal without any penalty. You could choose to double up on principal payments or make an occasional lump-sum prepayment of principal (say, when you are paid a bonus). That will speed up the time until you're free and clear—and slash your overall tab for interest. You can play around with the what-ifs using the free calculators available on the Internet. (Again, be sure to check out the calculators *at www.hsh.com.*)

## Pay Less with an Adjustable-Rate Mortgage (ARM)

Not everybody needs thirty years of predictability from a mortgage. With an adjustable-rate mortgage (ARM), your interest rate fluctuates from year to year, or at even shorter intervals, depending on the specifics of your loan. This increases your risk, given that no one can predict if interest rates in the future will be higher or lower than they are now. In exchange for that risk, lenders offer you a lower interest rate at the beginning of the loan.

There are some very good reasons to take out an ARM. If you're all but certain you will move within the next decade (or refinance into another loan), why should you pay extra to lock down your mortgage payments another two decades beyond that point? It's a waste of money. Alternately, if you're in the early years of your career—when four-for-a-dollar ramen noodles are a diet staple—you need to go for a cheap interest rate. Later, when you're earning enough to add beef and chicken to your diet, you'll probably be able to handle a higher interest rate, too.

Many buyers who might prefer the predictability of a 30-year fixed-rate mortgage—especially when interest rates are rising—find they have to use an ARM because the lower payments it offers in the early years are all they can afford. Lenders base their qualification decisions on the payment level during the second year so keeping that payment as low as possible with an ARM will help you qualify if you're right on the edge.

## How Adjustable-Rate Mortgages Work

Let's look at the traditional choice in adjustables, the one-year ARM. Each year, your rate is adjusted according to the specific *index* plus a *margin* (or markup) to arrive at your new rate. Most one-year ARMs are pegged to an index of one-year Treasury securities. To that index, the lender adds a margin of about 2.75 percentage points to arrive at the interest rate charged to the borrower. (Treasury rates are published daily in the *Wall Street Journal*.) Be sure to compare the margins when shopping for an ARM; that's what really determines how expensive a loan is. But lenders usually sweeten the deal for the first year, offering an interest rate that is lower than the index plus margin would call for. Because of this, ARM borrowers can usually expect a rate increase in the second year, even if the economy is not experiencing rising interest rates.

Your risk is limited significantly by two crucial caps. One cap limits how much your rate can rise (or fall!) from year to year. The other cap sets an absolute limit on the rate you can be charged at any time during the overall 15- to 30-year term of the loan. Most one-year ARMs carry interest-rate caps of 2 percentage points per year and 6 percentage points over the life of the loan. If you were to take out an ARM with a 4 percent initial rate, the interest could go no higher than 6 percent after one year. The highest it could ever go would be 10 percent. Always, always double-check that the caps are in this reasonable range (2 points annually/6 points over the life of the loan) before you sign the loan documents. This is especially important if you've had some credit problems and can only qualify for special, higher-interest loans designed for risky borrowers.

Beware of loans that cap the *payment* but not the interest rate. If rates rise quickly, your payment might not be enough to pay down your loan balance. This situation is called "negative amortization," and it means you could face a big sum of interest that still needs to be paid off after your loan was scheduled to end. Insist on a loan that caps both your payment and the interest charged.

You may encounter an ARM that adjusts every six months. While you would face rate adjustments twice a year, you also should have lower rate caps. Caps of 1 percentage point at each change and 6 percentage points over the life of the loan are typical. If the economy were to go through a period of rapidly rising interest rates, six-month ARM borrowers would feel the pinch faster. Of course, they'd be the first ones to feel relief when rates decline, as well.

## Which Index?

In addition to the one-year Treasury index, there are a couple of other common ARM indexes, namely the London Interbank Offered Rate (called the LIBOR) and the Federal Reserve Cost of Funds Index (or COFI). These indexes tend to rise and fall somewhat faster (for the LIBOR) or slower (for the COFI) than the Treasury securities, but they all end up going in the same direction. Six-month and one-year LIBOR and COFI indexes are used mainly to set six-month and one-year ARMs.

While you'll find that some of the new, low-payment ARMs (which we'll get to shortly) are pegged to the LIBOR or COFI indexes, you shouldn't let a loan officer convince you that you're getting some special deal on an "exotic" LIBOR or COFI ARM. Remember, money costs what money costs. If you lock in a rate for a long time, you will be charged more interest at the outset; if you let your rate change frequently, you will be charged less interest to compensate you for the greater risk you take on.

When rates are rising, the rate you pay on ARMs pegged to Treasuries, LIBORs, and COFIs all rise at roughly the same pace, thanks to differences in the adjustment periods on these loans. Rate adjustments on an ARM work pretty much like a roulette wheel. The only thing that matters is the specific number you hit on your spin of the wheel. Your interest rate will be based on the prevailing rate the day your loan adjusts, subject to the limits imposed by your caps. When evaluating any type of ARM, the most important things to judge are the margin and your interest-rate and payment caps.

## Loan Features You Should Avoid

Amid all the paperwork involved with taking out a mortgage, it's easy to let your mind wander and simply sign on the dotted line. But you should read through the loan documents. (If the loan officer is tapping his toe with impatience, so be it.) In particular, you want to ask about—and watch out for—these hazards to your financial health. Although these are most commonly found in loans offered to borrowers with poor credit scores, these days they're being included in more loans marketed to borrowers with strong credit, particularly the newer ARMs with ultra-low payments. You should be on the lookout for them in any type of mortgage.

### Balloon Payments

Some ARMs aren't scheduled to be paid off entirely by the end of the loan. They call for a final balloon payment, which is usually a very large amount of unpaid principal. You're expected to refinance that balloon into a new loan, at whatever interest rate prevails at the time. When problems come up with balloons, it's usually because the borrower's situation has changed since taking out the loan. If a balloon comes due while you're temporarily laid off, you're in a tough situation. If you have a need for long-term financing (as most homebuyers do) avoid balloons.

## Negative Amortization

There's nothing positive to be said about negative amortization, which is an increasingly common feature associated with ARMs. You'll find it when interest rate is not capped, but the payment is. Watch for the words "payment caps" in the advertising; that's your clue that the *interest rate* is probably not capped. The interest rate may, indeed, rise faster than your capped payment. If that happens, the unpaid interest is added to your principal balance. You end up borrowing more money instead of paying off the loan. (Imagine borrowing against your credit card to make your mortgage payment each month. That insanity comes close to what you're doing with a negative-amortization loan.) Unless home prices continue to rise strongly (and you cannot bet on that continuing) you could end up having to write a check for tens of thousands of dollars when you sell the home—a prospect that could keep you trapped there when you'd prefer to move on.

## Prepayment Penalties

Most mortgages do not limit prepayment of your principal. If you'd like to pay twice the principal due each month, with the goal of paying off your loan early, you're free to do so without penalty. If rates fall and you'd like to refinance to a better loan after a year or two, you don't owe anything extra. But some mortgages don't treat borrowers so kindly. Some mortgages will impose a prepayment penalty on borrowers who try to pay off all or part of the loan balance earlier than scheduled. These penalties can run into thousands of dollars. Prepayment penalties are found often on loans made to borrowers with credit problems, but, increasingly, they're found on loans offered to borrowers with better credit.

Sometimes borrowers with good credit ratings will *choose* to accept a prepayment penalty in exchange for a discount on the interest rate. If you reasonably expect to stay in the home for at least the five years or so when a prepayment penalty applies, that can be a sound move. But be careful. Prepayment penalties are being included in some of the most noxious mortgages being sold today—the loans that all but guarantee a future of sharply rising home payments. Avoid those loans (called "option ARMs," which I will discuss shortly) and be on the lookout for prepayment penalties in any other type of loan. If you accept a penalty, you should be well-paid for it with a lower interest rate.

## Hybrids, Jumbos and Other Creatures in the Mortgage Zoo

Today, lenders offer a dizzying array of home loans beyond the old reliable thirty-year fixed rate and the classic one-year adjustable-rate mortgage. Depending on your circumstances, it might be worthwhile to investigate some of these alternatives. Hybrid loans, jumbo mortgages and stated-income loans have been commonplace for years, and millions of borrowers have taken advantage of them successfully. But some of the newer loan varieties, particularly the interest-only ARMs and option ARMs, are all but certain to lead overextended borrowers to the foreclosure court. In fact, as this text was being written, federal regulators were looking into the need to rein in lenders offering such loans. Here's how you can tell the domesticated critters from the wild beasts in today's new lending zoo.

## The Brilliant Compromise: Hybrid Loans

Hybrid loans won't save you quite as much money as a pure ARM, but they're cheaper than a 30-year fixed rate mortgage *and* they limit your risk. They're especially popular among buyers who don't plan to be in their new home for more than ten years.

Hybrids give you a fixed interest rate for the first three, five, seven, or ten years of the mortgage. At the end of that fixed-rate period, the loan converts to a one-year ARM for the rest of its life. These loans are often referred to numerically, like so: 3/1, 5/1, 7/1, or 10/1. The first number specifies the number of years the rate is fixed, and the second indicates the adjustment period of the ARM that follows. Usually it's a one-year. That first adjustment can be pretty sizable; a typical cap is 5 or 6 percentage points over the original, fixed rate. (For a hybrid with only a three-year fixed-rate period, that initial cap is a little lower, just 2 percentage points over the starting rate.) In following years, annual caps limit changes to 2 percentage points per year. The life-of-loan cap is 5 percentage points above your starting rate. If interest rates were to increase rapidly, you could reach the loan's absolute top interest rate at the very first adjustment! But if you think you will only live in this house five years, a 5/1 ARM could be the perfect loan; if you think you might live there longer, the 7/1 or 10/1 might be the better match.

## Jumbo Loans

Jumbo loan is the term for loan amounts greater than $359,650, as of 2005. To understand jumbos, and why they have higher interest rates than smaller loans, you first need to understand a bit about two large corporations with the folksy names Fannie Mae and Freddie Mac.

Fannie and Freddie buy mortgages from approved lenders and repackage them as bonds which are sold to investors around the world. But they can buy only conforming loans that meet certain standards, which include limits on borrowers' creditworthiness, the existence of consumer protections on the loans (such as ARM caps), and on the dollar amount of the mortgage. That dollar amount ($359,650 in 2005) is called the conforming loan limit. Anything larger is a jumbo.

Although they cannot buy jumbos, other investors will—and they demand higher interest rates. Translation for the homebuyer: Your interest rate on a jumbo will be 1/8 to 3/8 percentage points higher than on a conforming loan. Some buyers arrange piggyback loans (discussed in Chapter Three), using a second mortgage for the amount above $359,650 to keep most of their borrowing below the jumbo cutoff.

Every November, Fannie and Freddie announce the new limit that will go into effect at the beginning of the coming year. If you're buying a home in November or December and are just above the current jumbo threshold, it could pay to put off closing until the higher loan limits go into effect January 1. You can then stay under that jumbo threshold and pay less interest.

## Stated-Income Mortgages

If you don't want to (or cannot) give a loan officer documentation to prove your income, you can get a stated-income mortgage (also called a low-documentation mortgage). This type of loan is based

## Fannie Mae and Freddie Mac

These two publicly traded corporations have an unusual
relationship with the federal government. They are not
government agencies, even though they must report to a
federal regulator. Both were created by a charter from the
federal government, which wanted them to bring Wall
Street and global capital to the home-mortgage market
and to transfer some of the risk of lending away from individual banks and other mortgage-lending institutions. Their
formal names are the Federal National Mortgage Assn.,
with the acronym FNMA having morphed into "Fannie Mae"
and the Federal Home Loan Mortgage Corp., FHLMC,
dubbed "Freddie Mac." These days they go strictly by
their nicknames, which helps downplay their federal roots.
That unusual federal tie remains, however, and it helps
Fannie and Freddie borrow money more cheaply than
their competitors can.

on little more than your word. You need a high credit score to
qualify, but you can get by without providing as much
documentation as borrowers using traditional loans. With a stated-
income mortgage, the lender verifies the source of your income,
but not the amount. You even can get a loan without the amount of
your income—or your assets—being verified by the lender. The less
you disclose, however, the more interest you can expect to pay.

While some cynics within the industry call them "liars' loans,"
they can be a life-saver for borrowers who clearly have the money to
qualify for the loan, but who have problems with the paperwork.

Candidates include people who've had their jobs for only a short time, people in sales or other occupations in which income varies tremendously from month to month, and people who are self-employed. These folks may find it worth the extra interest to get a stated-income mortgage.

## Interest-Only Loans

Welcome to one of the most controversial areas of mortgage lending these days. These loans are the scary spawn of the boom in housing prices, and they are being pushed hard by mortgage lenders. Unfortunately, many of the borrowers I've spoken with really didn't understand the risks that loom down the road, when they must start paying back the principal or refinance to another mortgage.

An interest-only loan is usually an ARM or hybrid mortgage that allows you to pay only interest during the first few years. Five years is the typical interest-only payment period. After that, for the remaining twenty-five years (on a 30-year loan) you repay interest *and* principal. Sounds good, doesn't it?

Unfortunately, even if interest rates remain steady, your payment will jump sharply after the interest-only period. That's because you delayed paying any principal. If you've been making interest-only payments for five years, for instance, you have to pay off the entire amount you borrowed in twenty-five years instead of thirty. If interest rates rise, you're in for an even bigger payment shock. (By the way, interest rates run a little bit higher on these loans than on ordinary ARMs or hybrids. You'll pay about ⅛ to ¼ percentage points more.)

You're taking on a lot of risk with this type of mortgage. During those interest-only years, the only equity you build up will come from your down payment and any appreciation in local real estate values. While price increases have been very strong in recent years, you always must be prepared for the idea that real estate prices could lose steam at any time. If you needed to sell the home unexpectedly, would you get enough from the sale (after paying off the big mortgage) to cover the real estate broker's commission, or would you have to bring cash to the closing table?

These loans *can* be a reasonable choice for the financially sophisticated investor—in other words the investor who already is sitting on a pot of money that they could tap should times get tough. Those savvy souls may indeed take the savings from their interest-only payments and invest them in other assets, and barely bat an eyelash when the interest-only option expires. I, however, like to keep things more straightforward when I'm talking about financing the roof over my head. I want my loan payments to actually *pay off the loan.*

Unfortunately, these interest-only loans are not being pitched solely to the Donald Trumps of the world. They're being sold—and sold hard—to homebuyers who are stretching their dollars to the snapping point in order to buy homes in outrageously expensive markets. Don't even consider one of these loans unless you have a plan to deal with the payment jolt at the end of the interest-only period. And don't let any loan officer get away with implying that you're unsophisticated if you recoil from the risk. You're simply being wise with your hard-earned money.

## Option ARMs

If you've ever gotten in financial trouble with your credit card, you'll have an idea of what's in store for you with the newest version of mortgages, the "Option ARM," also being sold with the attractive

73

names "minimum payment mortgage," or "cash-flow ARM," among others. Basically, the lenders who dreamed up these horrors chose almost every consumer-threatening feature available in the mortgage world and wrapped them into one package. I cannot say this strongly enough: If using an option ARM is the only way for you to afford a home payment, then you're better off paying rent.

Here's how they work. Each month, you are given four payment options: the minimum payment, an interest-only payment, the fully amortized payment on a 30- or 40-year payoff schedule or the fully amortized payment on a 15-year schedule. The last two options are fairly clear-cut—and they're *not* the reason many people would choose an option ARM. After all, with an ordinary 30- or 40-year fixed-rate mortgage, you are required to make a fully amortizing payment, and most allow you to prepay principal on a 15-year payoff schedule, if you wish. The hazards involved with the second option, making interest-only payments, have already been discussed. It's the first option, the minimum monthly payment that can really get you in trouble.

These loans have an artificially low interest rate to start. Recently, when ordinary one-year ARMs were charging about 4.5 percent, these were as low as 1 percent. But that intro rate was guaranteed for one measly month! (Some versions fix the rate for three months.)

After that, your interest rate will change monthly, with a cap as high as 9 or 10 percent. The minimum payment, however, usually stays the same for 12 months at a time (with one important exception). When the rate rises, as it is bound to, seeing as it's artificially low to begin with, if you choose to make the minimum payment, the unpaid interest will be added to your loan amount.

That's the negative amortization feature discussed earlier in this chapter. Each year, your minimum payment will change, but it can only differ by a maximum of 7.5 percent from the previous year's payment. (Unfortunately, few people can look forward to 7.5 percent annual pay raises to keep up with this escalating cost of living.)

Every month you choose to make the minimum payment, you effectively borrow more money because the unpaid interest charge is added to your outstanding loan balance. This can't go on forever, of course, so the lender sets limits. At least every five years your loan is "recast" and you get a new set of monthly payment choices that will pay off your loan on time. You are *not* going to like what happens at a recast point! And you can hit a recast point even earlier if interest rates are rising. At any time your indebtedness increases to between 10 and 25 percent above the amount you originally borrowed (depending on the rules for that particular loan) payments will be reset. That means you could face a recast if your debt reached $220,000 on a loan you originally took out for $200,000. According to an interest-rate projection by HSH Associates, borrowers could very realistically face a 54 percent increase in their monthly payment within less than five years of taking out one of these loans! As a final grace note to this sorry song, option ARMs often carry prepayment penalties, so they'll dun you if you try to escape to a better loan. You deserve a better deal than this.

# Razzi's Rules to Live By

### ⌂ Match your mortgage to your time frame.

The traditional 30-year fixed-rate mortgage is a favorite because it offers unbeatable predictability. But if you expect to move or refinance within the next ten years, you can save with an adjustable or hybrid loan.

### 🏠 It's the margin that counts.

Interest rates on ARMs are determined by your index plus the *margin*, or markup. Pay close attention—that margin reveals the true cost of your loan.

### 🏠 Save big by paying off early.

You can save hundreds of thousands of dollars of interest by paying off your loan in fifteen years instead of thirty. The bigger your loan amount and the higher your interest rate, the greater are the savings you get from prepayment.

### 🏠 Money costs what money costs.

When interest rates rise or fall, the indexes used to determine ARM rates will follow, all in step. There's nothing special about COFI or LIBOR indexes compared to the more common Treasury security index.

### 🏠 Watch for these mortgage menaces.

These three mortgage features could threaten your long-term financial health: balloon payments, negative amortization, and prepayment penalties. Always check your loan documents for them.

### 🏠 Just say no to interest-only ARMs and option ARMs.

Your payments are certain to rise, but your ability to profit from homeownership is anything but certain.

# CHAPTER FOUR

# Shopping Is Shopping: Get the Best Loan

"As a house, Barton Cottage, though small, was comfortable and compact; but as a cottage it was defective, for the building was regular, the roof was tiled, the window-shutters were not painted green, nor were the walls covered with honeysuckles."

JANE AUSTEN, *Sense and Sensibility*

T HERE ARE TWO BASIC RULES TO REMEMBER when you're in the market for a home loan. First, there are a lot of lenders out there competing for your business, so shop aggressively for the best deal. Second, never forget that the loan officer is a salesperson. While a good salesperson knows his or her products inside out and can help you find the one that fits best, you must never confuse a loan officer with a financial counselor. That loan officer wants to *sell* you a mortgage, the larger the better. And he or she earns more profit on some loans than on others.

That's especially important to remember if you're dealing with a mortgage broker. In an era when homebuyers can get a mortgage from local banks, credit unions, specialized mortgage banks, and the always-open Internet mortgage sites, mortgage brokers continue to exist by promising extra service. They work with a number of loan originators (the companies that actually lend the money) and can shop among them to get you the best deal. In exchange for the mortgage broker's services, the originators give them a cut of what you will pay for the loan.

The idea is that a mortgage broker has an inside track to lenders, as well as access to loans you couldn't get on your own. That's especially appealing to borrowers with credit problems who, indeed, may have been turned down by another lender already. But don't forget rule number two: Loan officers are salespeople. Mortgage brokers are loan officers, and loan officers are salespeople. Unfortunately, some of those salespeople are determined to sell the deal that is best for *them*. There is no requirement that a mortgage broker look out for your best interest. The good ones do—but many do not. Some will steer you into whichever mortgage earns them the greatest profit. And the truly despicable among them will steer you into a high-rate loan designed for borrowers with bad credit, even if your credit scores could have earned you a higher rate.

In all my years of writing about personal finance, I've heard many stories of borrowers who ran into trouble with mortgages. Lost documents. Expired interest-rate lock-ins. Unanswered telephone calls. Great, promised deals morphing into so-so deals. Most often, there was a mortgage broker involved in those deals. While I also have had many people tell me they got great service from their mortgage broker, the worst stories usually involved a mortgage broker. Everything rests on the reputation of the individual broker.

Unless you personally know the mortgage broker and trust his or her reputation, my advice is to hunt for a mortgage on your own. Skip the intermediary, roll up your sleeves, and do your own shopping. Even if you do use the services of a mortgage broker, take some time to shop on your own, just so you can recognize a good deal when you see it. Here's how to go about shopping for your mortgage.

## Start with Your Credit History and Scores

Remember when your fifth-grade teacher threatened to place that little spit-ball incident on your "permanent record?" You managed to survive that scare relatively unscathed. But, as adults, we really do have a permanent record, namely our credit reports and the numerical credit scores that are derived from them. These very important records will determine the interest rates that lenders offer us, and even if they will be willing to approve a mortgage at all. You need to find out what's on them, and go about fixing any mistakes, pronto. It's best if you start requesting these reports six months before you plan to apply for a loan (or even earlier if you've had some credit problems in the past) so you have plenty of time to fix mistakes and perhaps even boost your scores a bit.

Your credit history is contained in reports from three separate credit bureaus: Experian, TransUnion, and Equifax. Whenever you take out a loan the lender makes regular reports to these credit bureaus. The credit bureaus then compile that data into a credit report, which lists all payments you make on your loans and credit cards. The reports include info on late payments, missed payments, the number of times you have requested credit, and the reason any accounts have been closed (by your request or on the request of the lender, which usually happens because of a problem with your payment history).

Although all three credit bureaus are supposed to receive identical data from lenders, their reports are not necessarily the same. They aren't always accurate, either. Give yourself time to clear the record, keeping in mind that all changes involve an exchange of paperwork between you and the lender in question. We'll get to the details on how you can accomplish these fixes in just a bit.

The other key component of your permanent record is your credit score. This is the mighty number that lenders will use as their most important bit of info in making a decision about whether to give you credit. Scores very directly influence the interest rates lenders will offer you.

The Fair Isaac Credit Corp. is the keeper of the credit scores. Fair Isaac has developed its own method of interpreting borrowers' credit histories and distilling the information into a single number, called your FICO score. FICO scores are reported in a range from 300, for the worst credit profiles, to 850 for the best.

This number is available to any lender whom you authorized to access your credit history. (Now you know what the car dealer is checking while you're out for a test drive.) Because Fair Isaac owns the methodology for calculating these very influential scores—and the company is not keen to give up the secret recipe—there's little way for consumers to check on the validity of these scores. The best you can do is to evaluate the raw material that goes into them, namely the info on your credit reports, and make sure that it is accurate and up-to-date.

## Getting Your Credit Reports

The Federal Trade Commission (FTC) requires each of the credit bureaus Experian, TransUnion, and Equifax to give consumers one free credit report per year (for a total of three free reports each year). But you have to ask for them. You can get your free reports by going online to *www.annualcreditreport.com*. (Don't go directly to the credit report companies; they're geared toward *selling* you reports.) You'll have to supply your Social Security number and answer personal questions to validate that you really are the person you claim to be, but you should get the reports—and an explanation of them—instantly. (Be sure to print them out before you leave the site!) You also can get your free reports by calling toll-free 877-322-8228 or by printing out a copy of the Annual Credit Report Request Form (available on *www.ftc.gov*) and mailing it in. The phone and mail routes may take fifteen days or longer before you get your reply.

If you've already taken advantage of your free credit reports for the year but you want to confirm that the information is still current, you can buy updated copies. Each company may charge you up to $9.50 per copy. To purchase reports, go directly to the credit bureau Web sites, at *www.equifax.com*, *www.experian.com*, and *www.transunion.com*. But you'll actually be better off buying the reports in conjunction with your credit scores.

## Getting Your FICO Credit Score

Because Fair Isaac owns the method for determining FICO scores, the government has not forced them to give consumers a free peek each year. You'll have to buy a report. To buy your FICO score, go online to *www.myfico.com*. Unless you also need to buy updated copies of your three credit reports (perhaps because you ordered your free copies eleven months ago and aren't due for another free copy yet), go with the cheapest package advertised on their site, the FICO Standard, priced at $14.95. The standard package gives you the credit report and score from only one of the three bureaus, but if you already have a recent, free copy of your credit report—and the info looks good—you can save a few dollars by going with that single FICO score. If your score turns out to be borderline, go back and buy your other two credit scores to see if one is significantly better. That's the one you will urge lenders to use! Buying scores a la carte brings your expenditure up to $44.90, only five cents more than the "FICO Deluxe" package that contains all three reports and the three scores based on them. Unless you've experienced identity-theft problems, skip the annual subscription to your scores. Requesting free annual reports of your credit reports will keep you up to date.

Steer clear of Web sites that offer you free credit reports or approximations of your FICO scores. While these are not necessarily scams, the free offers do come with strings attached, such as a requirement that you accept a free trial of a credit-monitoring service. They will start to charge a monthly fee to your credit card after the several-month trial period is over. It can be a hassle to get them to discontinue the service and to quit charging your credit card. You're much better off doing business directly with the credit bureaus and Fair Isaac Corp.

## Correcting Your Credit Report

Even if you're scrupulous about paying your bills, mistakes can crop up in your credit reports and lower your FICO score. A common mistake is for your credit report to list credit accounts that belong to a stranger (or a relative!) with the same last name as yours. Resolved disputes with a creditor may still turn up on your record. Ancient accounts you never actually got around to closing may still be there, making it look as if you have too many open lines of credit. Each credit bureau has its own directions for fixing mistakes, and you need to make sure all three reports are correct. Lower scores mean higher interest rates—and fewer loan choices.

## Don't Fall for Phishing

There's one crucial caveat when it comes to buying credit reports and FICO scores online: *Never* reply to an e-mail that asks you for sensitive financial information, such as your bank account numbers, mother's maiden name, computer passwords, PIN codes, or your Social Security number. Even if the e-mail links you to a site that looks absolutely legitimate, it could very well be a type of fraud known as a "phishing" scam. The e-mail contains a link to a site that *looks* as if it belongs to a legitimate financial company. The logos look right; the slogans are there; practically everything looks legit. But it's not legit at all—the linked site is run by con artists, who take the information people supply and use it to steal from their accounts. It's safe to put information in legitimate Web sites run by banks and credit reporting companies, but *always* type in the Web site addresses yourself!

## Help with Credit Trouble

According to the National Foundation for Credit Counseling, signs of early-stage credit trouble include being near the limit of your lines of credit, being able to make only the minimum payments on credit cards, and having credit card payments take up more than 15 percent of your take-home pay. If credit-card payments consume 20 percent of your take-home pay, you're skipping some bill payments so you can meet others, or you're getting calls from bill collectors, you're in outright crisis. If you're truly in trouble, you can get high-quality, free help to get back on track—and eventually to buy a home. Contact the National Foundation for Credit Counseling through their Web site, at *www.debtadvice.org*.

# Credit Scores and Interest Rates

Your credit score is hugely important in determining the variety of mortgages you qualify for and the interest rates you will be offered. A high credit score demonstrates a borrower's history of being responsible about handling credit. Borrowers with good track records in these areas represent lower risk to lenders and are rewarded with more mortgage choices at lower interest rates than those offered to borrowers with less-attractive histories.

## Top-of-the-Line Credit

The best interest rates are available to borrowers with a FICO score between 720 and 850. The Web site *www.myfico.com* also will tell you the average interest rate you should expect to be quoted if you have a score that high. Let's say you have top-rate credit, 720 or above. The actual rates lenders will quote vary all the time, of course, but let's look at a snapshot on how they compared on one day when, for a 30-year fixed-rate mortgage for $200,000, lenders might quote 5.76 percent for such a creditworthy borrower, which translates to a monthly principal and interest payment of $1,168.

## Next-Tier Borrowers

The next tier consists of those with a credit score ranging from 700 to 719. If your scores were in this range on that day, lenders would quote you a slightly higher interest rate, 5.88 percent. This, of course, would boost the payment, but not by much. You would pay $1,184 each month, just $16 more than a borrower with the very best score. You still would be offered a broad assortment of loan types.

Although the difference between a perfect and a good-enough FICO score isn't that great, the difference between a good-enough score and a poor one can be huge. If your score ranged from 620 to 674 on that day, you could expect to pay much more in interest: 6.42 percent. This translates to a monthly payment of $1,254. That's $86 more than a borrower with a top score would be paying, month after month. In addition to being required to pay a higher rate, you would be offered fewer loan choices. It could mean being offered only adjustable-rate loans, even though you might prefer fixed. You also might be stuck with a nasty prepayment penalty if you try to refinance to a better loan within two or three years.

## Subprime Mortgages

With a score of 620 or lower, it gets worse. You're stuck in the subprime mortgage market. That means your scores aren't high enough to qualify for a mortgage that can be purchased by Fannie Mae or Freddie Mac, the government-sponsored corporations that buy mortgages and resell them on Wall Street. Other investors will buy those loans—but they'll demand higher interest rates than Fannie and Freddie. That low credit score would jack your rate up to 9.29 percent and your monthly payment to $1,651. That's a whopping $483 more each month than a borrower with the best credit scores could expect to pay for the same mortgage. Think of it this way: To borrow the same amount of money, you'd be required to make a house payment *plus* the equivalent of a loan payment on a very lovely new car. That's what a poor credit score will cost you.

Lenders actually like making high-rate subprime loans. They're profitable. But, as a borrower, you need to beware. When loans aren't being sold to Fannie Mae and Freddie Mac, they don't have to include the consumer protections (like reasonable interest rate caps) that Fannie and Freddie demand. Subprime loans are the wild west of mortgage lending, and borrowers with poor credit are the most susceptible to predatory lenders who charge outrageous interest rates and demand stiff prepayment penalties if borrowers' fortunes improve and they try to refinance into a better loan.

The lowest score that can still qualify for a mortgage is about 500–520. If your scores are lower than that, spend the next year overhauling the family budget, getting rid of debts (attack those with the highest interest rates first), and making payments on time.

## Get All the Credit You're Due

If you know your credit score, you should have a good idea of the range of mortgages and interest rates available to you. Without this knowledge, it is possible for some loan officers to take advantage of you and steer you toward more expensive loans, even when your credit score qualifies you for a better deal.

You're actually most at risk of being taken advantage of if you're right on the cusp of having good credit, say with scores in the 600 to 640 range. Because subprime loans are so profitable for lenders, even if you might be able to qualify for one of Fannie and Freddie's approved loans, an unscrupulous loan officer might stick you into a high-rate subprime loan. If you're in that range, be sure to ask the loan officer to try running your application through the Fannie and Freddie underwriting programs. Make sure you've really been rejected for both programs before you settle for a higher-rate loan.

There are some offsetting factors that can help make you a better credit risk, despite FICO scores that are on the edge. Having a large down payment, maybe 25 or 30 percent of the home's price, is a big one. So is having a significant amount of savings still in the bank after you've closed on the home. A stable job with a good income is another selling point you should highlight for the loan officer.

Remember that everyone has three different FICO scores, based on the credit reports maintained by three separate companies. Which score will your lender chose? It's a critical question if you're on the edge of qualifying for a better loan. According to the Fair Isaac Corp., a lot of lenders simply choose the middle score, but some go with the lowest of the three. Clearly that's not a lender you want to work with. Be sure to know your scores and ask the loan officer which one he or she plans to use.

People with weak credit histories often feel grateful to get any mortgage at all. Don't let an unscrupulous loan officer or mortgage broker take advantage of that gratitude and push you into a bad loan. Remember, loan officers are sales people. You're paying top-dollar on the interest rate, and you can afford to be as pushy and demanding as anyone else.

## Internet or Hometown Lenders?

You should shop both local and Internet mortgage lenders before you decide where you'd like to make your loan application. Mortgages are commodities these days, so you can be fairly ruthless in your quest for the best combination of rates, points, and terms. What you want from a lender is businesslike efficiency and good rates. Keep in mind that even if you work with a local lender, you may end up handling part of the process over the Internet. The last time I refinanced a mortgage, for example, I used the same local lender who had given me our original mortgage. I filled out the application online, answered a few questions over the phone, and followed up with one face-to-face meeting to supply documents. I actually like the comfort of entering my own data into the application. I figure I'm more likely to spot a misplaced decimal point or scrambled account number than a stranger would be.

Start your search broadly. If you belong to a credit union, by all means check out their mortgage offerings. Often they're better deals than you can get elsewhere. Also check the rates and loans offered by the bank that handles your checking account. They may offer a slight break to current customers. Take a peek also at the offerings of one or two other local lenders. Search online as well. Take a look at loans offered by some of the big online lenders, including *www.countrywide.com* (which also has local store-front offices), *www.eloan.com*, *www.gmacmortgage.com*, and *www.wellsfargo.com/mortgage*.

Don't get sentimental about the idea of doing business with a hometown bank or with the idea of keeping all your business at one institution. The odds are high that shortly after you close on the loan, the loan itself will be sold off to another company, and the right to service the loan—that is, collect your payments, manage your escrow account, and otherwise take care of your needs—will be sold off to yet a different company. You will have no say in the matter. You'll find more on that in Chapter Nineteen.

Each November, J.D. Power and Associates, a market research company best known for its surveys of consumer satisfactions with automobiles, releases a survey of consumer satisfaction with mortgage companies. Go online to *www.jdpower.com* to find the latest mortgage survey (along with many others related to personal finance). While they don't survey mortgage lenders' competitiveness with interest rates, they do ask about how happy consumers were with the service they received during the loan application process and after closing. (The hands-down favorite, year after year, has been USAA, a company that offers financial services only to members of the military, veterans, and military families. If you qualify, you can reach the company online at *www.usaa.com*.) It's worthwhile to check out the latest version of the J.D. Power survey, if only to spot which companies rank significantly *below* average in consumer satisfaction.

## Get a Feel for Rates

Take a week to compare how several lenders' interest rates (and points) compare each day. Go ahead and make yourself a little chart. Rates and points are constantly changing. The change might be as small as ⅛ percentage point a day, but they're still always moving. At the end of the week you can see which of the lenders tends to offer a better deal compared to the others.

To be even more complete, you can compare these rates to the average interest rates that are updated each day on *www.hsh.com*. You'll soon know the price of credit as well as you know the price of a gallon of milk and a loaf of whole wheat. And it will become clear that one or two of those lenders tend to have the most competitive rates on most days.

There's one thing to keep in mind about the interest-rate quotes you find in newspaper real estate sections and on some Web sites. The quotes in the newspapers are several days to a week old. Rates can change a lot in just a few days, so they're almost certainly *not* the rate you will be quoted. Second, these rates are come-ons. Sometimes those rock-bottom rates call for paying 3 or more points, and almost always they reflect the rates offered to borrowers with top credit scores. That's why it pays to know your credit scores. Many of the Web sites will give you a customized rate quote based on your credit scores. Take the time to get real rate quotes; don't rely on published "Today's Rates" boxes for guidance.

## Pay Me Now or Pay Me Later: Rates Versus Points

As you track rates, you'll find that one thing blocks easy comparisons: Each lender quotes different combinations of rates and points. But you can compensate for this to make comparison easier.

Points are simply prepaid interest, paid when you close on the mortgage. You don't actually have to fork over cash; often the points are rolled over into the mortgage amount. Basically, that means you're borrowing the money that you will use to pay the very same lender in cash at the closing table. (The lender who dreamed up that scheme certainly must have patted himself on the back with satisfaction. The lender gets cash *plus* interest on the cash.) The only reason for you to agree to such a double-dip plan is because there's a pretty attractive payoff; it can reduce the monthly payment significantly. One point equals 1 percent of the mortgage amount.

Each point shaves ⅛ percentage point off your interest rate, so the more points you pay, the lower your interest rate will be. Even if you end up borrowing the points (that is, rolling them into your loan amount), you reduce your monthly payment.

You may even encounter something called negative points, in which a lender reimburses you money at closing in return for a higher interest rate. Typically, though, loans are quoted with 0 to 3 points.

Mortgage lenders are required to tell you the annualized percentage rate, or APR, on your loan, which translates the interest rate/points combination into a single number that represents the true cost of credit. Unfortunately, the APR isn't as useful a comparison for mortgages as it is for credit cards and other types of loans. That's because most people don't hold on to their mortgage for the full fifteen to thirty years.

To figure out which is the better choice, low points or low interest rate, you have to look at how long you expect to hold on to that mortgage. If you expect to keep that mortgage for only a few years before moving or refinancing, then you want to pay as few points as possible. You wouldn't be around long enough to benefit from the lower interest rate. If you have profit from the sale of your old home that could be put toward points and want to keep your monthly payment as low as possible (especially if you're about to start writing college tuition checks or are going into retirement and need to minimize monthly expenses), then load up on the points and cut your interest rate.

As discussed in Chapter Two, points are tax-deductible for the tax year when you bought a home. (Points paid on a refinance can only be deducted over the life of the loan. So, if you pay 1 point on

## What's the Point?

Consider this example. For simplicity's sake, let's say you want a 30-year fixed-rate loan for $100,000. The lender gives you three choices: A loan with 6 percent interest and 2 points, which would require you to pay the lender $2,000 in cash at closing and $599.60 every month. Your second choice would be to add those points to the loan amount, bumping it up to $102,000. You wouldn't have to pay the lender any cash at closing, but your monthly payment would increase by $11.90 to $611.50. Your third choice would be to accept a loan with a higher interest rate, 6.25 percent, but with 0 points. You would not have to pay the lender at closing but your payment would go up by $4.20 to $615.70. Many loans, of course, are for amounts far greater than $100,000, and that's when the differences between small changes in the interest rate really add up. Notice how adding

a 30-year refinance loan for $200,000, you can deduct one-thirtieth of that $2,000—a whopping $66.67—each year.) New-home builders often offer to pay points to sweeten the deal for buyers. If homes are selling slowly when you happen to be buying, you may have some luck convincing a seller to pay a point or two when you're bargaining over an existing home. From the seller's perspective, there's absolutely no financial difference between cutting $4,000 off the home's price or agreeing to subsidize the buyer for up to 2 points on a loan for $200,000. The seller is out $4,000 either way. But prideful sellers sometimes find it easier to swallow paying points than accepting a lower price. They can brag to the neighbors that they got full price for their home. Remember:

the points to the mortgage amount saves a bit of money each month, compared to accepting a higher interest rate?

The cheapest option, over the long term, would be to pay the 2 points in cash in exchange for the lowest rate. But it's a pretty long time to wait for your payoff, roughly ten years in this example. Here's how you figure out your break-even point. You would save about $16 per month by choosing the 6 percent/2 points combination instead of 6.25 percent/0 points. Take the dollar amount of the points, $2,000, and divide it by the monthly savings, $16, to arrive at the number of months it would take to save enough to make up for the points you paid. That's 124 months or nearly ten and a half years. You have to ask yourself if you will hold on to this mortgage (or even this home) long enough to make the up-front points pay off.

Even if the seller actually pays the points, the buyer always gets the tax deduction.

## Applying for the Loan

Before you even go shopping for a home, you want to have your financing lined up. You wouldn't go to the mall without your wallet, would you? Now that you've singled out one or two lenders who usually offer the best rates, it's time to become preapproved for a mortgage. In hot housing markets, where there may be several buyers competing for the same home, sellers won't even consider an offer from someone who is not preapproved. To get preapproved for a loan, you go through practically all of the loan-application process before you make an offer on a home. You will have to give the lender all your financial information and perhaps pay a loan-application fee. The lender will pull your credit scores. Everything will be complete except for the information on the home itself. Make sure to get that preapproval in writing! Get yourself in the habit of thinking that if it isn't in writing, it doesn't exist. That philosophy will serve you well in every step of the home-purchase process—and to all your future dealings with contractors, repair people, and sales clerks.

Don't settle for getting "prequalified" for a loan. That's a near-meaningless review of your income and debts, with little follow-up. Real estate agents used to do this commonly before they would take you out to look at properties. What you want is a full-blown pre-approval letter from your lender.

## Information Needed for a Loan Application

According to Freddie Mac, you should be prepared to give your lender the following information for *each* borrower:

- Social Security numbers

- Birth dates

- W-2 statements stating your income

- Tax returns for the past two years (particularly if you are self-employed)

- Previous employer contacts. Have names, addresses and telephone numbers for employers going back two years. If you don't have two years' employment history because you were still in school for part of that time, bring your school transcripts or diploma.

- Bank-account statements. Account numbers and current balances for checking, savings, and any other accounts.

- Statement of current assets, including IRAs, CDs, stocks, bonds, mutual funds. A recent brokerage statement is useful.

- Personal property documentation. You may be asked for information on other assets, including cars and boats.

- Loan information, including the name and address of current creditors, such as your auto loan and credit card companies. Know the total amount of debt outstanding for each line of credit, and the monthly payment.

- Current housing information. If you already own a home, be able to estimate its current value (if you have a real estate agent's written estimate of value, an appraisal or tax assessment, bring that). Know the address, phone number, outstanding balance and monthly payment for your current mortgage lender. Bring a copy of your lease, if you're a renter.

- Contract and deposit. As soon as you have a ratified sales contract on your new home, get that and copies of receipts for the earnest-money deposit you offered the seller when you presented your offer to buy the home.

- Gift letter. If you're getting down payment money from a relative or employer, you need a letter verifying that the money really is a gift, and does not have to be paid back.

- Profit-and-loss statements for the past two years if you're self-employed.

- Divorce decree or maintenance agreement, along with amendments, if you're divorced or separated. If money you receive for child support or alimony will help you qualify for the mortgage, you should bring a 12-month history of those payments. (Regular deposits on your bank statement can help verify that payment history.)

- Current lease and a complete copy of your federal tax return, plus the account number for your mortgage and the name and address of the lender, if you own rental properties.

The more documentation you have handy, the faster your loan application will be approved. The lender will pull your credit reports and scores. You may be asked to pay a nonrefundable loan-application fee of $50 or $60. But check out those fees before you apply. Some lenders, including big Internet companies, such as *www.Eloan.com* and *www.Countrywide.com,* don't charge any application fees, but others can be quite high — Citibank recently required a $250 nonrefundable fee, for example.

## The Fee Circus

Before you finally choose a mortgage lender and pay an application fee, ask a few questions about the whole range of fees that lender charges on a mortgage loan. In addition to points, some lenders charge a loan-origination fee. From the borrower's perspective, this fee is the same as points. The loan origination fee is tax-deductible, as are points. When you read lenders' rate quotes, check to see that their quote of "7 percent and 0 points" doesn't carry a 1 or 2 percent origination fee.

When you apply for a mortgage, the lender is supposed to give you (or mail within three days) a form known as a good-faith estimate, which is supposed to be a reasonably reliable preview of the closing costs involved with the transaction. Some lenders pile on dubious fees for photocopying, document delivery, everything but their takeout lunch bill, while others pare the fees down to those absolutely required to move the transaction along, such as those for the appraisal and title search. Of course, you want to pay as few fees as possible, as long as the lender's rates and points are good as well.

Unfortunately, there isn't always a lot of good faith put into the good faith estimate. The numbers you finally see on the closing documents can be quite a bit higher than those disclosed in the estimate—and there's no government penalty in place to halt the practice. Certainly, some numbers can change legitimately. Your property taxes, for example, will be prorated according to your closing date. But there's little to prevent lenders from springing extra fees on you at closing. Much like the back-office guy at the auto showroom who sells you high-profit, unnecessary rust-proofing at the last minute, some lenders pad their profits with pure-profit, unnecessary junk fees.

## Avoiding Unnecessary Fees

There are two ways lenders can pad fees: by charging important-sounding processing fees, and by inflating the amount they pass along to you for a legitimate service, such as for pulling your credit report. *www.Bankrate.com*, an excellent Web site that publishes daily interest rates for mortgages and other types of credit, surveyed 306 good-faith estimates from lenders doing business in all fifty states and the District of Columbia. They compared fees for a loan of $180,000 with a 20 percent down payment and found the average loan had fees totaling $3,350. But, oh the difference it makes in choosing a lender! The cheapest tally for fees was $1,020, some $2,330 less than average. What was truly shocking, however, was what their survey found to be the most fee-infested bill. That tally hit $11,395, some $8,045 more than average. Same loan, same down payment, same hypothetical borrower.

Don't panic. Nobody expects you to know the actual price of every single service that goes into putting a loan transaction together. Simply keep an eye out for some of the telltale signs of fee gouging, and feel free to demand answers of your loan officer. Appendix Five lists a typical range for closing costs that you can use as a comparison.

Here are a few areas to give special attention:

- Question fees for "document preparation," "processing," "funding," "administration," and "underwriting." These are the lender's back-office expenses, and if you are paying a 1- to 2-point loan-origination fee, they should already be covered. You may be able, at least, to negotiate them lower.

- Be dubious about inflated fees if those familiar to you seem unexpectedly high on your good-faith estimate. For example, if you know that anybody can get their credit report for about $15, why would a high-volume lender (who presumably could get a discount on credit reports) charge you more? If the fee for termite inspection looks unreasonably high, whip out your mobile phone—right there at the closing table, if necessary—and call the exterminator to double-check for a "mistake."

- Save your good-faith estimate and take it to closing. Compare the final list of fees to those on that estimate, and challenge any brand-new ones. They *may* be legitimate, but they may not be. Remember, the lender wants to wrap up this deal as much as you do, and you're entitled to a reasonable explanation of everything you pay for.

- Take advantage of your right to choose who will handle the closing of your mortgage. (You'll make that choice after you have a contract on the home.) Look for a closing agent that promises good service and low fees; you'll find one the same way you find a good dentist or hair stylist, by asking around. Ask for recommendations from your loan officer and real estate agent and especially from friends who've bought homes or refinanced recently. (You'll find more on closing in Chapters Seventeen and Eighteen.)

## Once You're Preapproved

Once you're preapproved, the only thing lacking is information about the property itself. You'll supply that after a seller has accepted your offer to buy his or her home. The lender will insist on an appraisal and a title search (to verify that the seller actually is the legal owner of the home) before finally making the loan. The lender then will commit to giving you a loan up to a top-dollar amount. Everything is ready to go once you find the house and get it appraised. Be sure to nail down how long your preapproval will remain valid. Six months is common, and lenders usually will extend that period at your request.

Finally, don't do anything drastic with your finances—like buy a car or quit your job—after you have the preapproval letter in hand!

Lenders will usually take another peek at your credit just before you go to closing, and you can't afford to mess it up now.

## How Many Loan Applications?

Your strategy should be to shop a lot and then apply to only a few lenders, and preferably to only one. Aside from the nonrefundable fees that some lenders charge for a preapproval, there's another reason you need to be careful about applying with many different lenders. Every time you apply for credit, the inquiry is noted on your credit report, and too many inquiries will scare off lenders who fear you're about to plunge deep into debt. Mortgage loan inquiries made within a two-week period are counted as only one transaction, so if you're going to apply to more than one lender, stay within that two-week limit. They know you may be shopping for the best loan. But don't even think about going to the car dealer to take the new models out for a test drive during the weeks when you're shopping for a home and a loan. The car salesman will pull your credit when you go on that test drive—and such inquiries could nudge up your mortgage interest rate. And when the department store sales clerk asks if you'd like to save 10 percent on your bill by opening a new credit card account, politely say no. This is not the time to muddy up your credit record. (Getting your free credit reports from the government, or pulling your own FICO scores does not hurt your record.)

By all means, switch to a different lender if your first choice disappoints you with poor service or tries to spring surprise fees. But take your time choosing which lender to ask for a preapproval. Doing business with just one is the fastest, easiest and usually, cheapest way.

## Locking in Your Interest Rate

When you have a contract in hand on the house you intend to buy, you will contact your lender again to get things moving on your preapproved loan. You'll face the big question: Do you want to lock in your interest rate, or let it float? And the only way to answer that question is with another question: Do you like to gamble?

Not a soul on Earth can predict changes in interest rates with any accuracy (though that doesn't stop people from trying). Most of the economists I've talked to over the years cringe when asked about interest rates. They know it's a crapshoot. Here's how to make your decision about whether you should roll the dice:

- If even a slight rise in interest rates could keep you from qualifying for your mortgage, lock in the rate immediately.

- If worrying about the daily ups and downs of interest rates causes you to lose sleep at night, lock in your rate.

- If it would grate on you for years that you didn't nab the very lowest rate, and your gambler's gut tells you rates are going to go down, let it float.

In other words, it's all about you and your tolerance for risk. In most cases, it's wise to lock in early and make sure your loan goes to closing before that lock expires.

Most lenders will lock your rate for 30–60 days or so without charge. For longer lock periods, you'll have to pay as much as 1 point for the security. That can be a wise move, however, for people buying homes still under construction, because finish dates are always at the mercy of the weather and other complications.

It's especially important to be clear about your intentions to lock a rate when you're dealing with a mortgage broker. After all, it's the *lender* who is locking the rate, not the broker. Unfortunately, brokers sometimes promise locks they can't deliver when rates start rising. Always get your lock confirmation in writing—and push everyone to the closing table in a hurry if your closing bumps up against your expiration date. It's not unheard of for lenders to drag their feet on closings when rates are rising and rate-lock commitments are about to expire. They stand to profit quite a bit from dallying.

## Razzi's Rules to Live By

### 🏠 Shopping is shopping.

The process of finding the right home, the right mortgage, the right insurance policy is fundamentally the same as finding the right business suit or new car. Figure out what you need; zero in on what you really want; scour the marketplace to find out what's available; brace yourself for sales pitches; choose the most appropriate, comfortable option; hold out for the best price.

### 🏠 There are many lenders competing for your business.

It's true even if you have a weak credit history. Shop aggressively.

### 🏠 Never forget the loan officer is a salesperson.

He or she wants to sell you a mortgage, the larger the better.

### 🏠 A mortgage broker is not necessarily searching for the best loan for you.

He or she may point you toward the loan that earns him or her the biggest fee.

### 🏠 Get your FICO credit scores and your credit reports.

Do it at least six months before you shop for a mortgage, so you have time to fix mistakes.

### 🏠 Resist being pushed into a loan for high-risk borrowers.

You're most at risk of being taken advantage of if your credit scores are between 600 and 640. Unscrupulous lenders may push you into a loan for high-risk borrowers because it earns them more profit.

### 🏠 Ask which of your three FICO scores the lender will use.

Do they routinely use the highest, middle, or lowest score (based on reports from the three different credit bureaus)? If your credit is questionable, obviously you will want to avoid those that go with the lowest score.

### 🏠 Track interest rates every day for a week.

You'll learn to recognize a good deal when you see it.

### 🏠 Don't pay points if you expect to move in a few years.

You won't benefit from the lower payments long enough to recover the upfront cost.

### 🏠 Get preapproved for a mortgage.

Get your loan lined up before you even start shopping for a home.

### 🏠 Compare lenders' fees as well as the points and interest rates they quote.

Later, at closing, compare the actual fees they charge with their good-faith estimate and question anything that's unexpected. Go ahead, be a pest—at least until lenders display a little more good faith in their good-faith estimates!

## 🏠 Never click on an e-mail link to a financial-services company.

Con artists can whisk you off to a fake Web site that looks very convincing, complete with familiar logos, brand names, and slogans. *Always* type in the Web address yourself before you disclose any sensitive financial information over the Internet.

## 🏠 If it isn't in writing, it doesn't exist.

Make sure to get your loan preapproval in writing, along with any other assurances from lenders and sales people.

## 🏠 Guard your interest-rate lock.

Make sure your lock lasts long enough for you to close, get the commitment in writing, and push everybody to close before it expires.

# CHAPTER FIVE

# Special Challenges for the Move-up Buyer

"I thought you would never come back to this horrible place! What am I saying? I didn't mean to say that. I meant to be nice about it and say—Oh what a convenient location and such."

TENNESSEE WILLIAMS, *A Streetcar Named Desire*

YOU MIGHT FIND YOURSELF LONGING FOR THE DAYS when you were a renter. Sure, it may have been a struggle to get together the money for a down payment and closing costs on your first home, but when you finally found the right deal, all you had to do was give notice to the landlord and be on your way. Not so when you're a move-up buyer. You have the nest egg for a down payment now—namely, the built-up equity in your current home—but everything else is so much more complicated!

Your first obstacle is inertia. Unless there's job relocation or other life event that forces you into the housing market, you're making this jump entirely at will. You want more space, better schools, a shorter commute, or perhaps more prestige. But there's probably something you really love about your current home and will hate to give up. The last thing you want to do is take on a bigger payment for a new home that is not substantially better than the old one. And, heaven forbid, what if it turns out to be worse?

Then there's the ultimate fear: What if a buyer snaps up your lovely current home and you can't find anything decent to move into?

## Buy First or Sell First?

It's the classic move-up dilemma: Which should you do first, buy the new home or sell the old one? The way you work through that problem will depend on your finances and on local market conditions.

In a world made perfect for every home buyer, you would be able to sell the old house but make the deal contingent on your finding a suitable replacement home. In a strong seller's market—where there are many more buyers than homes available for sale—you may get away with it. Be sure to get that contingency clause into the sales contract *before* you sign your acceptance.

In a balanced market, on the other hand, it would be rare for buyers to agree to put their deal on hold while you shop. Conversely, if your local real estate market is so weak that you as a seller are desperate to find *any* willing and able buyer, you're not going to be foolish enough to try to win such a juicy contingency. At the same time, you will have some negotiating clout when purchasing the new home. You might be able to make your purchase contingent on your ability to unload the old one. That's a pretty feeble deal you're offering the seller—resting on your ability to sell your old house in that same weak market—and it could easily fall through if a more stable buyer comes along and offers the seller a better deal.

You may need to buy before you sell, if you're determined not to give up your current home unless you find just the right move-up place. You face a very real possibility of having to pay mortgages on both homes for awhile, but if you have some built up equity and room in your monthly budget, you can pull it off.

## Bridge Loans and Other Helps

A bridge loan can allow you to dip into your current home equity to make the down payment on your new home. One of the easiest ways to do this is to set up a home-equity line of credit at a bank. Typically, these loans charge the prime interest rate plus a 1 percentage point markup. They allow you to make interest-only payments during the early years of the loan. Banks compete heavily for these loans and may offer to pick up all your closing costs (which add up to a couple of hundred dollars). However, if you pay off the line of credit within a year or two of taking it out (as you almost certainly will if you're using the line of credit as your bridge loan), they will demand that you reimburse them for those charges.

# Why It's So Hard to Move up From a Nice Townhouse

Townhouses offer tremendous value for the money. Whether they're modest starter homes or stately residences geared to forty- and fifty-year-olds in their peak earning years, townhouses give owners the most house for the least cash because very little of the investment is going into land. And land is expensive.

But moving from a nice townhouse to a nice detached home with a yard can be tricky. Something has to give. Remember, around most metropolitan areas you can have your choice of two—and only two—of three things: low price, big wonderful house, or short commute. You *can* get a wonderful, big house with a short commute, but it will be very expensive. You *can* get a low price and wonderful, big house, but you will have to live far away from jobs in the city. You *can* get an affordable house with a short commute, but you can be sure it will be very small and perhaps in disrepair. In many cases, it's a condo apartment or a modest townhouse.

Unless you're willing to move farther out into the suburbs (or perhaps into rural towns beyond the suburbs), you will be forced to pay much, much more for a house with a yard that has the same living space and amenities that you've grown used to in a townhouse. Moving farther into the suburbs may be just what you're after—they're many people's ideal for a place to raise a family. Safe schools, quiet cul-de-sacs, roomy houses, and big lawns remain, for many, the picture of the American Dream.

But if you like the convenience of in-town (or close-to-town) living, you'll have to make some compromises when moving to a detached house from a townhouse. You may have to accept an older house with fewer closets, fewer electrical outlets, and smaller rooms. (It may require remodeling, eventually, to get the conveniences to which you've grown accustomed.) Or you could simply pay a whole lot more money to get the same amenities in a close-in address. Remember, it's two of the three, and only two.

## The Kid Perspective

You might not be alone when you hunt for a move-up house. If you have children who are at least old enough to talk, they're going to want a say in where you live. Even if they're destined to move out of the nest in a year or two, they want a say. (They also want a guarantee that their bedrooms will become eternal shrines to their childhood.) Certainly you want to hang on to your adult prerogative to make decisions, but you'd be wise to at least consider what they have to say. Kids pick up on things adults often miss.

You might even give your children some age-appropriate tasks in your house hunt. They might check out the back yard, for example, or report on whether the neighbors have barking dogs. Ask them to size up each house in terms of how they would use it. Where would they set up the computer? do homework? lay out a Hot Wheels track? work on crafts? hang out with friends?

Listen to the kids, of course, but do *not* let them drive your decision. Kids can be more conservative and resistant to change than the worst adult stick-in-the mud. (One friend of mine says his kids claimed the food tasted better in their old house.) Then, once the decision is made and they've settled in, they might turn around and say the new house they criticized so vehemently is now the greatest place in the world. They're kids—and kids do that. You're the grownup, and grownups make the hard decisions.

Meanwhile, as the grownup, you'll want to apply your seasoned judgment to the things that will be important to them. The quality of local schools, of course, is paramount, and is covered fully in Chapter Eight.

But other amenities count, too. Is the yard fenced? If not, and you would like to add a fence after you move in, make sure they're not prohibited by a homeowners' association (HOA) or local zoning laws. While you're at it, check to make sure the kids' basketball hoop is not prohibited by a homeowners' association. Some associations even squawk if the kids leave their toys and bicycles in the driveway too long. Are there parks, swimming pools, and playgrounds nearby? Can older kids walk or bicycle to anything? Are there hazards nearby, like water retention ponds or busy highways? Finally, pay attention to traffic as you drive home from your visit. Would you (and your kids) have to cross a death-defying intersection every time you left the neighborhood?

## The New Rules for Capital Gains

Since 1997, the tax laws have allowed home owners to sell their main residence (as long as they've lived there for two of the five years leading up to the sale) and keep a huge chunk of the profit tax-free. Married couples can rack up as much as $500,000 tax-free; singles get up to $250,000. It doesn't matter if you sell the house and move into a more expensive mansion or a less expensive cottage or even a rental apartment. Heck, you could pitch a tent in the woods and call that home. The profit is yours, tax-free. And you can take advantage of this wonderful tax break as often as once every two years.

But the old tax rules were in effect for many, many years, and they still linger in the back of the minds of many people. It used to be that the only way to shield your capital gain from a home sale was to buy a more expensive home and roll your profit over into that. Once—and only once—in a lifetime could you downsize to a smaller home and shield some of the profit from taxes. The old law put an awful lot of pressure on people approaching or in the early years of retirement. You had one chance to downsize, and you didn't want to do it prematurely and then face a big tax bill if you needed to move to an even less expensive home (or a rental) sometime later. Rest assured, the old law is dead, dead, dead. The tax collector has very little say now in how expensive your next home must be.

## Preserving Future Profit by Moving Now

But with the huge run-up in housing values in recent years, half a million dollars in home-sale profit ain't the huge sum it used to be. If you've been a homeowner for many years and, under the old tax rules, you rolled your profit over from previous home sales into your current home, you might want to look at selling just to preserve future home appreciation from taxes.

Here's how it works: Say you owned a couple of homes before the tax laws changed in 1997. Looking back, it's amazing how little you paid for your very first home. Over the years, property values rose steadily, and you ended up with $250,000 of capital gains (or profit) from all your previous sales. Back in 1996 (or earlier), when you bought your current home, the tax laws dictated that you roll that profit over into the new one. You do that with a process called adjusting your basis. Let's take a closer look at that example. Say you paid $500,000 for your lovely home in 1996, before the new tax rule took effect. (For simplicity's sake, let's say you bought it without any down payment.) For tax purposes, you had to roll over your $250,000 from the sale of your old home into the new home. On paper, you reduced the investment in your new home by that $250,000 profit you racked up from various home sales over the years. Because you shrunk the cost of your new home ($500,000 minus $250,000) you have what's called an "adjusted basis" of $250,000. As a result, you'll reap a bigger profit (at least on paper) when you sell.

Let's also assume prices in your neighborhood have soared since 1996, and that lovely home is now worth $750,000. If you were to sell now, your capital gain would be $500,000 ($750,000 minus your adjusted basis of $250,000)—for simplicity's sake, we'll assume you didn't give up some of your profit to a real estate agent's commission. You and your spouse could shelter every penny of that half-million dollar profit from taxes. But what if property values keep rising? What if you sell five years from now, when your home's value is $10,000 higher? You can expect to pay capital gains tax on that full $10,000. It might be in your financial interest to sell now and reset the meter on your capital gains so future profits will be tax-free as well.

## Moving from the Too-Big House

Many homeowners find themselves heading into retirement with more house than they really need or want. One reason for the huge boom in sales of homes and condos in vacation spots and retirement communities is the growing number of mature homeowners, who have been selling off their big homes close to the city and reinvesting the money in one (or two!) smaller homes in less expensive communities. They get a lower-maintenance home (especially if they go into a condo apartment or a townhouse), a more comfortable lifestyle, *and*, sometimes, money in the bank.

# Razzi's Rules to Live By

### 🏠 A bridge will take you there.
If you're truly determined not to give up your current home unless you find the perfect replacement, you may have to buy first. A bridge loan (often simply a home-equity line of credit) can help you make the jump.

### 🏠 It's tough to get out of a townhouse.
Townhouses offer a lot of house for the money (because you own so little land), and it can be difficult to find a detached house that offers a comparable lifestyle. You may have to settle for less house, a longer commute, or a very high price.

### 🏠 Kids see the darndest things.
Children can spot things about a new home or neighborhood that you might miss. Listen to their opinions—but don't let them drive the decision.

### 🏠 You might not believe what's "verboten" at your own home.
Check to see if a homeowners' association or local zoning laws prohibit something important to your family, like a fenced yard or basketball hoops.

### 🏠 You can keep your cash.
Forget the old "rollover" rules. Old tax laws that required you to buy ever-more-expensive homes to shelter your profit are dead, dead, dead. You can now pocket up to $500,000 as a married couple or $250,000 as a single as often as every two years without paying tax on that home-sale profit.

# hunting for your new home

# CHAPTER SIX

# What Kind of Home? Special Issues to Consider

"I walked closer and stared at the house that would be my home for the rest of my life. The house had been in the family for many generations. It was not really so old or remarkable, but I could see it had grown up along with the family."

AMY TAN, *The Joy Luck Club*

A YOUNG CHILD'S DRAWING OF A HOME looks pretty much like the drawing made by any other child the same age. They draw a face, basically, with two upstairs windows for eyes and a front-door mouth. A peaked roof and chimney make a jaunty chapeau with feather. They may even give it little arms and legs, just to drive home the point. While we all start out with a similar vision of home, we grow up to a wide range of accommodations from which we choose to make home. This includes apartment condominiums and cooperatives, townhouses and rowhouses (as the in-city version of townhouses are still known), partially attached homes and, finally, that original vision, the detached single-family home proudly dominating its own front and back yards.

You may notice I tend to use the word "home" throughout this book, rather than the word "house." Many real estate agents do the same in the hope of conjuring up warm hearthside feelings (and opening the buyers' pocketbooks). I choose to use the word for a different reason, namely because it encompasses all these different version of shelter in which we live today. A tenth-story apartment condo is every bit as much a home as a brick house in the suburbs. By living in it, decorating it, and welcoming our friends and families into it, we make the place our home. Let's review the different types available in most markets.

# Condominiums and Co-ops

Normally we think of a condo or a co-op as being an apartment that you own rather than rent. But the words actually refer to a form of ownership. A condo or co-op can be an apartment, a townhouse, or even a detached house. In fact, you'll often find these latter forms as condos in resort or retirement developments.

## What Is a Condominium?

Condominium refers to a form of ownership in which you own and hold title to the interior of a specific residence. You own the interior of a condo apartment, for example, including the floor and the ceiling and the indoor face of the walls, which you are free to carpet or paint or wallpaper as you wish. The condo association owns the roof and the exterior walls, the plumbing and wiring inside those walls, the sidewalk and shrubs outside, plus any common facilities, such as the gym or pool. (Your condo documents will detail *exactly* what you own—and therefore are responsible for repairing—versus what the association owns and must maintain.)

As a unit owner, you belong to that condo association and own a fraction of those common facilities. Each owner is assessed a condominium fee (also called a maintenance fee), usually paid monthly, which pays for upkeep of common areas, pool management and lifeguards, property taxes, insurance premiums owed on the common areas and, usually, the services of a property manager who keeps it all running smoothly. In fact, give the condo some bonus points for hiring a professional property manager; you really don't want amateurs (that is, you and your neighbors) trying to manage a big property in their spare time. Your property value is at stake!

Pay very close attention to association fees when you're weighing the purchase of a condo. (The same is true of homeowners' associations, where you own your home and yard completely, but pay into a pool to manage common neighborhood areas.) They can be hefty, especially if the development boasts a lot of common-area features such as pools, gyms, playgrounds, tennis courts, clubhouses, or full-time security people. And there's no limit on how high your fees might rise over the years. While you could lock-down your mortgage payment for three decades with a low-interest mortgage, your association fee could ratchet higher year after year.

And if your association doesn't manage its money carefully, you can be hit with special assessments to pay for big repairs. Unlike your mortgage interest, condo and homeowner association fees are *not* tax-deductible.

## What Is a Co-op?

Cooperatives, known as co-ops, are a bit different. First, they aren't as common as condos. You'll run across some elsewhere, but New York City is the undisputed national champion of co-op living. Still, many cities are seeing increased development of limited-equity co-ops designed to provide affordable housing for people with modest incomes.

In the cooperative form of ownership, whether it's a high-priced apartment building on the Upper West Side of Manhattan or a limited-equity co-op apartment in Chicago, you don't actually own the unit in which you live. Instead, you own shares in the corporation that owns the building, and ownership of those shares gives you the right to live in a particular unit.

## Becoming a Co-op Member

Buying a co-op can be tricky. You don't just *buy* a co-op. You *apply for membership* in the corporation that owns and manages an apartment building or complex. Essentially, you are going into business with the other owners of that building. If any of the partners turns deadbeat, a portion of that person's bills will land at the other partners' feet. In evaluating you as a potential partner in that business, board members can—and will—ask to see your financial statements. They can—and will—interview you before deciding whether to let you in. They'll want references. They may demand that you make a large down payment. With an expensive market-rate co-op, boards are famous for turning down applicants if their financials aren't lustrous enough, if their Yorkies yap too much, or if the applicants are so famous that their entourage could threaten other owners' peace and quiet. Federal fair housing laws say co-op boards are not supposed to discriminate on the basis of race, religion, nationality, or family status, but it's more difficult to pin down an illegal act of housing discrimination when a co-op board is legally entitled to reject you on a whim.

Exclusivity is what makes some co-op lovers love their buildings. The same exclusivity, however, can make it much more difficult for you to sell your co-op when it's time to move on. Not only do you have to find a willing and able buyer, but that buyer has to pass the co-op board gauntlet before the deal goes through. In fact, if you belong to a notoriously picky co-op, their tendency to reject buyers could even limit your property's price gains in the future.

As a co-op owner, you will pay interest on your own mortgage, which is the "share loan" you take out to pay for your shares in the co-op. You also will pay a monthly maintenance fee to cover your portion of the building's expenses, including property taxes and the underlying mortgage the corporation has taken out to pay for the building. At the end of the year, you'll get a statement from the co-op board detailing what your share of the property taxes and interest were, which you then can claim as an income-tax deduction.

It will be in your interest to be involved with your co-op's board of directors and its committees, just to make sure the property remains at least at the same level of quality as when you bought into it. When you sell a market-rate co-op, you get to keep all the capital gain that has built up since you bought your shares.

## Benefits of Co-op Ownership

Once you're in, owning a co-op gives you most of the same benefits of ownership that you get with any other type of owned residence. You get a tax deduction for mortgage interest and property taxes (including the interest on your share loan and your portion of the building's mortgage interest and property taxes). You qualify for that wonderful tax break that allows married couples to keep as much as $500,000 in home-sale profits tax-free and singles to keep up to $250,000.

## Financing a Co-op

You may fare best if you go to a lender that specializes in co-op financing. Because your collateral for the loan will be your shares in the corporation, the lender will want to review the corporation's financials to make sure there's real value there. Your loan will be referred to as a "share loan," a "co-op mortgage," a "co-op apartment loan," or "end-unit financing." One good place to look for financing (and for more information about co-ops) is the National Cooperative Bank, based in Washington, D.C. (online at *www.ncb.com*). Another good source of information is the National Association of Housing Cooperatives (*www.coophousing.org*).

Because you're buying into a fairly complicated business when you buy into a co-op, you really need to pick apart the governing documents, financial statements, and minutes of previous board meetings. If the corporation has committed itself to a balloon mortgage (with a big balance due in the future) or it doesn't actually own the land underneath the building and instead holds a lease that someday will expire—yes, people build multimillion dollar structures on rented land!—you could be buying into a big liability. If the board is about to launch a fabulous remodeling of the lobby, guess who's going to be expected to help pay the bill? If you're not completely comfortable doing such a due diligence investigation by yourself, you really should pay a lawyer or accountant to review the documents for you. Real estate agents can be helpful advisors, but never forget their real role in this deal: They're sales people who have a motive for you to say yes to the investment.

## Limited-Equity Co-ops

Limited-equity co-ops are quite different from their fancy market-rate kin. Limited-equity co-ops are designed to be a way for people with low or moderate incomes to become homeowners, especially in expensive cities. Often they're organized by community development activists who using government and private grants to acquire an apartment building. Existing renters in that building and others are given an opportunity to buy shares in the co-op. Although residents own their co-op home, their ability to profit from owning is limited; resale value of their shares most likely is capped by the corporation's bylaws. The idea is not for one resident to ride a wave of property appreciation and make a windfall profit, but rather to keep a building as part of the community's affordable housing stock and enable residents to enjoy well-run, affordable housing for the long term.

## Common Condo/Co-op Concerns

There are several things you should consider before buying into a condo or co-op. If it is an older building, originally intended to contain rental apartments, it may not have been built with the soundproofing in the walls and floors that you'll find in newer buildings. That's especially true of the many buildings that were converted from rental apartments to condos during the 1970s and 1980s. Many of these buildings were built cheaply in the first place, with little attention to niceties like insulation for sound and heat retention. It's bad enough to live in a noisy, drafty apartment for a year or two, but do you really want to own one?

Excess sound may very well be the number-one peeve of apartment owners! When shopping for your unit, try to visit in the early evening, when most residents are home. Listen for sounds of footsteps, blaring televisions, and flushing toilets. Storage space (particularly for your unwieldy stuff) can be another issue. Is there space available to you in the basement, perhaps? Also take a good look at security available for you and your car. You want to see that there's someone or something in place to keep strangers out, even in a safe neighborhood! How do they handle package deliveries when you're not home? Give extra points to doorman or concierge services—they go a long way in providing the carefree lock-it and leave-it lifestyle so attractive to condo and co-op owners.

If you're moving into an amenity-laden community, be prepared to pay high fees. That's especially true if your condo or co-op association is small, because there will be only a few members to share bills for the services of a doorman or on-site superintendent, swimming pool maintenance, elevator repairs or lobby decorations. Remember, high maintenance fees to pay for amenities can drive off buyers and hold down your resale value. On the other hand, amenities make life so much more comfortable.

You'd be wise to take a look at the various rules put in place by the condo or co-op board. Associations have different personalities—

permissive to rigid—and you'll be happiest in one that mirrors your own. You may find a host of rules governing how long visitors can stay with residents, the type of furniture allowed on balconies and patios, allowable window coverings, appropriate hours for moving-in or moving-out, allowable house pets and other particulars. Only you can decide if the rules strike you as reassuring or repressive.

A huge concern for people planning to live in a condo or co-op is the number of renters living in the development. It's not that renters are riff-raff; it's fundamentally a matter of money. Absentee owners who rent their units out to others usually aren't as diligent about going to association meetings and volunteering on committees—and their renters aren't going to participate either. (Renters don't get to vote.) Some landlord-owners will fight *any* extra expenditures for maintenance or improvements because they cut into their bottom line. Tenants may resist complying with association rules that they don't like, say, those prohibiting them from storing bicycles on balconies. They're more likely to neglect small fix-it jobs, perhaps allowing a stuck toilet valve to someday cause a flood that damages neighboring units. These nuisances can make your condo or co-op feel an awful lot like a rental apartment, except it's an apartment into which you've invested a lot of your hard-earned money. Values tend not to appreciate as fast when a complex is filled with renters.

Not least, there's a very direct financial effect of having too many renters in your condo or co-op building. Once the share of renters reaches about 30 percent, lenders will balk at making new mortgage loans in the complex. They're worried about their equity (also known as your property value) declining as the building starts to take on a rental atmosphere. If you need to sell, your prospective buyers could have trouble getting financing! Always check the renter/owner ratio when you're reviewing the association's legal documents. If the renter share is approaching 30 percent, beware of buying.

## Townhouses

Townhouses (also known as rowhouses in their older, in-city incarnation) can be owned either as a condo or co-op, or they can be owned 100 percent inside and out, just like a detached house. Ask your real estate agent (and confirm the information when you read the association documents) about just where your ownership starts and ends. You need to know if in coming years you can expect to pay for roof repairs and repainting, or whether that will be paid for through the association. Even if you own the whole thing without any condominium setup, you most likely will be part of a homeowners' association (especially if it's a newer development) that tends to the streets, trash and snow removal, parking lots, and other common needs.

Townhouses are popular because they're a wonderful compromise. You get most of the benefits of owning a detached single-family house (especially if you own an end unit) without the expense of buying a lot of pricey land. (And the less land you own, the less weekend time you must spend on mowing and weeding!) They can be as roomy as a detached house, complete with garage and a small, private yard or patio. In fact, townhouses often have more luxurious finishes than nearby houses in the same price range, because more of the money goes into the *inside*, and not into acreage.

## Purchase Considerations

Before buying, though, there are a few things to consider. If you have an interior unit in a long row of houses, you may have to walk around the block just to get from the front yard to the back. (My husband carried his garden hose through our old townhouse so frequently that I bought him a special compact hose on a reel, just to keep things tidy.) Interior units can be dark unless they are very well designed with well-placed windows. Soundproofing in common walls dividing you from your neighbors is another small detail that will go a long way toward making you a happy owner.

You also should review parking arrangements carefully. Surprisingly, parking problems can be worse in places in which each townhouse has its own garage. All those driveways take away a lot of curbside parking. When applying for a building permit, the developer may have counted on owners parking one car in the garage and one in the driveway. (Owners in these neighborhoods often prefer to put their extra car in a guest space—leading to tight parking.) Just make sure there are enough spaces for you—and for your guests.

## The Quarter-Acre Land Baron

When you purchase a freestanding home with its own front and back yards, you take on a tiny portion of the joys and tribulations of land ownership that our ancestors knew back on the farm. You can make a hobby out of raising lush lawns and the kind of tomatoes that don't exist in grocery stores (namely, ripe ones). You may also be taking on the need to concern yourself with proper drainage, the health of tall trees, and the constant threat that nature, in all its glorious forms ranging from mold to white-tailed deer, will set up housekeeping on your land, welcome or not.

That potential for growing things (and a bit of distance from your neighbors) is one of the reasons Americans have so loved the house in the suburbs or the country. But you owe it to yourself to check out the land as well as the house. That's true if you're buying a quarter-acre in the 'burbs, but it's absolutely critical when your little spot of land actually amounts to acreage.

Walk the property. Look for mushy spots in the yard or extraordinarily green patches of lawn. Those are both potential signs that a septic tank needs attention, and that's a costly proposition you want to avoid. Regardless of apparent problems (or the apparent lack of problems), you should have the tank inspected before you close the deal. If you're buying undeveloped land in the country (or an old home that you intend to tear down and replace with a bigger one), make absolutely sure the land can handle the size septic system you will need. Pay for your own "perc" test by an evaluator who is licensed in your area. (Local zoning or health-department officials can to tell you how to find an evaluator who is qualified in that jurisdiction.) That test measures how easily fluid drains from the soil and therefore whether the land can accommodate a septic system. It's a do-or-die factor in determining whether you are allowed to build a home on that land. A successful perc test decides whether you're buying a home site in the country—or your own little bit of perpetual park land.

If you're buying waterfront land with thoughts of docking your boat along your shore, confirm for yourself how deep the water is. Take a stick and measure the water's depth, just to make sure. You shouldn't rely on the word of the seller or the real estate agent.

Check the condition of fences and retaining walls to be sure their repair bill won't land on your lap. If the property has mature trees, especially if they're close to the house, it may be worthwhile to add a contingency to your purchase offer allowing you to have a licensed tree surgeon evaluate their health before you commit to buying the home.

A seller is supposed to tell you, and your title search company is supposed to discover when researching the history of the land's ownership, any easements that will affect your use and ownership of the property. Easements are legal restrictions recorded on the title that give someone else, say a neighbor, a utility company, or a government agency, the right to use your land. A landowner behind your home might not have access to the street, for example, but he or she may have an easement granting the right to drive over your property to reach the street. The gas company may have an easement allowing it to run its gas line along the edge of your land—and allowing the company to bring in a backhoe and dig up your land to fix a leak. Easements reduce the value of your land, and you have a right to know about them when you're negotiating the price.

## Owners' Associations: The Clubs You Can't Quit

Before you move into any neighborhood governed by a community association—including detached homes in a neighborhood governed by a homeowners' association, as well as townhouses and apartments owned separately or as condos or co-ops—it's critical that you review the association's financial statements as well as its governing documents, known as "Codes, Covenants, and Restrictions," or CCRs. Sure, they're boring, but associations are clubs you can't quit, and belonging to a badly run association can make your life miserable. Some jurisdictions require that buyers have two or three days to review those documents, during which they can back out of their purchase contract. Just in case yours doesn't, it's wise to write a contingency into your purchase contract allowing two or three days for you to review and approve of the documents. Community associations typically charge $100 or more for a set of documents.

## Codes, Covenants, and Restrictions (CCRs)

You don't have to be a certified public accountant to evaluate the association's financial statement and CCRs (most are less complicated than co-op documents). Basically, you want to see that the association has been spending something regularly on maintenance. You especially want to see that the association consistently has been accumulating a reserve fund for major repairs and replacements. Roads, sidewalks, and clubhouse air conditioners all wear out—at fairly predictable rates, too. A well-run association will have a plan to replace roofs over any commonly owned buildings every so many years, depending on the roof material and climate, for example, and will be setting aside some money each year to pay for it. But not all associations are run well and yours may lack those funds, raising the odds that you will get hit with a special assessment.

Occasionally, even in well-run associations, surprises happen. Association members can get hit with a special assessment (sometimes amounting to several thousand dollars) to cover an unexpected, large bill. Let's say a drainage problem is causing a retaining wall on the property to buckle, and it's going to cost thousands to reroute the water that's causing the problem and rebuild the wall. You may not want to buy into the neighborhood just as that bill comes due. The sellers and property managers are supposed to disclose to you any special assessments that are looming, but you should ask about them as well.

## Know the Restrictions!

It's extremely important for you to dig into the association's rules; you need to make sure the association does not prohibit anything that you hold dear. Homeowners have all but gone to war over some of the restrictions in their communities! In addition to the very common restrictions on exterior paint color, you might run into some of these prohibitions: no wreaths or decorative flags; no basketball hoops or kids' bicycles in the driveway; no fences; no unusual plantings; no boat or truck parking.

Of course, the prime attraction of living in a controlled environment such as a neighborhood or condo association is the ability to keep the *neighbors* from adopting unsightly habits that might drag down property values. Just make sure the rules suit your lifestyle *before* you buy into the neighborhood, because they can be nearly impossible to change. Keep in mind that associations can levy a fine on you—and they have the power to place a lien against your title to collect that fine, should you violate the rules.

As you tour any community governed by an owners' association, whether it's a condo, co-op, or a neighborhood of freestanding homes, try to gauge how happy the residents are. You can glean a lot of intelligence from reading back issues of their newsletter and even by reading notes on a bulletin board in the clubhouse. Are people sniping about parking problems or pool rules? Are they complaining about heavy-handed enforcement by volunteer owners who prowl the community looking for violations of the association's rules? Or are owners organizing poker games and pot-luck dinners? You'll be happiest, of course, living in a community that is as rule-oriented—or freewheeling—as you are.

# Razzi's Rules to Live By

### 🏠 Soundproofing is the key to happiness.

At least it is in condo/co-op apartments and townhouses. Be careful buying older condos; many that went condo in the 1970s and 80s were originally built as rentals, with scant attention to insulation for sound and heat-retention. Visit close to dinner time, when residents are likely to be at their noisiest.

### 🏠 Beware of renters.

If the share of renters in a condo or townhouse development hits 30 percent or more, subsequent buyers can have difficulty getting a mortgage, making it more difficult to sell units.

### 🏠 If it doesn't perc, take a pass.

With a rural or near-rural lot, you will not be allowed to build unless the land drains well enough to support a septic system. Pay for your own evaluation, to be sure.

### 🏠 Test the waters.

If you plan to dock a boat along your own shoreline, measure the water depth yourself. Don't rely simply on the word of the seller or real estate agent.

### 🏠 Read the dreary documents.

You must read the association documents—the financial statements and the Codes, Covenants, and Restrictions—when you buy a condo, co-op, or a detached house in a neighborhood association. You want to see that they've been setting aside money for predictable repairs and replacements to common areas.

## 🏠 Love the rules you're with.

If you're going to chafe at restrictions on your ability to keep a boat, play basketball in the driveway, or paint your front door blue, make sure those activities aren't prohibited *before* you buy. Those dreary documents sometimes spark fights.

# CHAPTER SEVEN

# Home Styles: What They're Like to Live In

> "Dad said of the house that it had no style, it was styles, a quick history of American architecture."
>
> JOYCE CAROL OATES, *We Were the Mulvaneys*

W E JUDGE HOUSES BY THE WAY THEY *LOOK* from the curbside and by the way they *feel* once we're indoors. Starting in childhood, most of us develop very strong tastes about what style of home we find appealing. But as you search for a new home, it would be worthwhile to step back and examine just what it is you like and dislike about certain styles. Knowing which features you really like and dislike might open you up to more types of home in more neighborhoods. The features that give a Craftsman the earthiness you love might also be found in a special Cape Cod that you might not have thought to look at.

From the curb, a house conveys quite a few messages. Its expense gives everybody who cares to look a rough estimate of your net worth. It also conveys a very strong message about your personal taste and style. The people living in a massive brick colonial with heavy curtains over the windows and a long, winding driveway are saying something very different about themselves than are people living in a clapboard cottage with a swing on the porch and a front yard full of wildflowers.

The prevalence of certain styles varies across the United States. The roots of styles that traditionally dominated an area were determined by history and climate. In New England, for example, you once found simple houses built of wooden clapboard or shingle with small windows and steeply pitched roofs. These hardy houses were influenced by English traditions, built from the materials abundant in the area (namely wood) and were made to withstand harsh winds and heavy loads of snow on the roof. The Southeast had a lot of brick homes, which took advantage of the abundant red clay and resisted the termites that plague that hot, humid region. In the Southwest, you found many homes built following Spanish traditions, often with courtyards or covered walkways, made with materials abundant in the area, namely stone or stucco. Often the tiled roofs had large overhangs to shield windows from the midday sun.

Today, however, we find mix-and-match styles. Sometimes the exterior of a house may look traditional, keeping with the neighborhood's colonial tastes, while indoors it has modern, open rooms and a back wall full of oversized windows that seem to bring the outdoors inside, in a very non-colonial way.

We ask an awful lot from our homes, and sometimes those desires conflict with each other. Our overriding desire is for the home to achieve its fundamental purpose and shelter us from cold, midday heat, wind, and water in all its forms, including rain, snow, hail, sleet, and the dampness that seeps up from the ground. A bunker would do nicely to provide such protection.

But then there are the *other* things we want from our homes. We want fresh air and sunlight to flow into our living space, so we cut holes in those safe, solid walls and put in windows and doors, both of which can be weak spots for letting in water, wind, cold and heat. We even cut into the roof to put in windows or skylights, all but daring the forces of nature to dump water on our heads! We cut still more holes into the roof and walls to make our space more comfortable, accommodating ventilation fans and fireplace chimneys, even if those fireplaces don't throw nearly as much heat as our central heating system does. We even take our basements, places originally built as a dead space to insulate our cozy living areas from the cold, damp ground and any occasional seepage of water from the outside, and we build family rooms down there, complete with expensive televisions, computers, and stereo systems.

Today, innovative building products allow us to muscle our way past many of the obstacles to getting what we want, even if home builders of a hundred years ago would have scratched their heads and wondered at the craziness of it. Thanks to double- and triple-paned windows filled with insulating gas, we can have giant walls of windows on the windy side of homes in Minnesota and Maine. Even in California and Arizona, we can cut holes in the ceiling and put in well-insulated skylights because a flick of a switch can draw the built-in shades to keep out the noontime July sun. Across the country, the availability of central air conditioning allows us to build houses without thinking of the need for cross-ventilation, a now-quaint notion that used to cause builders to add windows on two sides of every room, in hopes a breeze might find its way through.

That progress in technology (along with our broadened tastes) is one reason that you'll sometimes find houses that don't quite relate to their location. You can build a Tudor-style house with a steep roof and small windows in Florida. Just turn on the air conditioning and pretend you see snow sliding off that steep roof.

There are benefits and drawbacks to any style of house. What's cozy to one is cramped to another. But here's an overview of some of the more common house styles, with some ideas on what it's really like to live there. An architectural historian could tell you the nuances that set apart the variations within these very broad categories (a New England colonial versus a Dutch colonial versus a colonial revival, for example). The following sections describe some of the most commonly found schemes, which you'll find in detached houses and sometimes translated to townhouses as well.

## Center-Hall Colonial-Style Homes

As the name implies, colonial-style homes have been built in this country since before the Boston Tea Party, back in the early days of the 1600s and 1700s. The style has never really gone out of favor. One of its nicest variations is the center-hall colonial, which has a roomy area inside the front door for receiving guests. The hallway cutting through the center of the house provides wonderful traffic flow through the house. The kids' friends can go straight back to the kitchen while formal visitors can be escorted to the living room or library in the front of the house. It's a formal style of house, but it's also generally quite comfortable. However, traditional colonial-style homes may not have the large windows that you'll typically find in more contemporary homes.

Exteriors can tend to look a bit cookie-cutter with this very traditional style. You'll find a big variety in exterior building materials used on these homes. More expensive homes may have exteriors of brick, or fiber-cement siding (Hardee Plank is one popular brand) which looks like wood clapboard but is much more resistant to damage from water or insects and needs painting less frequently than wood. More affordable homes may have aluminum or vinyl siding. An attached garage can negate some of the traffic-flow benefits of that center hall, so pay close attention to the spot where you enter the house from the garage. That will actually be your route in and out of the house, more so than the front door. Will traffic still flow so nicely in the morning if the garage opens directly into the kitchen or family room? Many colonials don't have much of an eave or roof extending over the front door. You may regret that when the rain trickles down the back of your neck as you fumble for the front-door key.

## Spanish/Mediterranean-Style Homes

The British weren't the only ones to establish colonies in the New World, of course. In areas from Florida westward to Texas and on through most of California, where the Spanish language prevailed among early settlers, Spanish also is the language of the architecture. Homes built with a Spanish/Mediterranean flair still are among the most popular home styles being built in these states, and they work well with the local vegetation and climate.

You'll find lots of tile, flowing from the indoors to the outdoors, and perhaps more tile (sometimes in rich hues of orange or blue) on the roof. Front doors may feature elaborate wooden carving, and you can find fancy wrought-iron (or another metal made to look like iron) grilles on banisters, fences, balconies or windows. Homes may wrap around a courtyard or feature covered walkways.

The seamless transition from indoors to outdoors (aided by the same flooring and views out to the garden or courtyard) is one of the nicest features of Spanish/Mediterranean-style homes, making them particularly suitable for places with a mild year-round climate. All those hard surfaces, however, can lead to harsh echoes unless you soften the rooms with throw rugs and plush furniture. The exterior finish often is stucco. These days, you also will find a faux stucco (called EIFS, an acronym for exterior insulation and finish systems, or by the brand-name Dryvit) made essentially of foam and plastic. Both real and faux stucco are great insulators, useful for hot climates, and are resistant to the termites that plague the South. However, stucco tends to crack over time (a particular concern in earthquake zones), and faux stucco can trap dampness inside the walls if it was not applied with competence and care, leading to mold or rot. Make sure your home inspector pays particular attention to this point if you buy a home made with faux stucco.

## Victorian/Gothic Revival-Style Homes

The original detached houses and townhouses built in the Victorian/Gothic style date back to the latter half of the 1800s. The most striking element of these homes is that they're teeming with ornamentation, with arches and frills made of wood or stone extending from the front door to the eaves beneath the roof, even further up to, perhaps, an elaborate finial topping the peaked roof of a tower. Usually there's a porch, sometimes one that wraps around the front half of the house.

Victorian houses can be a hobby as much as a home, offering seemingly unending opportunity for owners to paint and wallpaper and restore. A central hallway ties the home's public rooms (a parlor and maybe a library in the front) together with a dining room in the heart of the home, and the private space (an eat-in kitchen and maybe a tiny family room) in the rear. Many of these homes have two upper levels for bedrooms. What you won't find much in a genuine Victorian is closet space. Back in those days, they used armoires instead.

Victorian homes often aren't as spacious inside as they appear to be from the street. Porches, especially if they wrap around to the side, make the homes appear bigger than they really are. Quite a bit of the interior space may be taken up by hallway and a grand stairway. Rooms largely are separate from each other, reached from the hallway, and that lack of openness can lead to dark interiors.

## Craftsman-Style Homes

Very popular in new construction and remodeling today, Craftsman styles earned their first popularity around 1900 and remained a common choice until the Great Depression in the 1930s. (Relatively few homes of any style were built during the hard times of the Depression and World War II.) These are sturdy houses, usually anchored by a generous porch supported by chunky columns of wood or stone. Roof lines are steeply pitched with large overhangs, and often you have multiple roofs, thanks to one or more windowed dormers jutting out from the second floor, first floor, or sometimes as a small wing attached to the main floor. Indoors, a good Craftsman-style house will have lots of prominent woodwork and molding, especially around the fireplace.

Like so many houses with porches, a Craftsman may not be as big inside as it appears to be from the outside. That porch also may make adjoining rooms dark during the daytime. With their heavy use of woodwork and molding, rooms tend to have an earthy, cozy feel . . . or a dark, claustrophobic feel, depending on your tastes.

## Tudor-Style Homes

Many Tudor-style homes were built in the first half of the 1900s as the first "streetcar suburbs" sprang up outside major cities, allowing the financially comfortable to escape the city yet keep their in-town jobs. The hallmarks are heavy exposed half-timbering in the frame; steeply pitched roofs; tall, narrow windows, and prominent chimneys (not to mention the prominent hearths at the base of those chimneys). The exterior may be of stucco, stone, or brick. Some of the most beautiful Tudor-style homes have lattice windows with small diamond-shaped glass panes joined together by lead glazing, harkening back to medieval England when glassmakers weren't able to produce large panes of glass.

Small Tudor-style homes made of brick or stucco have a cottage feel to them, while the larger stone and brick versions carry a scent of the English stately manor and can be practically castle-like. Cottage-size Tudors often have a full-size second story for bedrooms, though the ceilings may be sloped along the lines of the attic. These second stories may sport dormer windows that all but beg for a window seat. Grand Tudors (and colonials of a similar size and expense) offer expanses of space for entertaining, including spaces for home theaters, pool tables, and a guest bedroom or two. Large Tudors (and colonials), however, can throw off an institutional feel if you're not careful about décor and landscaping.

Those tall narrow windows on a Tudor may be lovely to look at, but they're about the worst when it comes to letting in daylight. And getting all those corners clean in lattice windows isn't something you want to think about often. And, remember, with any style of home, a complicated roof that has many ridge lines and valleys, can be expensive to replace, which can be necessary every 15 to 20 years for an asphalt-shingle roof. (Tile, steel, slate and other materials may last much longer.)

## Ranch-Style Homes

Ranch-style homes started to be built during the 1940s, but they became *the* house of the postwar baby boom of the 1950s and 60s. The suburbs were expanding, and land was still cheap enough that homeowners didn't feel compelled to stack the bedrooms on top of the living space. Homeowners' Manifest Destiny would be to settle in clean-lined new homes spreading out across suburbia, each stretching from lot-line to lot-line. Attached garages can make these homes appear to sprawl even farther across the lot.

The relative simplicity of most ranch houses built during that time make them a wonderfully blank canvas for remodeling. Wings can be added, making an L-shaped or U-shaped house, and a few tweaks to the roofline and windows can give a basic ranch a very modern flavor. Because of the one-level living, it can be easy to open a ranch out to the patio or pool in back; they're also easily adapted for the needs of disabled people. They remain very desirable homes to grow old in. Depending on the layout, though, there can be little privacy for bedrooms. And you may face big re-roofing bills for a sprawling ranch-style home.

## Split-Level Homes

Television's *Brady Bunch* family lived in a split-level house, at least as viewed from the outside. (Indoors, the set showed a two-story house with a striking open staircase.) These homes, built mainly in the 1950s, 60s, and 70s, are an outgrowth of the ranch-style home. They usually feature a staggered set of three levels, each only a half flight of stairs away from the other. One single-story side typically holds the living room, dining room, and kitchen; on the other side of the split, you'll find a family room below and bedrooms upstairs. By putting the bedrooms on an upper level, you get more privacy than with a one-story ranch house. (A common variation is a split-foyer house. The entry is halfway up a flight of stairs. A half-flight up takes you upstairs to the basic ranch layout, with living and dining rooms, kitchen, and bedrooms all on one level; a half flight down takes you to a family room and garage.)

Split-level houses tend to have a cozy feel, and everything is not as far-flung as in a ranch. But your happiness will depend on your relationship with stairs. Does stair-climbing make you think of firm muscles . . . or sore knees? That one answer dictates whether you'll like living in a split-level. Going from room to room in a split-level almost always means climbing or descending a couple of stairs. Families may find that yelling—downstairs to the family room and upstairs to the bedrooms—becomes the default form of in-house communication.

## Cape Cod/Cottage Homes

Cape Cod–style homes were built as early as the 1700s, but their modern heyday was in the first half of the 1900s. These are modest but comfy family homes, typically with only one or one-and-a-half stories, as the second floor is actually converted attic space with dormer windows to let in extra light and air. Often you'll find a simple first floor with a living room, kitchen, and adjacent dining area, plus one or two bedrooms off to the side that share a common bathroom. Upstairs in the attic space, you may find one to three bedrooms with another bath or two.

These homes can have a romantic feel, with window seats in upstairs dormers and slant ceilings upstairs to follow the rooflines. Rooms tend not to be very large in a Cape Cod–style home, and tall people may particularly dislike the lack of overhead space upstairs. These homes can be especially nice choices for singles or older homeowners who would like to live on one floor but still have room upstairs for guests. Parents with young children, however, may balk at the bedroom arrangements, which may separate them from children who have bedrooms on a different level.

## Modern/International-Style Homes

The greatest of these homes are truly works of art that have come into creation when a wealthy owner commissioned an architect to produce a masterpiece. They first appeared in the United States during the 1930s and 40s. One of the best examples of a true International-style home is the late architect Philip Johnson's Glass House, a see-through box of glass with a steel frame that he built for himself in 1949 in New Canaan, Connecticut. Ornamentation is shunned in these homes, and clean lines are worshipped, inside and out.

The homes are built to highlight their integration with the outdoor space surrounding them. There may be relatively few examples of high-design International-style homes, but the design elements from this style can be found in many modern-looking homes across the country. Big expanses of glass are one of their most noticeable hallmarks.

You won't spend a lot of time dusting frou-frou and painting wooden scrollwork in a home like this; there isn't any to be found. The simplicity casts a yoga-like feel of calm and tranquility inside these homes. You'd better be tidy, though. Clutter destroys that tranquility. And, unless your glass-walled International style home is surrounded by lush woods, you may feel like you're perpetually on display.

## Contemporary-Style Homes

This catch-all describes the homes you'll find on many builders' lots today. Even if the exterior looks like a colonial-, Craftsman-, or Tudor-style home or a Mediterranean villa, inside you're very likely to find a medley of greatest hits. Among the highlights: Showplace kitchens that are fully open to an expansive, high-ceilinged family room; master bedroom-bath suites that practically count as their own apartment within the home; flowing spaces from room to room, with maybe only a single step or a bit of floating wall to differentiate one room from another. They may have very small formal dining and living rooms, or those little-used formal rooms might even be eliminated altogether.

Contemporary-style homes are thoughtfully designed to accommodate the way we live today. Our entertaining space is near the hearth—the kitchen and family room—because everybody knows a good party always ends up in the kitchen. Large rooms accommodate our big televisions (and our increasingly big selves). Self-contained master suites allow a desperately needed retreat from the bustle of our workdays, not to mention the bustle of a house full of teenagers enjoying the big television or pool table downstairs.

Though they've been designed to meet our every need (with the help of buyer-preference surveys and focus group studies), some aspects of contemporary-style homes still take getting used to. First, with the open kitchen/family room arrangement, it can seem you're *always* in the kitchen. The family cook(s) had better be tidy, because there's no place to hide your mess. (And imagine trying to limit the roaming range of a toddler or a not-yet-housebroken puppy!)

Decorating can be another challenge with an open floor plan. How do you paint one room without painting *all* of them, if they all flow together? Big, open spaces with high ceilings can be noisy and hard to keep clean. And if everyone in the household has a self-contained bedroom-bath area with their own television, computer, and phone, you may find that you don't talk to each other so much any more.

## Razzi's Rules to Live By

### 🏠 Technology makes crazy things possible.

We can have giant windows facing the wind and rain. Air conditioning allows us to build homes without good natural ventilation. Just make sure your home's features really do have technology that's up to the job.

### 🏠 All homes have trade-offs.

Quaint, old homes may lack closets. An attached garage is convenient, but it may thwart the efficient traffic flow of a traditionally styled home.

145

## 🏠 Porches distort your perception.

Often, a large porch will make a home look much bigger from the outside than it really is on the inside.

## 🏠 Wide, open spaces have limits.

They can be gorgeous to look at and wonderful to live in. But wide-open floor plans can be noisy and hard to decorate and may lack privacy.

# CHAPTER EIGHT

# How to Size up a Neighborhood

"These neighborhoods are never as empty as they look."

TOM WOLFE, *A Man in Full*

J UST BECAUSE IT'S CLICHÉ DOESN'T MEAN IT ISN'T TRUE. The three most important things in real estate really *are* location, location, and location. Almost anything about a particular home can be changed. You can tear the whole darn thing down and start over. But almost nothing can be done to change your neighborhood. Ideally, you should search first for a few neighborhoods where you would like to live, and then narrow your hunt to homes that come on the market in those well-researched neighborhoods. Never allow yourself to be seduced by a lovely home in a neighborhood that doesn't feel right.

Real estate agents sometimes can be frustrating when you talk with them about neighborhoods. First of all, remember that real estate agents are salespeople. They sell houses in lots of different neighborhoods. They may just *love* a neighborhood because they happen to have a house listed for sale there. At the same time, we should be fair to agents. The law limits their freedom to express personal opinions about a neighborhood, and they can pay a stiff price for saying the wrong thing—even if they thought they were saying something positive.

In the bad old days before fair housing laws were passed in the 1960s, some agents would steer buyers toward (or away from) neighborhoods based on the buyers' race, religion, or ethnicity. Today, the penalties for steering buyers (or otherwise discriminating against them) based on race, color, religion, sex, national origin, disability, or the presence of children in the household are severe. (Some state and local laws add sexual orientation to the list of federally protected categories.) These penalties can be levied even if the agent didn't really mean to dissuade a buyer from a certain neighborhood, as long as the agent's actions had the *effect* of discriminating. That's why an agent is likely to make a pained face and give you a noncommittal answer if you ask if there is a synagogue within walking distance or whether there are many children in the neighborhood. They could get in serious trouble for talking about it. Even calling a place "a nice, quiet neighborhood," might be taken as code that children would not be welcome there.

There is nothing illegal or unsavory about wanting to live in a neighborhood close to your place of worship, or where your children will have an easy time finding playmates. Just don't expect the real estate agent to be of much help.

# Get Out of the Car:
## The Pedestrian's Detailed View

It's absolutely critical that you get out of the car and walk (or bicycle) around a neighborhood before you buy into it. Even if it's a thoroughly modern labyrinth of quiet cul-de-sacs, where everyone drives straight into the garage and rarely leaves their property except by car, you need to get the pedestrian view. Take your dog (or borrow one), if it will make you feel less conspicuous, and take a good walk around.

On foot, you learn so much! You see if the neighbors give their homes enough TLC, weeding their flowerbeds and keeping their homes in good repair. Often (but certainly not always) an unkempt home is the sure sign of a rental. In general, renters tend not to fuss over their homes the way an owner would, particularly over the exteriors. Landlords, in turn, may not fuss over their rental properties the way they do about the roofs over their heads. And so, slowly, the rental property may start to look shabby. The people renting the home may be the salt of the earth, but you should hesitate before buying into a neighborhood that is heavy with renters. If those properties decline over the years, they will hinder the appreciation of your homestead as well.

Walking around gives you information you might miss otherwise. You see signs posted for zoning changes or pot-luck block parties. You see the telltale signs of children living nearby—swing sets in the back yard, basketball hoops, bicycles left in the driveway. You hear things, too: barking dogs, the hum of a nearby highway, or the roar from the local airport's flight path. You might discover that the scent of a nearby fast-food place would become your constant

149

companion should you move in. And you might even meet a few of the people who would become your neighbors. A visit after dark can be particularly revealing—and critical if you're moving to an urban neighborhood. Do you feel safe? Is there enough on-street parking in the evening? Do streetlights cast a harsh glare through the bedroom windows?

## Spotting Coming Changes

While you're walking a neighborhood, take notice of nearby areas that remain unbuilt, especially if you're in a fast-growing community. Those lovely woods behind your new home could disappear in a single day. I have known people who left for work in the morning without a clue that the woods behind their home would be razed by the time they returned home in the evening. If you don't own the woods, meadow, or vacant lot in question, you should consider that land fair game for eventual development. Depending on the strength of local zoning laws, that development might be other homes or some other type of use that you find less desirable.

You can learn a lot about upcoming changes to a neighborhood by visiting the local zoning office. A friendly little chat with the government employee might reveal that there's consternation in the community about a huge, new discount store that might be built on that side of town, for example. While this would probably be overkill if you're moving from one side of town to the other, or you already know people who live near the area you're considering making home, it's a very worthwhile extra step if you're moving from one part of the country to another. You just don't know what the local hot-button issues are from afar.

## Other Sources of Information

One of the best ways to learn about a new neighborhood is to follow its community newspaper for a while. The big city daily paper might not print much about a developer's quest to build a new McDonald's or an upcoming bond referendum to build a new school, but the tiny community newspapers will. You can ask local real estate agents if there are any small papers covering the community. (If there is one, it's a good bet the agent advertises there.) Or you can simply keep your eyes open at local shops, bookstores, and lunchtime restaurants. Often you can follow the papers online—particularly useful if the target neighborhood is far away. You'll glean a wealth of information about the neighborhood—and may even spot a house on the market that's "for sale by owner." You'll find more on such homes in Chapter Eleven.

A home buyer always should care about the quality of local schools, regardless of whether there are school-age children in the family. School quality is one of the biggest factors driving the difference in home prices from neighborhood to neighborhood. Year in, year out, families have proven that they're willing to pay top dollar to move into a great public-school district.

If a home is for sale in a popular school district, you can bet the real estate agent trying to sell that house will crow about it in advertising. If the home they're selling is just *outside* the popular school district, they simply won't mention schools. Never take the real estate agent's word that the home is within that school district's boundaries. Boundaries can change, and agents can make mistakes. Call the local school-board office to find out whether the address is indeed within their boundary. Ask if there are any proposals

## Schools Always Matter

What, exactly, are the hallmarks of a good school district? Academic excellence is certainly one sign of a good school, while pervasive drug use and high dropout rates are sign of a poor school. But in between the extremes, you'll find that different students thrive in different atmospheres. If your child has learning disabilities or special needs, finding a school that can best accommodate those needs will be most important. If the opportunity to play football motivates your child to tackle dreaded schoolwork, then athletic programs will be a top priority. There are a few commonly used measures you can use to grade schools, however. Small class sizes are usually prized, especially during the elementary years. Higher teacher salaries, compared to surrounding areas, probably indicate success at attracting top talent. And good performance on standardized tests, such as the SAT (Scholastic Aptitude Test) for college-bound seniors, indicates a system

pending that would change that boundary. School officials also can provide you information on the usual measuring points of school quality, class sizes, standardized test scores, dropout rates, and the variety of extracurricular activities offered.

You *will* pay more to get into a great school district. Your property taxes may be higher than in surrounding communities to pay for those great schools. (However, that's not always the case. There are plenty of bad schools to be found in high-tax communities.) But your home will appreciate faster than others, and it will be easier to sell than others should real estate markets go through a weak spell.

that has produced good students from the kindergarten years on up.

You can find a wealth of information on public school systems across the country through the SchoolMatch service. You can reach them at *www.schoolmatch.com* or 614-890-1573. They will give you three free "report cards" on schools of your choice which have easy-to-interpret info on how those schools compare to others nationwide on standardized tests, per-pupil spending and the income and education levels (along with other demographic data) of people in the community. You have to supply your contact information to get the three free reports, and the company may, if you don't object, refer you to real estate agents and other service-providers. If you prefer to stay anonymous, or you want report cards on more than three schools, they are available for $49 each if you request by phone, or $34 each online.

## Test the Commute

I'm convinced there are only two things honest people routinely lie about: their weight and their commute. If you ask them, they'll shave a bit off each. In both cases, the deception is usually based not in a desire to deceive others but from a protective need to deceive themselves. Promise yourself you will look at the real facts of your prospective commute when you're deciding on neighborhoods. You can fib all you like later.

Never rely on a real estate agent's sunny assurances about how long your commute will take after you move in. Also be skeptical of your own sunny assumptions about the commute—especially if you've done most of your house-hunting on weekends, when traffic usually is light. Before you decide on a neighborhood, you need to try out the real thing: a rush-hour commute. (If you're lucky, it will rain—giving you the true test.)

Go ahead, try it out. If at all possible, set your alarm early one morning, and get yourself to the prospective neighborhood just *before* you would need to leave for work if you lived there. Park at the train station and get a ticket for the commuter special; take the express park-and-ride bus; or ease your car onto the highway. Just be sure to give your real-life commute a test drive. One early morning will save many sleepless nights later—when you otherwise might lie awake wondering if you made a bad decision on a new home.

# Evaluating a Neighborhood Still Under Construction

It's a little trickier to size up a new neighborhood that's still under construction. Nonetheless, you should give the area a good look-see before signing a contract to buy a newly built house. If there literally is nothing to look at because construction has yet to start, get directions to two or three of the developer's previous sites and go visit them. You can get a good idea of the level of quality you can expect in your new neighborhood, especially if you focus on already-built developments that are close in price to the one you're thinking of buying into.

## Everyone Loves a Tidy Construction Site

There are some telling signs of quality that you can observe by walking or driving through a development under construction. Is the work site is organized and tidy? If it is, that's a reassuring sign that the developer runs a tight ship, and you can hope those standards will follow through to the workmanship on your new home. It's reasonable to see lumber, roof trusses, and other building materials stacked outside homes. But give the builder demerits if there are heaps of construction trash about, fast-food cups and wrappers blowing around like tumbleweeds, or stacks of drywall left unprotected from the rain. Somewhere, somehow, that sloppiness will cost you later.

## Check Out the Amenities

If they're installed, pay attention to the street lamps, signs, playground equipment, or park benches that the developer has added. Are they aesthetically pleasing or simply the minimum grade necessary to keep local government authorities satisfied? Pay particular attention to any areas where the developer plans to put in a retention pond to hold a rush of water after heavy rain. That could prove a danger to young children—or harbor mosquitoes in prolonged rainy spells—and not be something you want as a close neighbor.

Be especially skeptical when you're looking at a sales-office map of the development. Remember, it's a *sales* tool. It may include a conveniently located school that won't be built until years after your children have grown too old to need it, or grocery stores and other services that the developer is hoping to lure to the neighborhood. Opening day could be years off—if it ever occurs. Is work under way on amenities like pools, tennis courts, or clubhouses? Sometimes these extras are scrapped if a builder runs into financial trouble. Put your trust in what you see. Anything else is a salesman's promise.

# Razzi's Rules to Live By

### 🏠 Location really is the most important thing.

Never allow yourself to be seduced by a lovely house in a
neighborhood that doesn't feel right.

### 🏠 Get out of the car.

Walk or bicycle the neighborhood to get a true flavor of what it
would be like to live there.

### 🏠 See what creeps out after dark.

Visit in the evening, especially if you're buying in the city. Do you
feel safe? Is there enough parking? Are streetlights harsh?

### 🏠 Be wary of the woods.

Unless you own them, those lovely woods backing up to a home may
be developed someday. Once you buy the house, those woods could
transform into someone else's back yard—or even a commercial
building, depending on how strict local zoning rules are.

### 🏠 Try the commute on a Monday morning, and hope for rain.

Yes, indeed, you need to set the alarm early, hop in the car, and
drive to the neighborhood you're sizing up. Then get yourself to
work from there, by car or public transit, however you'd probably do
it if you owned a home there. Reverse the commute in the evening,
and then drive back home.

### 🏠 Trust only what you see.

Don't count on the proposed schools, shops, and places of worship
marked on the developer's map. They might never get built—at
least, not in your lifetime.

# CHAPTER NINE

# Buying Out of Town: How to Level the Playing Field

"For now here she was in what she was sure was the nicest and prettiest town in the whole wide country, in the happiest home that just fit the five of them like a glove for five fingers."

JOHN UPDIKE, *In the Beauty of the Lilies*

RELOCATING TO A NEW TOWN presents an extra set of challenges, especially if you're moving to a different part of the country. You will have to become accustomed to some obvious differences from your home turf: differences in the weather, in what plants will grow in your garden, and in the way locals go about their lives. But you'll also encounter important differences peculiar to real estate, such as whether the buyer or seller customarily pays certain closing costs. In this situation, it is particularly crucial to find a top-notch local real estate agent who can guide you through the process.

Under the old capital-gains tax laws, your home-sale profits were protected from tax *only* if you rolled them over into another home at least as expensive as the old one. Those laws practically demanded that people moving from one side of the country to the other *buy* some type of home in their new community instead of renting. But those tax laws are gone, and the pressure on relocating families has been relieved. You don't *have* to buy right away. If you're unsure about the relocation, or if you simply want to settle in and learn the area before you commit to a neighborhood, you can rent for a year or two—or even longer. Sure, it means you'll have to pack up your belongings and move twice, but it certainly takes the heat off the initial move.

## Finding a Relocation Specialist

Most large real estate companies have relocation specialists who are tuned in to the special needs of people who are moving great distances. If, for example, you're using a agent affiliated with one of the big, national franchise companies, such as Coldwell Banker, RE/MAX, or Century 21, to help you sell your old home, that agent can give you a referral to an agent who specializes in relocations in your new community. (Your agent will pick up a referral fee from the relocation specialist in the process.)

You also can dig up a contact to a relocation specialist yourself. RELO, a network of independent real estate companies around the United States and abroad, can link you to a referral specialist through its Web site, *www.relo.com.* I gave it a try (not identifying myself as a reporter) to see what kind of service I would get if I were relocating to the Washington, D.C., area (where, in fact, I already live). Within ten minutes of entering my info on the Web site, I got a phone call from a relocation specialist at Long and Foster Realtors, a major brokerage in the D.C. area. The specialist told me that if I really were moving, they would send me an information packet with maps, school information, and other material about the new community. With my permission they would direct me to a real estate agent in the area.

## Tuning in to the New Community

One of the best ways to tune into the daily rhythms of a new community from afar is to subscribe to its local newspaper. I'm talking not about the big metro dailies but the tiny, community-based publications. You may be able to get a subscription by mail or, even better, to follow the publication online. Little papers report the issues that their big-time brethren miss: changes to school boundaries and tax rates, new store openings, the controversy over a new sewer system, and the petty (or not-so-petty) crimes in the area. These tidbits are gold to someone thinking of moving to the area. Local neighborhood associations may be willing to add you to the mailing list for their community's newsletter, or to give you a password to their Web site. Ask your real estate agent for information about who to contact with your request.

You can find other good sources of local intelligence online. Go to *www.relocationessentials.com* for a wonderful trove of relocation information. You can plug in your current salary and see whether your dollars will buy a greater or lesser lifestyle in the new community, based on the local cost of living. Also, you can make direct comparisons to specific public schools in your old and new communities, including standardized test scores, teacher/student ratios, and the availability of extracurricular activities.

The message boards on *www.craigslist.org* are another great source of inside info on a community. (The Craigslist site also has other message boards, where you can browse the offerings of homes for sale or rent.) If you're sitting in Cleveland wondering whether a certain neighborhood in Las Vegas is safe or seedy, you can post your question on the Las Vegas board. Most likely, several locals will chime in with their opinions on the neighborhood.

## Review the Tax Picture

Your real estate agent can help you compare property-tax rates for different towns in the area. Make sure you compare *all* the taxes. Things may be done differently from the way you are accustomed. Property taxes, which are assessed by local governments, may not include trash removal, for example, requiring you to pay extra for that service. Or taxpayers might qualify for a break on their property taxes once they reach a certain age. State and local income taxes may also be very different from those back home.

## What's Not on the Agent's Tour

A real estate agent who specializes in relocation can give you a wonderful tour of the new community. If you're in town for a short house-hunting tour paid by the employer that is transferring you and your family, a relocation agent's tour is a lifesaver. They'll tend to highlight certain neighborhoods that are popular with relocating employees in your income range. But for a full assessment, you ought to make sure you at least take a look at the areas left out of the real estate agent's tour.

First of all, as the agent drives about town, follow the course on your own map. You might even highlight it with a marker. Later, you can take a little drive and check out the areas you didn't cover. (You might want to lock your car doors before you set out!) It's simply good salesmanship for a real estate agent to take the most scenic route to a neighborhood. After you move in, though, you might find that your actual daily commute is not quite so idyllic.

You'll probably find good and bad things on your extracurricular tour. For instance, you might discover that a long strip of auto-repair shops and vacant lots lies just down the road from the lovely community you're considering. But you could find a wonderful wildlife refuge there instead. The point is that you deserve to have a complete picture of the community that you're thinking of investing in—and where you plan to make a life for your family. You wouldn't want to base your decision solely on a well-delivered sales pitch.

## Razzi's Rules to Live By

### 🏠 You have the luxury of renting.

You no longer have to buy a home to protect your home-sale profits from tax. Renting for a year or longer could help if you're not completely convinced the relocation is wise, or if you simply want to learn more about the area before buying a home.

### 🏠 Get a relocation specialist to help.

They're better tuned to the needs of people moving from out of town. Get a referral from your local real estate agent, or from *www.relo.com*.

## 🏠 Tune in to local news.

Tiny community newspapers and local chat boards, such as those listed on *www.craigslist.org*, are great ways to get inside info on a new community. The Web site *www.relocationessentials.com* also provides good information on local schools and neighborhoods.

## 🏠 Go beyond the agent's tour.

It's good salesmanship to drive you to a new neighborhood via the scenic route. Drive around and get your own feel for areas not included on the agent's tour. You deserve the whole picture.

# CHAPTER TEN

# Get an Agent in Your Corner

"The house was not really a house, but a dream his father had. It was Clay's dream to build a house with his own hands, a house his wife and children could see being constructed, a house that would give strength and love to their lives because they would see the strength and love with which it was built."

EARL HAMNER, JR., *The Homecoming*

OST BUYERS SHOULD WORK with a good real estate agent when looking for a home. In fact, if you *don't* choose a real estate agent to work with, odds are quite high that an agent will choose *you*. You walk into an open house, write your name into the log book and, *boom*, you belong to that agent—that is, if you haven't signed on with a buyer's agent of your own. If you buy that house, that agent hosting the open house earns the buyer's agent share of the commission.

# Who Does Your Agent Really Represent?

Once upon a time, all real estate agents worked for the sellers. Trouble was, buyers didn't really understand that. And not all real estate agents fully understood their obligations, either. Sellers would contract with an agent to sell their home, agreeing to pay 5 to 7 percent of the sale price for the agent's services. The agent would list the information on that for-sale home on the local multiple listing service (MLS), an information-sharing system available only to Realtors (the name for real estate agents who belong to the National Association of Realtors) in that area.

But that MLS listing is more than advertising; it's an open invitation to all other Realtors belonging to that MLS. Basically, the listing says, "Bring me a buyer and we'll split the commission." Traditionally, the real estate agent working with the buyer actually represented the *seller* in the deal. But unaware buyers often ended up sharing sensitive negotiating information with the agent who drove them around from house to house, including, sometimes, the fact that they'd all but sell the fillings out of their teeth to afford the house they just fell in love with. Sometimes agents would pass that handy tidbit of negotiating intelligence on to the sellers (as, in truth, they were supposed to do), though buyers hardly expected to have their personal information spread about in that way.

## Getting Effective Representation

Today, one of the first things a real estate agent is supposed to do with you, a buyer, is to have a little conversation about whom he or she is going to represent in the deal. The agent will want your signature on a document confirming that you both had this little discussion about agency. Each state regulates its own real estate industry and has its own rules about agency. Some states allow a single real estate agent to represent buyer *and* seller in the same deal as a neutral, non-negotiating go-between; other states prohibit the very same thing. It gets legalistic and complicated, but you can clear up the babble by asking agents a straightforward question of your own: How can I be sure I have an advocate who will be able to keep my information confidential and negotiate aggressively on my behalf?

## Working with a Buyer's Agent

Today, most buyers choose to work with a buyer's agent who represents their interests. However, most of those agents also list properties for sale, and things can get muddy if you want to buy a home that happens to have been listed by your own real estate agent. That single agent now has a duty to obtain the highest price for the seller—*and* the lowest price for you. That's impossible to accomplish, of course. But both sides can—and must—be treated fairly. Before you ever start shopping, make sure you have an upfront discussion with your agent about how the agent intends to handle such a situation.

If state law allows, some agents will try to work as nonpartisan intermediaries in such situations. This arrangement may be legal, but your negotiating help evaporates as soon as you agree to such an arrangement. Another option is for the agent to hand you off to another agent who works for the same brokerage, and that agent can negotiate on your behalf. Because I believe negotiating help is one of the most valuable services an agent provides buyers *or* sellers, I believe most people are better off bringing in that other agent who can negotiate on their behalf.

For you, the buyer, this whole complicated issue of agency boils down to a single, simple sentence: "Who will keep my information private and negotiate on my behalf?" Don't hire a buyer's agent until you get a satisfactory answer.

Even after you have a buyer's agent in your corner, it pays to keep some things to yourself. Buyers agents aren't *supposed* to blab about how much you love the house, or about the big inheritance you could tap if you needed to, but it's human to let secrets slip sometimes. Even when it comes to negotiating help, you'll be better off if you can make the decisions and rely on the agent simply for tips and advice. Remember, *nobody* has as much at stake in this deal as you do.

# Choosing an Agent:
## Should You Work with the Listings King?

In a perfect world, there would be some agents who only worked with sellers and others who worked only with buyers. The "Who represents whom?" question simply wouldn't come up. But the real estate world doesn't work that way right now. Generally, there's more money to be made listing homes than in representing buyers because, thanks to the MLS, the listing agent has an army of helpers trying to sell that home. A buyer's agent is working largely on his or her own. Therefore, some of the best agents refuse to focus on buyers alone.

Having an agent who switch-hits between buyers and sellers can sometimes also work to the buyer's benefit. It's certainly more convenient to hire the same agent to help you sell your old home and find a new one at the same time. (And the prospect of two deals should give you a bit of ammo for negotiating a lower commission with that agent!) In a fierce seller's market, an agent who handles a lot of listings can give you an edge in finding new homes the minute they hit the market. Odds are high that, when the sellers were interviewing agents who could help them sell the house, that agent was invited in to make a listing presentation. Before the agent went for the listing presentation, which essentially is a job interview, he or she probably would have researched comparable prices and toured the home. Now, even if the agent didn't get that listing, he or she can give buyers a valuable heads-up that the home is soon coming on the market.

But not all agents like working with buyers. Oh, they'll do it, but they'd rather spend their time cultivating more listings. You'll recognize them by their impatience. They'd like you to see two or three homes (preferably their own listings!), fall in love with one, and buy it fast. You can avoid such agents by asking agents for references to recent buyers whom they have represented. Then phone those buyers and ask if they found the agent to be patient with their questions, willing to show them many properties, and aggressive in negotiations. Always conclude your chat with the simple, yet magic question: "Would you choose this agent again?" If they hesitate or make excuses for the agent, you should keep looking.

# Real Estate Commissions: Who Pays for All This Work?

Usually, your contract with a buyer's agent will stipulate that the agent's commission (typically about 3 percent) be paid out of the seller's proceeds at closing. Does that mean the seller pays? Well, it does and it doesn't. Since you, the buyer, are the one taking the cash to the table, and the seller is taking the cash away from the table, there's a pretty convincing argument to be made that *you* are paying for both real estate agents. Sellers, of course, usually don't see it that way.

## Negotiating the Commission

In practice, the real estate commission comes off the top of the sales price. On a $300,000 home, that's a commission of $15,000 to $21,000 (5 to 7 percent of the price) right off the top. That sum will be split among the sellers' and buyers' agents and their respective brokers. (Legally, real estate agents must work under the umbrella of a licensed broker.) The split is not necessarily fifty/fifty, depending on your market. Some sellers' agents will agree to discount their commission to 5 from 6 percent. But they'll offer buyers' agents the same split (3 percent of the sales price) that they'd get if they hadn't agreed to discount their own fee. If you decide to buy a home that's "For Sale by Owner" (known as a FSBO, pronounced "fizzbo")— that is, without an agent—you may be on the hook for paying the buyer's agent commission yourself, unless you can convince the seller to pick it up as a condition of the sale.

If your needs are unusual—say, you're intent on viewing lots of homes, maybe in several far-flung neighborhoods, and you don't want an agent to give up on you—try your hand at negotiating a different fee arrangement with your agent. For fear of violating federal antitrust laws, the real estate industry always stresses that commissions and fees are negotiable. So take them at their word, and try to negotiate a flat retainer or an hourly rate if that suits you better.

When signing a contract with a buyer's agent, keep your sights on the short term. A three-month agreement should be long enough. You always can extend it if you haven't found a home by the end of three months.

## Contracting with an Agent

Agents hate it when you work with more than one of them at the same time, and you can't really blame them. They could drive you all over the place looking at homes and spend hours researching tax records and recent sales prices for you . . . only to see you actually *buy* with one of their competitors. There goes their payday, despite all that work! In most cases, your contract with a buyer's agent will stipulate that they alone are representing you. If you find a home on your own, you're still on the hook for the commission.

There is one situation, however, in which you'd want to work with more than one agent. Make sure this is spelled out in any contract you sign! For example, move-up buyers may want to consider using different agents to help them buy their new home and to sell their old one. Oh, those agents will *want* to handle both deals. And if you're staying close to the same neighborhood, that's a wise choice.

But if you're looking to buy in a neighborhood five or ten miles away, look for a second, buyer's agent who's truly plugged in to *that* market. Just a few miles can mean a real difference! You want to work with someone who has a very accurate feel for prices in that neighborhood and who can get you in to see fabulous new listings *pronto*. Similarly, if you're looking for homes to buy in two distinct parts of a local metropolitan area, perhaps crossing state lines, you may need to use two real estate agents. Be careful that you're not under contract to pay two different real estate agents regardless of which home you buy! You need to have an up-front discussion with both agents before you sign any agreements, and make sure each agent is clear about which agent covers which territory, and make sure your agreement is noted in any contract you sign.

Not all buyers' agents require buyers to sign a contract for representation. Some will simply ask you to sign a document signifying that you've had a discussion about who the agent will represent in your transaction. But you should be aware of the obligations involved in signing a contract with a buyer's agent. Your agent may ask you to sign a representation agreement that obligates you to pay a commission, perhaps 3 percent of the home's price, if you buy *any* home during the three months or longer that the contract is in effect. Usually, the buyer's share of the commission comes out of the commission paid by the seller, but if you end up buying a home being sold FSBO, you could bear that burden yourself.

## The Power of Word-of-Mouth

MF (married female) ISO sensitive ABR, GRI (Accredited Buyer's Representative; Graduate, Realtor Institute) for committed, confidential relationship. Looking for a partner who's a good listener and tough negotiator for three-month fling, with possibility of LTR (i.e., three-month renewal). Send digital photos (360° tours preferred) ASAP.

Well, running such an "in search of" ad would be *one* way of searching for a good buyer's agent. But the better way is to find one the same way you find the best doctors, dry cleaners, and hair stylists—word of mouth. The best referrals come from people who have actually used that agent's services recently. Unfortunately, you'll also get plenty of referrals from people dying to hand you

# Real Estate Ad Decoder

Whether the ad is in the newspaper classifieds or posted on the Internet, real estate ads can be marvels of creative writing. You need to decipher the abbreviations *and* read between the lines. A sampler:

**BR:** Bedroom

**BA:** Bathroom, with toilet, sink and tub or shower

**1/2 BA:** Bathroom with toilet and sink

**TSK:** Table-space kitchen

**Must see inside!:** Dowdy—at best—from the curb

**Needs TLC:** It will need much more than tender loving care to be comfortable.

**Fixer-upper/Handyman special:** Needs major repairs

**Charming:** Small

**Dollhouse:** Shockingly small

**Jewel box:** Small for the price

**Gracious:** Expensive

**Light, bright:** That's the best they can say?

**Newer kitchen or bath:** Not original, but not that new, either

**Water access:** You have the right to use a pier or put-in, somewhere away from your property.

**Waterfront:** Property is along the shore.

**Water view:** You can see the water from the attic window.

**Seasonal water view:** You can see the water from the attic window when the trees are bare.

the business card of their son, daughter, father-in-law, or laid-off best buddy.

## Finding an Agent Who's One-in-a-Million

There's practically an army of real estate agents out there these days. With layoffs of mid-career professionals coinciding with a booming real estate market, a real estate license has looked like a lifeline to many folks. The National Association of Realtors, the main trade group representing agents and brokers, now has more than a *million* members nationwide. Members of NAR are called Realtors. The association sponsors continuing education programs and holds members to a code of ethics. There's really no reason you'd want to use a licensed real estate agent who is not a Realtor.

## Experience: The Best Credential

Not all of those million agents are serious pros. It's relatively easy to get into the real estate business, but it's tough to make a good living there. Some folks just dabble in real estate, and some inexperienced agents get precious little handholding from their brokers. (Brokers also are licensed by the state. They typically run the real estate office and have a number of agents working under their umbrella. Technically, buyers and sellers are under contract with the broker for real estate services, even though all your interactions may be with the agent.) You'll find that, in general, an agent with one week of experience charges the same commission as an agent with ten years of experience. You, of course, want a committed pro who can realistically promise to make your life easier.

One of the soundest pieces of advice I've ever heard about searching for a top-notch real estate agent came from a buyer in

Colorado. He found his buyer's agent by calling agents in his sister's hometown, some twenty miles away from the place where he wished to move, and asking them who *they* would want to work with if they were moving to the town he had his sights on. They weren't competitors, so they were willing to offer an honest opinion.

Real estate "for sale" signs can be a good indicator of who's active in the market, as well. If the same name pops up on a lot of signs, that's an indication of an agent who specializes in the neighborhood. It's worth a phone call to that agent to ask for references.

## Professional Designations

Real estate agents can earn a number of professional designations from NAR and its affiliates. Three of those designations, in particular, are good indicators that the agent has at least invested more than the minimum required amount of time and training in the real estate business. Look for the designations ABR (Accredited Buyer's Representative), GRI (Graduate, Realtor Institute), and CRS (Certified Residential Specialist). Earning them requires course work and evidence that the agent has completed a minimum number of sales transactions.

## Follow Your Gut

There's no magic to the designations, but they are a sign of an agent who has taken the time and trouble to get extra training. Give an agent bonus points for designations—but pay greater heed to the feedback you get from their references. And always pay greatest heed to your own gut. If you don't like the agent, for whatever reason, move along until you find one you do like. Remember, there are a million of them out there.

Buying a home is such a complicated and emotional process that personal chemistry with your agent really does matter. If you don't like the agent at the beginning of the deal, you will come to hate him or her by the end of it. Even when your personalities are compatible, there's so much stress involved in most home purchases that you can find yourself grinding your teeth at the sound of the agent's voice. Hitting it off with the agent is not a good reason to work with one—but *not* hitting it off is a very good reason to pass one by.

## Hallmarks of a Good Agent

Most buyers start their home shopping on the Internet. Once you've engaged the help of a buyer's agent, there's no reason you should abandon this valuable tool. You want to work with an agent who is completely plugged in and unafraid of technology.

A good agent will send you e-mails with links to new listings that have just popped up on the MLS. The agent will screen out homes you clearly aren't interested in because they're too big or too small, too expensive, or in a neighborhood that you dislike. A good agent will have seen the inside of the home with his or her own eyes. A lesser agent will send you an inbox-clogging download of half of the MLS every now and then.

A good agent will give you an office phone number, home phone number, and cell phone number. (The office number is the one where you're least likely to reach him or her. Most successful agents do the bulk of their work out of their home office and car.) A good agent will also give you phone numbers for an assistant and will make sure a competent, licensed agent can handle anything that comes up if the agent goes away for the weekend. A good agent returns your phone calls by the end of the day—and your e-mails within about a day, too. A good agent may have specific times of day for returning phone calls, because the heavy volume of business demands some limits. A lesser agent, of course, is hard to reach, and is downright laggard about answering e-mail.

There are several Internet sites that offer free matchmaking services to pair you up with a real estate agent. These services act as lead generators for the participating brokers, who pay for those leads. You go online and answer a few questions about your plans to buy or sell, including the price range and type of home you're interested in, and supply your e-mail address and phone numbers so they can get back in touch with you. (You can expect lots of "special offers" to come into your e-mail after filling out their forms!) Usually the sites promise you a significant discount or a gift card that you can use at a home-supply store in exchange for using one of their preselected agents.

I tried out the service on one of the better-known services, *www.homegain.com*. When I tried to take them up on the free estimate of my home's value, I found that my little town is not included in their automated service. However, within ten minutes of filling out the form, I got a phone call from the New Jersey headquarters of Weichert Realty, which is active in my market, offering to connect me to a local agent with at least a year of experience or $1 million in sales under his or her belt. (Given the real estate boom over the past few years, $1 million in sales is not that special a benchmark. Depending on the market, just one or two sales may do the trick!) Other referral services include *www.lendingtree.com* and *www.monstermoving.com*. You also can search the entire roster of local Realtors at *www.realtor.com*, though that site makes no attempt to differentiate between the experienced and inexperienced among its ranks.

It doesn't hurt to try one of these referral services, but I certainly wouldn't make it my only source of information. Direct recommendations from friends and acquaintances remain your best source of information. And you *always* should interview at least three agents and call up recent customers to get their opinion.

## Breaking Up Is Hard to Do

What if, despite your thorough search for a compatible, competent buyer's agent, you find the arrangement is just not working out? What if you want out of the contract so you can be free to engage the services of another agent? It happens sometimes, and it doesn't really matter very much why. Maybe the agent has simply been unavailable to you, didn't answer your calls or e-mails, or showed you only a few listings—and those few were completely out of line with what you said you needed. You're wasting precious time with such a dud, and you want out.

The first thing you should do is to speak with the real estate broker, preferably in person. Stay calm and unaccusatory, and explain that your arrangement with that specific agent has become unproductive and you would like to work with a different agent within that brokerage. Remember, your contract is actually with the brokerage, and most brokers will seek to keep you a satisfied client by switching your business to a different agent. Insist on it, explaining that it's not really in the interest of the original agent or of the broker to spend time with an unhappy buyer. Transferring you to another agent will keep you—and the commission on your sale—in the company.

If the transgression is greater than basic inattentiveness, you should file a complaint with your state's real estate board. Serious transgressions, such as taking your earnest-money deposit (the big check you've written to signify your serious intent to purchase the home, which is supposed to be held in a special escrow account until the deal closes) and mingling it with the agent's personal funds, can be cause for discipline, including having the agent's license yanked. Agents and brokers are licensed at the state level, and you can file a complaint with the licensing agency. You'll find a list of state authorities in Appendix Six.

If you believe you have not been treated fairly because of your race, color, national origin, religion, sex, family status, or disability, you should complain to the U.S. Department of Housing and Urban Development. You can learn more about fair housing laws and file a complaint online by going to *www.hud.gov*. The toll-free HUD telephone number is 800-669-9777. You also may write to the Office of Fair Housing and Equal Opportunity, Department of Housing and Urban Development, Room 5204, 451 Seventh St., SW, Washington, D.C., 20410-2000.

## Razzi's Rules to Live By

### 🏠 If they can't help negotiate, they're not much help.

If you do line up a top-notch negotiator as your buyer's agent, keep your personal info close to the vest—and don't abdicate your negotiating role completely to the agent.

### 🏠 No one likes a tattletale.

Ask a simple question of prospective agents: How will you make sure my information stays private and I have someone who can negotiate on my behalf?

### ⌂ Ask the magic question.

"Would you choose this agent again?" is the question to ask when interviewing an agent's previous clients. Then be quiet and listen. If they hesitate or make excuses, move on to another agent.

### ⌂ Two agents are better than one.

At least they are if you're considering two very different markets. But make sure you're not under obligation to pay both of them on the same deal!

### ⌂ Why pay top dollar to a rookie?

New agents and seasoned agents usually charge the same commission. Do you want to pay to be a new agent's learning experience?

### ⌂ If you want out, get out.

If things aren't working out with your buyer's agent, talk to the broker about being transferred to another agent in that same brokerage.

# CHAPTER ELEVEN

# For Sale by Owner (and Other Ways to Supplement Your Agent's Work)

"My own house was an eye-sore, but it was a small eye-sore and it had been overlooked, so I had a view of the water, a partial view of my neighbor's lawn and the consoling proximity of millionaires—all for eighty dollars a month."

F. SCOTT FITZGERALD, *The Great Gatsby*

IF YOU'RE IN A DEVILISH MOOD, try this little exercise: Say the word "FSBO" (for "For Sale by Owner," pronounced "fizzbo") in the presence of a real estate agent. Odds are your pleasant, professional real estate sales person will look at you as if you had just uttered a horribly obscene word during a church service. Most agents *hate* FSBO sellers—people who try to market their homes all by themselves. I've even heard agents make the argument that there should be laws preventing owners from trying to sell their homes without benefit of an agent because owners aren't well-versed in the legal forms and disclosures that local laws apply to real estate transactions. Some agents have similar contempt for the growing number of licensed agents who are willing to discount their commissions or to work on a fee-for-service basis, say charging only for placing a listing on the MLS and allowing sellers to show the home themselves.

## Finding FSBOs Through Your Agent

FSBOs attract a certain kind of attention from real estate agents, namely a barrage of phone calls asking for their listing once they (oh, so certainly!) fail at the endeavor and concede the need to list with an agent. The attention FSBOs often *fail to* attract is that of agents looking for homes on behalf of a buyer. Some agents will even avoid driving past a home with a FSBO sign (or the sign of a broker who charges lower fees for limited services) in the yard, so their clients don't see it. Seller's agents who do help buyers secure a FSBO home often grouse that, because the seller has no agent offering advice and legal documents, they end up doing twice as much work but receive only half the commission.

If you engage the services of a buyer's agent, that agent *should* show you FSBOs. But people *should* eat their vegetables and *should* extend charity toward the poor. And people don't always do as they should. Be sure to tell your agent you want to see FSBO homes along with those being sold by limited-service agents, but also keep your own eyes open!

# Find Your Own FSBO

In addition to keeping an eye out for FSBO homes as you drive through neighborhoods, you can search a number of Web sites where sellers post their home-sale advertisements. (Some of those FSBO sites also will post the listings on the local MLS, if the seller agrees to pay a fee for that service.) Because of the decentralized nature of the FSBO business, you should monitor several of the sites if you want to make sure you don't miss anything.

One of the most easily searched sites is *www.forsalebyowner.com*. This site allows you to search by community or zip code, and you can sign up to receive e-mail notifications when new properties are added for your search area. Other sites worth checking out are *www.homesbyowner.com* and *www.fsbo.com*.

Some buyers dealing with FSBO sellers think they ought to get a lower price because the seller doesn't have to pay a commission. Sellers, of course, resist that thought, wishing to keep the commission savings to themselves. There's no reason you shouldn't haggle with a FSBO seller as aggressively as you would with someone selling through an agent. But keep in mind that if you've signed a contract with a buyer's agent, and you decide to buy a home being sold FSBO, you may end up paying your buyer's agent fee out of your own pocket. Someone owes the buyer's agent a commission check, and it's a matter of negotiation whether that someone will be you or the seller. You're the one who hired the agent, of course, and ultimately remain on the hook if you can't convince the seller to pay.

Some FSBO sellers will agree to pay a buyer's agent commission; others are adamant about paying no commissions at all. What matters to you isn't who gets what commission. What matters is the bottom line: Does the price of the home, including the possible 3 percent commission (or thereabout) paid to your agent, fit your budget? Is it a fair price for the market? If the answers are yes, then go for it.

## Going Completely Agent-Free

If you happen upon the FSBO home of your dreams, and you haven't yet signed on with a buyer's agent, you have a more basic question to answer. Should you buy without any agents—or should you rush to the nearest real estate office and sign up a buyer's agent real quick? Well, it all depends.

The first thing to find out is how reasonable and businesslike the seller is being. You should also know ahead of time how comfortable you are haggling face-to-face over price and terms and other contract contingencies, such as who pays for the home warranty or what problems will be fixed before you agree to buy.

Basically, the question of whether you hire a buyer's agent for a FSBO purchase depends on how comfortable you are handling the important details of a deal, such as lining up inspections and title searches. Some well-prepared FSBO sellers will have a sales contract on hand, which they will suggest you use for making your offer. But you'd be foolish to use that contract without having it first reviewed by your own real estate lawyer. Your best bet would be to hire a real estate lawyer (which will cost several hundred dollars) to help you prepare the necessary documents and to make sure everything that's put on paper represents your own best interest.

A FSBO seller is supposed to comply with all the state and federal rules requiring various disclosures that are supposed to be given to buyers. They include disclosures about the presence of lead-based paint or asbestos in the home and disclosures of significant flaws such as a leaky roof. They should give you copies of the condo/co-op or homeowners' association documents. But FSBO sellers may not know (or care) about their obligations, so you need to be especially diligent about asking questions and tracking down information. And be sure to get a good home inspection.

Without any real estate agents involved, you will have to line up the termite inspection, lender's appraisal, the title search, and the home inspection. Your lawyer or the title company may be able to handle your closing, but you will have to scurry to make sure all the pre-closing details fall into place.

## Keep an Eye out for a Good Deal

There are some common signs that can alert you to a home that is getting prepped for sale. If it's a particularly nice home or a particularly popular neighborhood, you could find that the home ends up being sold before it hits the MLS. The early bird catches the new birdhouse!

You can read more about shopping in a hot seller's market in Chapter Sixteen, but these telltale signs are worth watching for in any market:

- Fresh paint on the front door and shutters. That's a dead give-away, especially if the paint wasn't particularly shabby before. Real estate agents *always* advise freshening up the front door area. Betcha there's a new doormat, too.

- Newly planted flowers and fresh mulch all around the front yard. That's more of the usual real estate sales advice for boosting "curb appeal."

- A Dumpster in the driveway (in the absence of a remodeling job). This is a sign of massive de-cluttering.

- Yard sale. This is another indication of a higher level of de-cluttering. They often precede a listing by a couple of weeks.

- Estate sale. This is a sure-fire sign. You can tactfully ask what the heirs plan to do about the house.

## Scouting Potential Homes for Sale

Don't be shy about asking the owners if they're thinking of selling; your question and interest are actually quite a compliment! If you don't catch the owners in the act of mulching (when you might interrupt them for a friendly chat), you might compose a sincere, handwritten letter explaining how you (and your family, if relevant) admire the home and how much you would love to talk with them about the possibility of purchasing it. Some buyers even have enclosed photos of their family, to make the appeal more personal!

Even if you're in a balanced market or in one that has lots of homes for sale and therefore favors buyers, it pays to move quickly when you find a home you like. That's as true when there are no real estate agents involved as it is when there are agents representing each of the sellers' and the buyers' sides. The best homes, when priced fairly, always sell faster than run-of-the-mill homes. Even if it's the very first home you see, move fast if it meets all your criteria—and especially if it just *feels* like home. Other buyers may be falling in love with it, too.

# Razzi's Rules to Live By

### 🏠 Who cares if your agent hates FSBOs?

If it's the home you want, it's the home you want, and your buyer's agent should help you buy it. Tell your agent you want to see homes being sold by limited-service agents and FSBO sellers.

### 🏠 Search FSBO Web sites.

Some sites worth monitoring include *www.forsalebyowner.com*, *www.homesbyowner.com*, and *www.fsbo.com*.

### 🏠 Ask a lawyer for help.

If a FSBO seller hands you a contract and suggests you use it as your purchase contract, be sure to have it reviewed by your own real estate lawyer *before* you sign.

### 🏠 It never hurts to ask.

If you admire a home, and especially if you suspect it's being gussied up for sale, go ahead and ask the owners if they'd consider selling it to you. It's not an intrusion, it's a compliment!

### 🏠 The early bird catches the new birdhouse.

Move fast when you find a home you like, whether it's being sold FSBO or with an agent's help. Someone else may be falling in love with it too.

# CHAPTER TWELVE

# How to Tour a Home

"I scanned more narrowly the real aspect of the building. Its principal feature seemed to be that of an excessive antiquity . . . Perhaps the eye of a scrutinizing observer might have discovered a barely perceptible fissure, which, extending from the roof of the building in front, made its way down the wall in a zigzag direction, until it became lost in the sullen waters of the tarn."

EDGAR ALLAN POE, *The Fall of the House of Usher*

TOURING HOUSES CAN BE A LOT OF FUN, so much so that real estate agents derisively refer to some buyers as "looky-loos"—people who seem to be more interested in looking than actually in buying. Then again, some agents would like for you to decide on a house after looking at only two or three. There's no reason you should feel so rushed.

In fact, you should be aware of a classic sales tactic. Let's say you're on your first house-hunting expedition with an agent, and that agent has three listings that he or she thinks you might like. A wily agent is not going to show you the best one first. You're too likely to dismiss it, thinking you haven't seen enough to form an opinion. Nor will that agent show you the best house last. That might only encourage you to think that houses four, five, and six will only get better and better and better. No, Goldilocks, the wily agent will show you the house he or she thinks is best second, hoping you find it to be just right. Just keep in mind that house four, five, or six might indeed be the best one for you.

## Develop a Home-Touring System

You can make more effective use of your looking-around time if you adopt a system. In all likelihood, you'll be seeing a lot of homes, probably in a short period of time. Each one will seem perfectly memorable while you're looking at it, but when you get home, your memory will start sprouting leaks. Developing a system of touring homes will help maximize your time and house-hunting efficiency.

### Take Notes and Pictures

Take notes as you tour a home so you can keep the properties straight after you go home and start to mull over your options with your spouse or partner. This is a good way to avoid arguments over whether the home with the big, stone fireplace had a shabby shower stall or whether the bad shower was actually in the home with the big back yard. All you have to do is check your notes.

You might take along a digital camera or a video camera to help you document the homes. This is an especially helpful method if only one member of the family is available to preview homes and will be reporting the details to the others. You don't have to ask anyone's permission to photograph the outside of a home, but it's courteous to ask the seller's agent for permission to photograph indoors.

## Use a Cheat Sheet

Go ahead and make yourself a little cheat sheet. There's an example at the end of this book, in Appendix Two. Use it as a guide, but customize it with your own hot-button wants and needs. If you absolutely have to have a sunny room for sewing, put that down on your cheat sheet. If you hate electric heat, mark that down. You're the one who'll be living there. In fact, you and your spouse could even draw up your own versions of a cheat sheet, allowing each of you to focus on the features most important to you.

## Don't Sweat the Small Stuff

It's surprisingly tough to do, but try to steel yourself against being influenced by the seller's furnishings while you tour a home, whether you find them fabulously tasteful or frighteningly tacky. Their furniture is not going to stay. You can paint the walls and rip out shabby carpet. It's only human to be affected by what you see, but try your best to imagine the house naked, as it were.

Be particularly skeptical when you tour a house that is decorated so perfectly that it betrays the hand of a professional brought in simply to "stage" the house for sale. I remember one home where the riding boots were perfectly posed next to the fireplace and the straw hat was casually draped over the bedpost. It looked as if Ralph Lauren himself lived there. It's easy to gloss over a home's flaws when everything looks so good. I almost didn't notice the terrible kitchen layout that put the cooktop directly under the elbow of anyone working at the sink—a flaw that will irritate future owners long after the smell of boot leather has faded.

Similarly, try not to be swayed by the presence (or lack) of top-of-the-line appliances. Sure, they add up to significant dollars, but, remember, these things can be changed. Anybody can buy a fabulous top-of-the line refrigerator or professional-style range for a couple of thousand dollars. Don't let it influence your decision on a house that costs *hundreds* of thousands of dollars. Again, it's only common sense, but it can be hard to put into practice.

## The True Value of a Home Warranty

Don't let yourself be terribly impressed (or comforted) by the fact that a seller is offering a fully paid warranty on the home and its appliances. Certainly, having the warranty beats not having it, but don't let a $400 warranty sway your decision. A seller-paid warranty promises repair or replacement of covered systems during your first year in the home. They typically cover heating, cooling, plumbing, and electrical systems plus major built-in appliances such as the range, dishwasher, and refrigerator. If something breaks due to normal wear-and-tear during the first year, you simply call their toll-free number to arrange for service and pay a fee of about $50 for the visit.

Most warranties, however, have significant exceptions (leaks from a shower enclosure or broken handles on a microwave or refrigerator may not be covered, for example). Even more important to remember is that the presence of a warranty should not dissuade you from inspecting a home thoroughly and bargaining on price. Consider this selling point contained in promotional material published by American Home Shield, one of the big warranty companies: "Sell for a higher price because when the buyer has confidence in your home, it discourages downward price bargaining."

# Hallmarks of a Well-Built Home

If you were to compare a suit coat from discount retailer with a more expensive version from an exclusive store, you'd notice obvious differences in quality. The more expensive suit would have a fabric that drapes better, neater seams, and better shoulder padding, for example. Similar quality differences can be found in homes. Look for the telltale signs of good tailoring as you tour a home.

## Windows

Windows are my favorite signal of quality. They're one of the most expensive components of a home, and a builder looking to cut costs can really trim his budget by falling back to a cheaper window. In high-end new construction, builders often crow about the high-quality windows they feature. In older homes, it sometimes can be harder to discern the brand used. Among the top-quality brands are Kolbe and Pella. Look for the little brand name in the corner of the glass. Andersen windows, while less expensive, still offer quite good value. Other brands can offer very good quality as well.

In addition to the brand name, there are specific features you can look for. In most climates, a double-paned window with an invisible gas (argon or krypton gas) between the panes offers good insulation in summer and winter. Look for neatly mitered corners in the window (you should barely see the joint); it's a sign of careful construction. Tilt-in features make it much easier to keep the windows clean. And vinyl outdoor trim will reduce your need to paint over the years. Look at the windowsill and the wall below to see if there are any water stains or softness in the wall—a sign that there could be a condensation or leakage problem with the windows. If the windows are cheap, you can be sure the things you can't see are cheap as well. You'll live in a drafty, uncomfortable house that's harder to maintain, too.

## Bathrooms and Plumbing

Bathrooms are another area where big amounts of money can be spent—or saved—during construction. Fortunately, money spent (or skimped) on a bathroom shows quite obviously. Tile, of course, beats vinyl as flooring or for the walls surrounding a tub or shower. Workmanship during construction and maintenance afterward show up later as neatly caulked tubs, showers, and faucets, as well as drains that work smoothly.

Especially in older homes, pay special attention to the floors and walls around (and downstairs from) a shower stall. Look for any sign of recent painting, a spongy feel, or mold. Leaks in a shower pan are terribly destructive—and hard to fix. Water that leaks from a tub or shower over time can rot the subflooring, a common problem in older homes, homes built from inferior materials, or places that have served as rentals (or that otherwise have not been carefully maintained).

## Exterior Finish

Step outside and take a good look at the exterior of the home. Give a home bonus points for an exterior finish that is resistant to rot, termites and fire such as brick, stone, or a fiber-cement siding (it's often referred to by the brand name Hardee Plank). Not only will your maintenance costs be lower over the years, but you may qualify for a discount on your homeowners' insurance as well.

Stucco and faux stucco (known as EIFS, short for Exterior Insulation and Finish System) require more maintenance, but they also are fire-resistant. Faux stucco, if it was improperly applied, can allow water to get trapped inside the wall, where it can cause rot, mildew or mold, so you (and your home inspector) need to examine it carefully for signs of water intrusion.

Homes with wood siding, while often beautiful, require routine re-painting, which grows costly.

Vinyl or aluminum siding are economical and long-lasting, but check it for dings, tears and fading. Some older homes are still clad in asbestos shingles. You still find it because it was durable, but those durable little asbestos fibers are now known to cause cancer. You can leave asbestos siding intact if it's doing its job, but be aware that asbestos siding is now classified as hazardous waste, and if you remodel you will pay extra for contractors to handle and dispose of it safely.

Take a good look at any porches or decks attached to the home. Porches, unless they were built with adequate ventilation underneath, can suffer rotting wood from trapped dampness. And many older decks (especially those built by not-so-handy homeowners) are not attached to the home securely. Eyeball it yourself—and then make sure your home inspector gives it a good professional examination.

## Red Flags and Hidden Problems

Watch for signs of rooms that are smaller than they appear to be. The decorators who dress up model homes have a few favorite tricks to dress up undersized rooms so they make a bigger first impression. Be on the lookout for this trick in older homes as well. Baby furniture is one. Not only does seeing one bedroom furnished as a nursery ring emotional bells with some buyers, but baby furniture also happens to be small! If the home you're considering has baby furniture in one room (or a twin-bed setup), measure it to make sure your larger furniture will fit. Mirrors are another tried-and-true decorator trick to make a space appear larger. If you see a mirrored wall, make sure to measure the room.

If you have any particularly large furniture, make sure it can be moved into the new home with you. A king-size mattress might not be able to make the turn in a tight stairwell, for example. Measure your behemoths, and make sure you could actually get them into the new home (or consider sacrificing them, if you really love the place). If you're moving into an apartment building, make sure the freight elevator is big enough to haul your big pieces up to your floor—or count on paying the moving company hundreds of dollars in extra fees to haul your stuff upstairs.

Fresh paint isn't always a good thing in a house that's up for sale. Sure, smart sellers know to paint the front door and to freshen up any tired rooms with a quick coat. But fresh paint also can hide problems that the seller *should* disclose to buyers. Be skeptical of fresh paint on basement walls, for example, because that could be an attempt to clean up mold or signs of leakage. A freshly painted ceiling? Same thing. Ceilings are a pain in the neck to paint! You should be especially skeptical if these areas have recently been painted while the walls in heavy-use areas (like the stairway or family room) have older paint. It's always wise to ask the sellers or their agent point blank whether there has there been any water seepage, condensation, flooding, or leakage in this house? Make sure your home inspector takes a good look at those areas, too.

Put your nose to work as you tour a home. Damp, musty smells are a pretty reliable sign of moisture problems. But other smells indicate trouble, too. I have toured entire neighborhoods that had a faint scent of natural gas, certainly not something you want to live with! And residents of new neighborhoods near working farms can be in for an olfactory shock when they open their windows!

## The Little Things

Finally, a well-built home will have little touches that are lacking in a lesser home. You may find heavier, more-detailed molding and wood-work around windows and doorways. Check if interior doors are solid wood instead of hollow-core, which are flimsy with no soundproofing capability. Wood shelving in closets is far preferable to wire shelves. Even heavier door hinges and knobs are a subtle sign of quality.

You don't have to be a carpenter to spot signs or quality—or the lack of it. Stand back and take a look at the walls. Look past the paint—is the surface consistent and even? Or can you see the faint lines where one sheet of drywall butts up against the next? New paint can only hide so much. What about the configuration of that all-important room, the kitchen? Is there room for the tools you can't live without? What about basic ergonomics—can two people work side by side in this space without driving each other crazy? Is cabinet space sufficient and within easy reach?

It's tempting to rush through the house tour. If you let that happen, you'll miss the small details that could make or break a deal. Give yourself time to stop and really look at each room of the house. Use as many things as you can—open and close windows and doors, test the strength of shelves and closet rods, run the water, make sure the outlets work. If you end up living in a place, you're

# Get a CLUE: Homeowners' Insurance

Eventually, practically everyone can get an insurance policy, but getting a homeowners' insurance policy isn't as cut-and-dried as it used to be. Insurance companies have become much pickier about what houses they will insure. After all, mortgage lenders will demand a policy before they give you a loan. But if the insurance companies get the notion that either you or the house you're buying will be likely to generate insurance claims, they may charge you a very stiff premium for the privilege of doing business with them.

The insurance industry now uses a centralized database for homeowners' insurance claims called the Comprehensive Loss Underwriting Exchange, or CLUE, database. CLUE reports track your history of submitting claims *and* the history of claims filed for a specific property. Both records go back five years. If either you or the property has a history of frequent claims—and some companies consider *two* claims in a couple of years to be frequent—they may decline to offer coverage. This might force you to get a policy from a company that specializes in expensive policies for borrowers at high risk of submitting claims.

Fine, you think. You've never even submitted a claim on your previous homeowners' policies. You'll have no trouble getting a policy on the new place. Not so fast; the simple act of placing a phone call to your insurance agent asking if some hail damage to your roof would be covered under your policy might be reported on your history, even if you never filed a claim. Also, the house itself could have some

## Get a CLUE: Homeowners' Insurance

black marks on its record. If the sellers of that home filed a couple of claims over the past few years, that home has a rap sheet that could cause insurers to balk at giving you a policy.

You do have the power to check out your CLUE report — and that of the house. Go to the Web site of the database keepers, at *www.choicetrust.com*. You also can reach them by phone at 866-312-8076. Everyone is entitled to one free report of their insurance scores each year. Extras cost $19.50 each.

You cannot order a report for a house you're just thinking of buying. Only the owner (and insurance companies) are supposed to have access to that info. But you can ask the seller to get a copy and show it to you. That's a particularly wise move if you are moving to an area where the home-owners' insurance market has had a lot of turmoil in recent years, or where strong storms tend to blow through with some regularity, damaging homes and creating insurance claims. This would include Texas and the Midwest, where hailstorms regularly pound homes, and coastal communities in Alabama, Florida, Louisiana, and the East Coast, where hurricanes and tropical storms are frequent visitors.

going to have plenty of time to notice things like shoddy carpentry or drafty doors—and plenty of time to kick yourself for not noticing the obvious when you still had the chance. Take full advantage of the house tour to take note of how a particular house is really put together—and how it will work for you.

## Questions That Can Haunt

In many places, sellers (and real estate agents) don't have to volunteer that there has been a death, suicide, or a crime committed on the property. But you always can ask. Some buyers simply won't consider making such a house their home, and so it becomes stigmatized. The superstitious among us will add ghosts to their list of turn-offs. Even if you don't care a whit about what happened under that roof in the past, be aware that a stigmatized property could be harder for you to resell someday and could lower your property's appreciation over the years. (If you plan to stay there a long time and won't be worrying about resale values any time soon, it could be a good excuse to bargain on the price.) Bottom line: If it matters to you, ask.

## Razzi's Rules to Live By

### 🏠 Be picky, but practical.

Do a self-check to make sure that the neighborhoods you're aiming for are realistic, given your budget, and that you *and* your spouse really have your heart in making this move. Go through your list of nice-to-haves and must-haves to see if there's any more room for compromise. Then hold on to your money until you find the right house.

### 🏠 Forget about the appliances.

Sure, they usually come with the house (though this varies according to local custom). But as you size up a home, keep in mind that for a couple of thousand dollars you could buy yourself some first-rate machines to cool, cook, and wash. Don't let the presence or absence of a chic cooktop sway your judgment on a house that costs *hundreds* of thousands of dollars.

### 🏠 Give your poor memory a break.

Take photos of houses as you tour. And prepare your own customized cheat sheet to help make sure you pay attention to all the things that matter most to you—and aren't sidetracked by the owner's lovely antiques and art work.

### 🏠 Beware of baby furniture.

Undersized furniture and wall-sized mirrors are tip-offs that a room is unusually small. Fresh paint (especially in odd places) can be a sign that the seller is hiding something. Bad smells never lie; they could be a sign of mold or other problems.

### 🏠 Get a CLUE.

Especially if you're buying a home in an area prone to hail, tropical storms, or hurricanes, you want to find out if the home has a history of insurance claims. If it does, you could have trouble getting an insurance policy at a decent price.

### 🏠 Judge the book by its cover.

Go outside and examine the materials and craftsmanship used for the home's exterior. Give bonus points to materials that resist water, rot, and termites.

### 🏠 Don't ask the Ouija board.

If you're spooked by the idea that someone has died in a home, that a crime has been committed there, or that it has a reputation for ghosts in the attic, speak up! Ask the seller or the seller's agent if any such things happened in the home. They're under no obligation to volunteer it. If there was a notorious event, it could actually stigmatize the property, limiting your ability to resell it later.

# PART THREE
# closing the deal

# CHAPTER THIRTEEN

# Making an Offer

"I want this house," Samuel said.

"What?"

"This house needs me, I can feel it."

"Maybe you should wait until the sun comes out to
     decide," she said.

ALICE SEBOLD, *The Lovely Bones*

Finally, you've found the right home! Now you have to find out if you and the seller can agree on the price and terms.

The right price for the home is not necessarily the listing price being asked by the sellers. In a balanced market, in which there are a reasonable amount of homes for sale and neither the seller nor buyer has the upper hand in negotiations, you may be able to offer a bit less than the list price and have it accepted by the seller. Many parts of the country have been experiencing sellers' markets, however, which offer buyers little to no negotiating room. In fact, competing buyers could drive the price higher than the list price. If you're in such a market, you're in for a head-spinning ordeal in which much of the tried-and-true advice simply doesn't work. Most of the usual protections (like professional home inspections) become luxuries that you cannot afford, at least not if you hope to be the victor in a bidding war. Special advice for these markets is offered in Chapter Fourteen-and-a-half, in addition to this one. We've given it a special "half-chapter" status to reflect the alternate universe facing buyers in a roaring seller's market.

The home's real price is determined by the market, not by how much the seller wants or needs to get from the deal or by what you can afford to pay. The combined actions of many buyers and many sellers set the market price. You have to find out what other recent real-life buyers and sellers have agreed are fair prices. Your buyer's agent can help you by looking up recent closed sales in the neighborhood. A good agent will focus on homes that truly are most comparable to the one you'd like to buy, and can help you adjust the prices up or down according to the special features of the home. If the home you have your eye on has an extra bedroom or a larger lot, the agent can help you estimate the added value that such features bring to the deal.

If you're not working with a buyer's broker, you need to do this research yourself. (If you're working with the *seller's* agent, keep in mind that the seller's agent is duty bound to get the highest price for the seller. You need to find out the real worth of that home by yourself.) Many communities have local property tax information available for you to look through at city hall or even from your home computer. In addition to the municipality's assessed value for the home (which usually is lower than current market prices), they often report previous sale prices. You can look up the tax records of homes similar to the one you'd like to buy.

Current MLS listings can give you an idea of the current *asking* prices for other homes in a certain market. Keep in mind that all of them could be inflated above what real buyers end up paying, at least in a balanced market or in a market that favors buyers. Web sites run by local real estate brokers (including the seller's broker) can be a good place to search current asking prices. Some MLS organizations also allow the public to search the entire database online.

Once you have a reasonable estimate of the correct price of that home, you have to decide how aggressively to negotiate with the seller. Your buyer's broker may have some insight on what's motivating the sellers, but there also are signs you can watch for that indicate a buyer might be receptive to a low offer. Here are a few to look out for:

- The home has been on the market longer than usual for that community. (Your buyer's broker can tell you the typical sales time for a reasonably priced listing.) If it's springtime and the photos online or printed in a sales brochure show bare winter branches, that's a tip-off that the home may have been on the market quite a while.

- Bad winter weather. People selling homes in December and January usually have few nibbles, especially when the snow and ice start to pile up.

- Signs that one or both owners have already moved out. If the home sale is being prompted by a divorce or job transfer, the owners may be eager to get out of the deal and to move on with their lives. Does the home look half furnished? Are closets empty?

- An estate sale. Heirs often just want to get the home sale over with so they can wrap up the estate.

If you don't anticipate a lot of other buyers competing with you for the home—or if there are other homes on the market that you'd consider buying—it doesn't hurt to make a low-ish offer on the home. The sellers can always counter with a higher proposal, and off you go into negotiations!

## How Much Earnest Money?

Sellers will expect your purchase offer to be accompanied by a sizable check. Known as "earnest money" or an earnest money deposit, this money signifies that you're serious about the deal. If you and the seller reach an agreement on a purchase contract, the seller's real estate broker will deposit your earnest money check in a special escrow account, where it will remain until the deal closes. At closing, the money will be applied toward your down payment. If you're buying directly from the seller, without the involvement of any real estate agents, you should give your earnest money check to the lawyer or to the title or escrow company that you will manage your closing. Don't give a check directly over to the sellers; that's asking for trouble.

While the deal is pending, if you should simply back away from your offer to buy the property, you would forfeit the earnest money. However, if your reasons for backing out of the deal are covered in contingencies included in your contract, you should get your earnest money back. This might happen, for example, if you make your offer contingent on receipt of a satisfactory home inspection report. Let's suppose the home inspection revealed significant problems. The seller won't fix them and won't lower the price to allow you to make repairs, so you decide not to buy the home. You should not forfeit your earnest money in such a situation.

Your buyer's agent can advise you on how much earnest money is expected in your community. By no means does it have to be your entire down payment! The amount should grow along with the price of a house, ranging from $1,000 to 5 or 10 percent of the home's price. Some sellers are impressed by a large earnest money check; if you're in a competitive market in which sellers have the upper hand, you may have to put down some serious earnest money just to get serious consideration of your offer.

But, it's not in your interest to put down a lot of earnest money if you don't have to. After all, that money is at risk if the deal should blow up before closing. Make sure your purchase contract spells out exactly what contingencies you want, such as for a home inspection, mortgage qualification, appraisal, or sale of your current home. Unless you can legitimately get out of the contract because one of these specific contingencies has not been satisfied, you stand to lose that money.

## The Offer: A Contract from the Start

It's important to treat your very first written purchase offer as if it's a binding contract that can't be tailored later. Get all your wants and needs into that document right from the start, because the minute the sellers sign that offer, bingo! Negotiations are over, you've bought yourself a new home, and all the terms are set.

Among the details you want to nail down are the exact items you expect to be included in (or to "convey with") the sale. Sellers often have a different notion than buyers about what is included with the home. Generally, a home sale is *supposed* to include any fixtures that are permanently attached to the structure. That would include chandeliers, gas ranges, fireplace doors, sconce lights, brass doorknockers, and anything else that is wired in or bolted on to the home. But sellers may have no intention of selling their fabulous crystal chandelier along with the home. You, understandably, might assume that the chandelier is part of the sale. These are details notorious for sparking squabbles between seller and buyer, and life will be much more pleasant if you can avoid them.

You have to get specific when preparing your purchase offer. Write down everything you can think of that you expect to convey with the home. That includes, if you want them, the chandeliers, kitchen appliances, window coverings, fireplace doors, and window-unit air conditioners. (Conversely, if you absolutely don't want those window units to remain after the sale, say so now.) If there's a children's gym set in the back yard, specify whether you expect it to remain or to be removed. You're not being greedy; you're just covering all your bases. If, for example, the sellers intend to take a $5,000 chandelier in the moving van with them, they can say so in their counteroffer, and you might then counteroffer with a price that's $5,000 lower.

## Important Contingencies: For Your Protection

There are several contingencies common to most purchase offers that give buyers important protections. Without them, you run the risk of buying a home that has defects you didn't expect, of digging into your savings far deeper than you had planned, or of forfeiting your earnest money check. It's true (scandalous, but true) that buyers find they have to do without these sensible protections if they have to buy in a superheated seller's market (see more on that in Chapter Fourteen-and-a-half). But don't give them up unless you're absolutely against the wall.

## Home Inspection

This contingency makes your purchase offer hinge upon receiving a home inspection report that is satisfactory to you. Specify how many days will be allowed for you to get the inspection report. (The standard purchase contract produced by the California Association of Realtors, for example, allows buyers to request a standard seventeen days or an alternative period to get the inspection.) In peak real estate sales season (generally the springtime), inspectors can get booked up; make sure you can get an inspector within the time you specify in the purchase offer.

You must also make sure the contract specifies what will happen if the inspector finds flaws. Sellers typically will want the opportunity to make repairs—that keeps you from having such an open-ended inspection contingency that it allows you to slip out of the deal on a whim. ("The inspector found loose doorknobs, so we'll pass on the house. Please return our earnest money.") If something significant turns up in the inspection that truly affects the livability or value of the home, like a foundation or water leakage problem, negotiations are still open with the sellers. You may want them to make the repairs or to credit you with enough money from the sale proceeds so you can have the repairs done yourself (which gives you more control over the quality of the work), or you might choose to call off the purchase altogether.

## Lead-based Paint Evaluation

If the home was built before 1978, it may contain lead-based paint. Sellers of homes built before 1978, when lead-based paint became illegal to use in homes, are required to disclose to buyers any information they have about the presence of lead-based paint. Federal law requires sellers to allow buyers up to ten days to get an inspection or risk assessment for the presence of lead in the home. Buyers and sellers can agree (in writing!) on a different period for inspection, or buyers can waive the requirement altogether.

It's especially wise to call in a pro to check for lead if your family includes (or will include) children or pregnant women, both of whom are especially at risk from lead poisoning; if paint is obviously chipping and peeling (although intact lead paint still presents risk); or if you plan to renovate. You could face a need to spend thousands of dollars for a qualified lead-mitigation company to come in and remove lead-based paint or to encapsulate it in a special type of paint. At a minimum, you will need to inform subsequent buyers of the home that it has lead-based paint, which could hurt your property value. For more info, you can reach the National Lead Information Center at 800-424-5323. You can also research the U.S. Environmental Protection Agency's regulations and recommendations online, at *www.epa.gov*.

## Radon Gas

The U.S. Environmental Protection Agency (EPA) and the U.S. Surgeon General recommend testing all homes for radon before they're bought or sold. Radon is an invisible, tasteless, odorless, radioactive gas. According to the EPA, radon in indoor air is estimated to cause about 21,000 lung cancer deaths per year in the

United States, making it the second leading cause of lung cancer. (Smoking remains the number-one cause.) The only way you'll know about radon is to test for it. Qualified radon testers can conduct quick tests, taking as little as forty-eight hours, which include measures to prevent or detect any tampering by the home's occupants that could result in an artificially low reading.

If the test shows a high reading, you can negotiate with the sellers about who will pay for a qualified contractor to install ventilation or another type of system that will lower radon levels. (The EPA estimates the average cost as ranging from $800 to about $2,500.) Because there are so many things that can affect a radon test, such as windows left open before or during the test, I prefer to have the test done *after* buying a home, even if the seller did a test before the sale. Then you can control the conditions and get a really good reading of your risk. You can find more information, including advice on finding qualified testers, from the EPA at *www.epa.gov.*

## Extra Inspections

Your home inspector might find some conditions that warrant further investigation. Wall cracks or sagging floors might require an inspection by a licensed structural engineer, for example. Or suspicious-looking insulation might warrant an inspection for asbestos. These should be permitted by your home-inspection contingency.

You may also want to add specific contingencies for other inspections, if they're important to you. If there are a lot of trees on the property, especially if they tower over the home, you might want to call in an arborist to find out if they threaten the home, or if they'll cost you thousands of dollars for needed trimming. If the swimming pool looks like it might be in disrepair, you might add a contingency that the pool be inspected by a qualified pool company as well. An older home with a septic system merits a look from a septic company, too, so cover that with a contingency clause.

## Finance Contingency

Of course, you can't buy a home if you can't get a mortgage. If you should have unexpected trouble qualifying for a mortgage, you at least want to make sure your purchase contract allows you to get your earnest money back. Even if you have a letter of preapproval letter from a mortgage lender, it's in your interest to include a finance contingency in your purchase offer. (Anything can happen, after all.) Such a contingency simply states that your deal is dependent on your qualifying for a mortgage with a reasonable interest rate (which you specify). The sellers, of course, will want to see language requiring you to apply for the mortgage within a week or two after your contract is accepted.

## Appraisal Contingency

Lenders always require an appraisal of a property before they will make a mortgage loan. Typically, your real estate agent will schedule an appraisal, which must be done by an appraiser who is acceptable to the lender. You most likely will be charged $300 or more for the service at closing. An appraisal contingency specifies that your deal is contingent on the appraisal (which will be required by your lender) saying the home is worth at least as much as you've agreed to pay for it. Without this contingency, if the appraisal should come in lower than your price, you're still committed to buying the home. You'd be expected to raid your savings to come up with the difference between the purchase price and the amount of money the lender will agree to loan you, given the appraised value of the home. If you can't (or won't) come up with the extra cash, you could have to walk away from the deal and forfeit your earnest money.

## Homeowners' Insurance

If you're in an area that's experiencing a troubled homeowners' insurance market, and it's not a slam-dunk certainty that you'll be able to get an affordable policy, you could include a contingency that hinges the deal on your getting coverage. Insurance availability crises have cropped up from time to time in places exposed to a lot of coastal storms or wild fires, including the East Coast, Florida, Texas, and California. If there's a chance that insurance costs could be so high as to make the home unaffordable to you, cover yourself with a contingency. (For more on how to guard against a homeowners' insurance problem, see Chapter Fifteen.)

## Home Sale Contingency

Sellers don't like to see this one in your purchase offer! But if they're having trouble finding a buyer, they may agree to a contingency that says the deal isn't firm until you have found someone willing to buy the home you are leaving.

You can make this contingency more palatable to them by including a "kick-out" clause, which allows them to continue to market their home while you search for someone to buy yours. If they find another buyer, you have seventy-two hours (or whatever period you specify in your contract) in which to remove your home-sale contingency and get the ball rolling toward closing day. If you don't remove the contingency, they can sell to the other buyer, and you should get back your earnest money.

## Setting the Date

Your purchase offer also should stipulate when you expect to be able to move into your new home. Usually, you get the keys and garage-door openers right at the closing table. But you might like to have access to the home before closing so you can paint or make repairs, especially if the home is vacant.

Sellers are understandably wary about letting you into the home before closing; what if you break something, or get hurt, or the deal falls through? If you really want such access, go ahead and ask for it in your purchase offer. More commonly, however, a purchase offer stipulates that the home will be available to you in broom-clean condition (that is, without the seller's junk inside, but still in need of a good scrubbing) at closing. It should state that you can walk through the property a day or so before closing, to verify that everything that should stay is, in fact, there, and that everything that should be removed is gone.

The sellers might come back to you with a counteroffer requesting that they be able to stay in the home for a time past the closing. In a seller's market, your acceptance of such a deal could make or break the deal! Of course this arrangement puts added risk on you. What if the sellers don't move out promptly? What if something breaks while they live there (but *you* own the home), due either to their actions or to sheer bad luck?

You can agree to let them remain, but you must protect yourself. You both will have to sign a rent-back agreement specifying how much rent they will pay you for each day they remain, the size of the security deposit they will post (which should be held in escrow by your real estate agent), and, most important, a firm move-out date. When setting your rent, take your new monthly mortgage payment (including tax, insurance, and any condo or homeowner association fees) and divide it by thirty to arrive at your daily cost for owning the home. Charge *at least* that amount per day they remain. You don't want to make it too comfortable for them to dawdle.

## New Construction

If you're buying straight from a new-home builder, you will be asked to use the builder's standard purchase contract. A salesperson may tell you that changes to that contract are not possible, but you should know that *all* contracts are negotiable, and you can be darn sure that contract favors the builder at every turn. Don't hesitate to write in any changes you decide are necessary. It's not a bad idea to have your lawyer look it over, either. If the builder doesn't like your terms, he can decline to sign the contract. Such are the ways of negotiation. Two areas of a new-home contract are particularly important: the language governing the materials used in the home, and the date set for delivery—that is, the date they finish the home and you can go to closing.

Builders' contracts typically state that the builder has the right to substitute different, but comparable, materials from the ones used in the model. To some extent, they need this protection; suppliers can go out of business, for example, and they may have to substitute Company B's roofing shingles when Company A's shingles become unavailable. You, on the other hand, have reason to expect that the Corian countertops you saw in the model will show up in your kitchen. Your best bet is to specify all of the finish materials that matter to you. Spell out that you want the Kohler nickel-plated bathtub faucets and the Lightolier over-sink lights, if they're what you expect.

Delivery dates are tricky as well. Rainy spells, labor shortages, supply backlogs, and slow government building inspectors can—and do—delay construction projects. A builder will leave himself plenty of wiggle room in the promised delivery date—as much as one year from the target date. Take note of how the delivery date is spelled out in your contract, and make sure you can live with the uncertainty of the timetable.

Builders loathe negotiating on price, but they will negotiate what's included in that price. You might try to include some upgrades in your purchase offer, such as a higher grade of carpet or the optional fireplace, for the standard price. Make sure you write it into your purchase offer (after you've done a little negotiating with the salesperson), because you have no chance of scoring such upgrades later. And that salesperson just might forget your conversation after the deal is signed.

## Razzi's Rules to Live By

### 🏠 Forget the asking price.
The *real* price of that home—the price you should pay—is set by the market. It may be lower (or occasionally higher) than the asking price.

### 🏠 Look for haggle potential.
Watch for signs that your buyer may be willing to settle for a lower price. These include a home that's been on the market longer than

213

usual, bad winter weather, signs that an owner already has moved out, and estate sales.

## 🏠 Treat earnest money carefully.

This chunk of cash that you present with your purchase offer, signifying your seriousness about buying, is at risk if you decide to back out of the deal. Don't make any bigger an earnest money payment than is necessary in your market.

## 🏠 When in doubt, spell it out.

With a swipe of the seller's pen, your purchase offer magically becomes a binding contract. Get everything you want written into that purchase offer right from the start. Include a list of all the things you expect to convey with the house, including light fixtures, window coverings, play sets and appliances.

## 🏠 Protect yourself with contingencies.

If the home turns out not to be as good a deal as it first appeared to be, or if your ability to get a decent mortgage is not as certain as you thought it was, you need an escape hatch from your contract to buy that home. Contingencies are your escape hatch. Include contingencies for home inspection, appraisal, and financing. Other contingencies can be used for special needs.

## 🏠 You can haggle with builders.

They'll try to dictate the terms of the contract, and it's tough to get them to budge from their asking price. But builders may be willing to throw in a few free upgrades if that's what it takes to seal your deal.

# CHAPTER FOURTEEN

# Anxiety Time: Negotiating Your Way to a Deal

"I need a drink and a place to rest my ankles,"
Serena said, blowing a kiss and sweeping past him
into the living room."

JOHN BERENDT, *Midnight in the
Garden of Good and Evil*

I T'S LIKE BEING A HIGH SCHOOL SENIOR all over again, waiting for
colleges to send you the thick envelope of acceptance or the thin
envelope of "We wish you well in your efforts . . . elsewhere." All
you can do is wait to hear whether the sellers will snap up your
fantastic offer to buy their home, or whether they'll come back with
a counteroffer for you to consider.

# How to Present Your Offer

Talk with your buyer's agent about how your offer will be presented to the sellers. A great agent has the poise and nuance to make sure your offer is presented in the best possible light; a lesser agent will just fax your purchase offer over to the seller's agent and wait for a reply. Proactive, experienced agents will ask the seller's agent (and thereby, the sellers) for permission to present the offer in person. That gives them the opportunity to sell your offer a little, pointing out, for example, that your price may be a tad lower than they were asking, but your promise of a quick closing more than makes up for it. Not all sellers and agents will agree to a personal presentation, but it's worth pursuing, especially if you've found yourself a charismatic, persuasive buyer's agent. It's so much easier for a seller to say no to a fax machine than to a friendly face.

Often, however, busy buyer's agents simply fax the purchase offer over to the seller's agent. There's no guarantee the seller's agent will present the offer immediately. If they're getting nibbles from more than one buyer, they may wait and consider them all at once. If you're in a raging seller's market, you may have to equip your agent with an escalation clause, which will increase your bid in small increments above competitors' bids, up to your top dollar. Your agent can unveil this clause if it becomes necessary to bid against others quickly. (You'll find more on the escalation clause in Chapter Fourteen-and-a-half.)

Brace yourself for the idea that the sellers' agent may try to shop your offer around, hoping to draw a higher bid from another buyer. You can try to limit this by putting an expiration date on your purchase offer, say forty-eight hours from the time your agent presents it. Creating a little bit of urgency is a tried-and-true retailing tool. It's as if you're slapping a "Limited time only!" sticker on your contract. You do have the right to withdraw your offer at any time before it has been signed by the sellers, but be sure to discuss this deadline strategy with your buyer's agent; an experienced agent may have some insight into the personality of the seller's agent, and can advise you on how that agent will react to a limited-time offer. If it's going to poison the climate, it's not worth it, but if you're dealing with people likely to shop your offer around, then you need to protect yourself.

## The Counteroffer

Don't be surprised or offended if you get a counteroffer from the sellers. That's a good sign—it means you've started negotiations. Often the changes are simply handwritten into the purchase offer you've already submitted, but if the offer is significantly different, the seller's agent will probably present a clean, new document for your approval. Can you live with the new terms, and possibly the new price? These changes may be in response to any aspect of your offer. Maybe the sellers wants to push the closing date back a few weeks, or maybe they are asking for a rent-back period after closing. Maybe they've agreed to your lower-than-list price but not your request to pay some of your closing costs. Or maybe they're taking a hard line, resubmitting their original list price and denying any of the concessions you asked for in your offer.

Your agent may be of limited help as you evaluate a counteroffer. The agent doesn't know what you're truly willing to live with. At the same time, the agent has a very keen interest in seeing you just sign the darn contract, which brings closing day and a commission check into view—and frees up that agent's time to focus on another buyer or seller.

Essentially, you find yourself facing the classic bird in the hand or the two in the bush decision when you evaluate a counteroffer. Sign that offer, even if it means giving up some things you really wanted, and you've got yourself a deal. Change anything in that offer, and you might get what you want, but you also risk losing the deal altogether. The sellers could just walk away. And there's always the possibility somebody else will swoop in and steal the home away from you.

## Principles of Negotiating an Offer

There are three principles to keep in mind about negotiating. First, the best deals happen when both parties really want the deal to happen. If both of you really want to come to terms, a few go-rounds of refining the deal through offers and counteroffers won't kill it. You can tell by the tone of your exchanges with the sellers and their agent. Have you agreed on the big picture (particularly price), but you're still straightening out the details about the scheduling of inspections and items that will convey with the house? (The sellers said yes to the window coverings, but they really want to keep the chandelier.) If so, you can continue your negotiations with confidence.

Second, seasoned negotiators say you always should get a little something for every concession you make. Not only does that strategy net more for you, but it sends a message to the other side that there's a price to be paid for anything they ask, and that tends to curtail requests. (You might offer, for example, to give up the chandelier, but they need to leave the refrigerator, which they had planned to remove. Or perhaps you'll ask them to contribute toward your closing costs as a trade-off.) There is a greater risk here of killing the deal, especially if you're dealing with a seller who expects you to make all the concessions. But some sellers can't stop nibbling away at negotiations. One way to curtail the nibbling is to insist that all counteroffers be made in writing, so you can get something in your hands that you can sign quickly and put an end to the nibbling.

Third, remember that the best negotiations leave both sides feeling satisfied. That doesn't necessarily mean triumphant—both parties should be satisfied that they've achieved their most important objectives and are being treated fairly. Remember, both parties still face several weeks of working together to get to that closing table. Problems can crop up (maybe your loan gets delayed or you have trouble getting an inspection scheduled in accordance with the timing called for in your contract). You even could wind up re-opening negotiations if the home inspection reveals a need for costly repairs. If you've bargained the other party into a corner already, you can't expect much cooperation if trouble crops up later. Seething sellers might even act against their own interest and call your deal off altogether, just to spite you.

## Find a Way to Make it Work—or Not

Most American consumers shy away from haggling. It seems impolite, somehow. We're used to seeing a price tag, and maybe waiting for a sale if that price is too dear. But negotiation over price and terms (which can be at least as important) are simply a fact of life in real estate transactions. And you can negotiate without playing hardball . . . although that remains an option, too.

219

Consider a few examples of how you might do your horse, uh, house-trading:

In the few months it has been on the market, the homeowners lowered their price twice, a good sign that they really must sell. In fact, you find out that they have already moved into a new home and are stuck with two mortgage payments. You make a fair offer, contingent on a home inspection, and they accept. The home inspection turns up some plumbing and siding problems that will be expensive to repair. Based on that report, you make a new, lower offer. The sellers acknowledge the problem but say the repairs will be cheaper than your estimate, and they counteroffer with a smaller price concession than you asked for. Neither of you wants to budge any further on the price. But maybe there's a win-win solution. What about all those hand tools and garden equipment stored in the garage? You've been renting and are not looking forward to buying new ladders and hoses and hammers. So you make another offer: You'll take the smaller price concession if you also get to keep all that equipment. They love this idea. You have yourselves a deal.

Another scenario: You're relocating to a different part of the country. To get your home ready for sale you spent $10,000 on a new roof. Your home was in tip-top shape and commanded top dollar. You find a lovely older home in your new community, and the sellers accept your offer for just $5,000 under their asking price. You go back and forth with counteroffers once or twice. They ask to push back your proposed closing date two weeks so they can attend their son's graduation. That won't be a hardship for you, so you agree. It's looking like this will be a smooth path to closing day. Suddenly you learn that the homeowners insurance company will only give you a policy if the house first gets a brand-new roof. It's in a part of the country prone to severe hailstorms, and they've become very strict about the quality of roofs on homes they insure. The cost of a new, hail-resistant roof: $15,000. But you just shelled out $10,000 on a roof for your old home! You ask the sellers to pay, but they balk. Suddenly, your whole deal hinges on $15,000. Knowing that this is a community where insurance availability has been a problem, you put an insurance contingency in your purchase offer . . . and the home inspection hasn't even been done. Surely you could get out of the deal on the basis of either contingency. Do you walk away and demand that your earnest-money be refunded? Not yet. You offer to split the cost with the seller, and not wanting to lose the deal at this late point, they agree.

But, at some point, concessions just cost too much. Consider this situation. At long last you've found a house in the school district you were hoping to get into. It's not the ideal house you had in mind at the start, but it has the four bedrooms your family needs, and it will be much more to your liking after you tear out the seller's dated choices in carpet and wallpaper. You offer $15,000 less than the asking price, an offer you think is fair based on recent sales in the neighborhood, and include a finance contingency, a home-inspection contingency, and a closing date that's one month away. Your offer notes that you expect the kitchen appliances, window coverings, fireplace doors, and ceiling fans to stay. Their counter-offer has a token price reduction of only $2,000 and says they want to take the refrigerator and rent-back the home for two weeks after closing. This isn't much progress, you think. You counter with an offer that's $10,000 less than their asking price and agree to their requests for the refrigerator and the rent back, specifying that they will pay rent equal to your new mortgage payment for that period.

In their counteroffer, they agree to everything except the price. They'll agree to $6,000 less than their asking price. You accept this offer; it's absolutely your top dollar. But the haggling isn't over yet. The home inspector's report shows that the floor under the dishwasher is spongy from water damage; there's insufficient insulation in the attic, and the stairs and railing on the backyard deck are unstable and need to be replaced. A contractor estimates that you'll spend at least $8,000 on the repairs. You ask the sellers to reduce the price by that amount and you'll have the repairs done to your liking after you move in. Nothing doing, say the sellers. That deck has been fine since they built it themselves 20 years ago, and you can just drive a few nails into it if you're concerned. They'll agree to only $1,000 to compensate you for the floor. But you've reached your limit. If you agree to their offer you'll be cutting into the money you had planned to use to redecorate the home. And it never exactly stirred your soul to begin with. The deal is off, you say, invoking your home inspection contingency. You ask to have your earnest money returned.

## Get It in Writing

These words ought to be embroidered in a cross-stitch sampler, framed and handed down through generations of your family: "Get it in writing." Absolutely everything involved in a real estate deal must be in writing. If your agent calls your cell phone with the great news that your offer has been accepted, go ahead and rejoice—but keep your joy tentative until you get a copy of that signed contract in your hands. (And make sure your agent gets it to you pronto!) If you agree to the sellers' request to remain in the home after closing, get that rent-back agreement written up and signed right away. When you're satisfied with the home inspection (the results of which, of course, should be written up and signed by the inspector), sign off on your release of the contingency right away to keep the deal on track. The "Get it in writing" mantra applies to everyone you work with in a real estate deal. When you call the lender to lock in your interest rate, ask for a written confirmation of that lock—and its expiration date. Paper is your friend in a real estate deal, and time is your enemy. Whatever needs to be done, make sure you do it as promptly as possible. Get the details in writing, and file the documents in a big accordion file so you can get your hands on everything quickly if questions arise.

At some point, you will finally have it: A purchase contract, signed by both seller and buyer! Jump up and down, call your extended family and friends, open the champagne, and celebrate. Buying a home is one of life's sweet moments, and you should savor it fully. Sure there are details to be tended to, and you'll tend to them as they come. But, for now, celebrate.

## Razzi's Rules to Live By

### It's easy to say no to a fax machine.

Proactive real estate agents like to present their offers in person whenever possible. It allows them to cast the offer in its best light and even sell it a bit. Urge your agent not to simply fax your offer in to the seller's agent if it can be avoided.

### Make it a limited-time offer.

Sellers may try to shop your offer around, hoping to drum up a better offer from someone else. Talk with your agent about putting an expiration date on your offer, to limit their ability to shop it—

and to create a bit of urgency. Remember, you can revoke your offer at any point before the sellers sign it.

### 🏠 Counteroffers pave the way to a deal.

Don't be surprised if you have to go through a round or two of counteroffers that tailor the deal to meet the needs of both buyer and seller.

### 🏠 Agents have their own interests.

Agents can get fretful about the back-and-forth of counteroffers. Remember, they have a keen interest in seeing you finally sign off on the deal (a deal whose terms *they* don't have to live with). An agent's commission check rests on getting a signed deal moving along swiftly toward the closing table.

### 🏠 Get as good as you give.

When negotiating, ask for a little something for every concession you make. Not only will that strategy net more for you, but it may limit the number of requests the sellers make, once they know each one carries a price.

### 🏠 Don't go in for the kill.

Even if you're in a position to wring the last drop out of negotiations, remember that the most successful negotiations leave *both* parties feeling they got what they needed and are being treated fairly. You still have several weeks of interaction ahead with those sellers, and you might need their cooperation later. Don't leave them feeling burned.

## 🏠 Paper is your friend; time is your enemy.

Document everything and keep all your papers in an accordion file
for easy reference. Jump on all the little tasks you have to perform
before closing; you literally cannot afford to waste any time.

## 🏠 Get it in writing.

Make it your policy, your mantra, your dogma: Get it in writing.
Every single agreement between you and the seller, you and your
lender, you and *everyone else* must be in writing or it doesn't exist.

# Special Tips for Surviving a Cutthroat Seller's Market

"What nonsense you talk, precious. No one can get
    into the home without knocking."
"I think he comes in by the window," she said.
"My love, it is three floors up."
"Were not the leaves at the foot of the window, mother?"

J.M. BARRIE, *Peter Pan*

CONDOLENCES TO YOU if you are trying to buy a home in a super-competitive seller's market. So much of the sensible advice about how to shop and how to negotiate simply doesn't apply to you. The commonsense precautions that buyers use to protect themselves, such as contingencies for home inspections, simply aren't available to buyers trying to survive a market where there are lots of buyers chasing scarce properties. You're dealing in a topsy-turvy world where much of the advice I just offered in Chapter Fourteen doesn't quite apply. That's the reason behind this little half chapter—it's full of exceptions to the rules.

The first caution, however, is a very important one. Make sure your local market still is one of those roaring sellers' markets. Markets can change quickly. What was a seller's market last month might have cooled off a bit this month. You don't want to throw money at a seller (and caution out the window) if it's not absolutely necessary. Be alert for signs that a torrid market is starting to cool. Ask your agent for info about how many homes are listed in the MLS compared to last month and the month before. Ask about the average time homes remain on the market. If the number of available listings and the time on the market are starting to inch up, the market is cooling. Are you starting to see fewer people at open houses? Are fewer homes attracting multiple offers? Sellers will be the last to sense any shift to a cooling market. If their neighbors sold for more than their asking price a few months ago, they expect to sell their lovely home for even more money now. They may be surprised when they don't get an offer after the first weekend on the market. Surprise will turn to shock if they receive just one offer— for a few thousand below their asking price. The burden is on you and your agent to be watchful for a saner market, where it's safe for you to offer a reasonable price and insist on common protections such as a home inspection.

Keep in mind that housing markets don't move in lockstep. Even within a single metropolitan area, different neighborhoods can run hot or cold. Frequently, when a local housing market is starting to cool, the prices stop accelerating first for the most expensive homes in town. Prices there simply reach a point where buyers cannot follow. But it's not always the case that prices weaken first at the top. Sometimes condos are the first to get the chill; sometimes it's new construction that weakens, thanks to a glut of new homes. Developers grow increasingly desperate to unload homes and drive down the price for all their competitors. (Homeowners trying to sell homes that are only a few years old can see their prices weaken terribly.) The only way they can compete with builders who offer free finished basements and other upgrades is to lower the price on their own home, sometimes below what they paid for it just a few years earlier.

The stakes are high for a buyer. You don't want to be the last fool to pay top dollar, only to have prices flatten out or even decline for a couple of years. When buying after years of a booming market, it's absolutely critical that you keep your ear to the ground for rumbles of change to your local economy. Is a big employer hinting about layoffs? Are companies slowing down their hiring? Is there a rumor of a big corporate merger that could siphon jobs away from your town? These are the types of things that usually bring a roaring housing market down to earth. Watch for them.

Once you conclude that the town, or even just the neighborhood where you're trying to buy a home is still a roaring seller's market, you have to act boldly. To simply find and buy a home, you will be forced to act like a predator. You must be the lion who beats the hyenas—all those other buyers—to the kill. You have to act swiftly and present the seller with a killer contract. But you have to be nice to your prey. Otherwise, that seller might give preference to one of those darned hyenas waiting in the background.

If you're reading this chapter, odds are you're already familiar with the signs of a seller's market. They're places where there are several buyers competing for each home that's put up for sale. Places where buyers get sucked into bidding wars, driving prices higher than the seller's asking price. Places where homes routinely sell after only a couple of days on the market. Places where buyers make full-price offers, or even higher than full price, and still lose out to another buyer with deeper pockets (or less common sense). Places where buyers offer free rent-backs to the seller after closing. Places where buyers throw in a free week at their family's vacation home, if the sellers will be kind enough to accept their greater-than-full-price offer. Places where buyers don't even ask for a home inspection, or an appraisal contingency. If you're a buyer, there's nothing worse than a raging seller's market.

How long these sellers' markets can continue to rage is anybody's guess. But even if the broader market cools enough to give buyers a fair shot at landing a home without kowtowing to sellers, one thing is certain: There always will be hot spots that remain seller's markets. Whether it's because the school district is fabulous, the address is chic, or the waterfront views are breathtaking, some neighborhoods will always remain difficult for buyers. If you find yourself in one of these squeezes, you will find this chapter will be the most important part of this book.

Will you end up overpaying for the home? Well, yes, you might. But, if this is to be your home for the next five to ten years, the risk of long-term financial damage from overpaying is lessened. As we discussed in Chapter One, you minimize your financial risk if you buy a home that is in a good location and that is big enough to accommodate your changing needs for years to come. Should prices level off or, shudder to think, decline in coming years, you can stay put and ride out the market until prices again start to rise.

If the neighborhood has been desirable for years—places like Georgetown in Washington, D.C., or Winnetka, Illinois, outside Chicago, come to mind—it's likely to remain desirable for years to come. Other buyers will follow in your footsteps, paying more than *they* should for homes in that chic community, and boosting your value further. But, if you're buying into a suddenly trendy community that's attracting a lot of investors who don't plan to live there themselves—such as some of the newly built condo communities or golf-course developments—then the risk of overpaying is greater. Investors don't stick around like owner-occupants do. And trendy doesn't stay trendy for long.

## The Naked Buyer

The ordinary recipe for successfully buying a home goes pretty much like this: Don't overextend your budget. Shop hard for the best home. Negotiate over the price and terms. And *always* include protective clauses in your purchase offer stipulating that the deal hinges on your ability to get an acceptable mortgage and on you being satisfied with the home after a professional home inspector has examined it on your behalf. Unfortunately, in a raging seller's market, if you followed that tried-and-true recipe, you simply wouldn't get the home. To win the home, you'll have to go naked—stripping your purchase offer of those valuable protections. And you very likely will have to pay *more* than the asking price.

The only protections you have in a raging seller's market come from the extra preparation you will do *before* starting the hunt and from the extra scrutiny you will apply as you evaluate a home. You may have only a few hours in which to decide whether to make an offer on the home, so advance work is crucial. It's your safety net.

## Discover Your *Real* Top Dollar

This is going to be a real gut-check. After going through the financial review covered in Chapters Two and Three, you should have a very good idea of how much you're comfortable spending on a home. But how much are you *really* willing (and able!) to part with? You don't want to find out the real number after you've been out-bid on the perfect home and then kick yourself because you know you could have bumped up your offer by $5,000 or $10,000 if only you'd had a second chance to bid.

I advise working backward to arrive at your real top-dollar. Let's say the home is listed at $400,000, which seems to you like a pretty fair price. But there were dozens of lookers swarming through the one-day-only open house on Saturday. The sellers' agent says they'll consider all offers on the Wednesday after the open house. You're facing a bidding war, and a full-price offer for $400,000 is probably not going to win it.

You really want this home. But what are you willing to pay? If the price rose to $500,000 (it *has* happened) would you still want it? Probably not at that price. You'd kiss that lovely home goodbye, wish the crazy, deep-pocketed victors well, and sleep soundly that night.

What if bidding drove the price close to $450,000? That's outrageous, you think. But do you start to think that, just maybe, it's feasible? "If we take some money out of this mutual fund and put off buying a new car, maybe we could do it," you think. Now you're closing in on your *real* top dollar. If the home were to sell for

$445,000 to someone else, would you kick yourself for not having offered $450,000?

Substitute your own numbers. Maybe your top dollar is $420,000 or $305,000 or $200,000, but the process is the same. At what price will you kick yourself for not having bought the home? At what price are you absolutely certain you should walk away? Somewhere in between those two figures lies your real top dollar. It's a poker-player's decision. Has the pot grown too rich for you? Each of us has our own cutoff point for folding. Try to learn yours before you get into the game.

*Knowing* your top dollar doesn't necessarily mean you'll have to *pay* your top dollar. Determined buyers in sellers' markets typically use an escalation clause to manage their bidding. Let's say you're willing to go as high as $420,000 on that home that's listed for $400,000. Your real estate agent can help you write an escalation clause into your purchase offer that raises your offer in increments of $1,000 above a competitor's offer, up to a cap of $420,000. Some aggressive buyers' agents will keep your signed escalation clause in their vest pocket. If it doesn't look like there will be other bidders, they don't need it. (And you don't have to signal to the sellers that you're willing to pay more.) But if other buyers unexpectedly appear, they can present the escalation clause.

## Make an Offer They Can't Refuse

You need to make your purchase offer irresistible. Simply throwing money at the sellers might not even be enough. You need to give them everything they want. A good real estate agent can help you find out just what will tickle the sellers. Sometimes their hot button is that they want to close quickly. Others want to put off closing for a few months while they shop for their new home. They might want to rent back for a few months after closing, until their kids get out of school. Some sellers have a soft spot for families who will bring children into the home where they once raised their own even though doing so risks running afoul of fair-housing laws. Whatever it is, you want to give it to them—short of borrowing youngsters to pass off as your own. You might even have to take up temporary lodgings in a short-term rental apartment if the sellers want to rent back after closing. Of course it stinks, but it's what you have to do to get the home.

Sellers like to see that you have enough money to swing the deal without hassle. A big earnest-money check helps reassure them that you're serious—and that you have some cash behind you. How big is big? That varies according to local custom and the price of the home, but it can go to 10 percent of the purchase price—or even more. Keep in mind that you stand to lose this money if you have to back out of the deal for any reason not covered by a contingency clause! And contingency clauses are a buyer's fantasy in markets like these.

Sellers also want to see that you already have your loan lined up. It's a good idea for you to do so in an ordinary, balanced market; it's crucial in a sellers' market. In fact, you should be suspect of any real estate agent who agrees to represent you without demanding that you get preapproved before looking at homes. A real pro wouldn't waste the time on you. And, as with everything involving the buying or selling of real estate, it's important that you get that preapproval *in writing*. Remember, if it's not in writing, it doesn't exist.

## Hire an Aggressive Agent

Do a lot of research before you sign up a buyer's agent. You want one who has a no-nonsense reputation for bringing sound contracts to the table that will close without headaches. Be aware that, even in big cities, the real estate community tends to be cliqueish. If you use an agent who has a reputation for presenting offers that fall apart before they close, or who's haphazard about paperwork, or who's simply unpleasant to work with, you could find that your strong purchase offers get rejected, time after time. Nothing requires a seller to take the highest-price offer. And if two offers are roughly equivalent, the buyer is likely to choose the one that looks most likely to close without hassle. Certainly the seller's real estate agent would prefer to avoid dealing with a flake, so he or she may pooh-pooh offers from your pesky agent, advising sellers that competing offers look stronger. You'll suffer for your agent's sloppy reputation—and you might never find out what the problem was. You can find more on choosing a good agent in Chapter Ten.

## Get the Listings King in Your Corner

It's counterintuitive, but you should consider engaging the local listings king to be your buyers' agent. Sure, in a perfect world some real estate agents would represent only buyers, while others would represent only sellers. Each would be a gladiator for his or her own side, minimizing the risk that your private information (like your real top dollar or your blinding love for a particular home) will fall into your opponent's hands during negotiations. But the system simply doesn't work that way right now, and we must deal with the fact that most of the best real estate agents focus heavily on the selling side of the deal. Many of them believe there's more money to be made that way.

But why would a buyer want to work with the listings king? Because that agent has his or her ear to the ground. That agent will hear about homes that are about to go on the sale *before* they ever hit the MLS. They'll get many of the best listings themselves—and will earn more if they don't have to split the commission with another agent. Even if they don't have the listing themselves, odds are they've been asked to make a listing presentation for the sellers. They've already toured the home, looked up sales prices on comparable properties and have met the sellers. Even if the sellers choose to list the home with another agent, *this* agent is primed and ready to show you the home the day it comes on the market. That's invaluable intelligence for a buyer in a hot market.

## Supplementing Your Agent's Work

While you're at it, keep your own ear to the ground for the distant rumblings of a home that's about to go up for sale. Review the telltale signs of a home that's being prepared for sale, outlined in Chapter Eleven. Of course, you'll want to enlist everyone you know in your house-hunt. If your friend notices that the couple down the street is having a yard sale (their first ever!) make sure either you or your friend manages to slip in a little question about whether they're thinking of selling. Your cousin spots the car of a hotshot local real estate agent parked outside a neighbor's lovely home? (Agents love Realtor bumper stickers and vanity license plates!) You need to find out if there's a home about to be put on the market!

If you detect one or more pre-sale rumblings, it doesn't hurt to knock on the door (or to compose a lovely handwritten letter) and ask the owners if they plan to sell their home. It's flattery, actually. Make sure to note that you want to buy it and live there yourself. You don't want them to think your letter is from just another real estate agent trawling for business. There's always the possibility that they'll agree to sell it to you before they've hired a real estate agent. If you have a strong offer at a tempting price, they could save a lot of money by not hiring a real estate agent. On that hypothetical $420,000 home, an agent would charge them about 6 percent, or $25,200. They could save that cash — if they'd agree to accept your juicy offer, right away. If you've already signed on with a buyer's agent, you can tell the seller you'll pay that agent out of your own pocket (probably 3 percent), to make the deal more attractive. It's at least worth your while to ask.

## The Same-day Decision

In a hot seller's market, you very likely will have to make a decision to buy the home the very day you first see it. That's preposterous, of course. I've taken longer than that to mull over the choice of a new toaster. But in roaring sellers' markets, you barely have time to think. I've shown up at first-day open houses only to find that the property has been sold already. As soon as you get an inkling that the home is for sale, decide whether you want it, and make your move. Even if the seller's agent says they aren't taking offers until a few days later, it's in your interest to have your agent at least *try* to present your juicy offer early. Remember, you're the lion, and all those other lookers are hyenas drooling over *your* kill.

Predator that you are, you already know the neighborhood. You've done a rush-hour trial commute. You know whether the schools are good and whether there's a suitable gym and grocery nearby. You know your top dollar; your real estate agent has given you some advice on prices, and you have your mortgage lined up and ready to go. All you have to do is tour the home and decide if you want to buy it. Using your customized cheat sheet (see

Appendix Two) can help you pore over that home like a detective. Never mind any hyenas who might be touring it at the same time. Be focused. Does the house have the rooms you need? Stand in the kitchen and imagine yourself preparing breakfast. Is it laid out efficiently? Are there enough closets? Whip out your tape measure to size up rooms, especially if you need to make sure Grandma's china cabinet will fit. (Measurements on listing sheets aren't always accurate.) Open the fridge, freezer, oven, and dishwasher to see if they seem to be in good repair. Turn on the hot and cold water faucets to gauge water pressure. Flush the toilets.

## Be Your Own Home Inspector

It's a shame, but you may not win a bidding war if your offer includes a home-inspection contingency. You will have to do your own mini-inspection right on the spot. (If you have a friend or relative in the construction business, now's the time to ask a favor and invite them to tour the home with you.) By no means does this replace the security of having a professional home inspector evaluate a home! But if you must buy naked, you'll have to look through the home for any obvious signs of big trouble. After you own the home, you still may want to hire a home inspector so you can get a good estimate of repairs to budget for in coming years. At a minimum, you should call in a heating contractor to inspect and clean the furnace and its flue, the hot water heater and the air conditioner. Before trying to use a fireplace, you need to have a chimney sweep inspect it and make sure it's safe. You can find more on hiring inspectors in Chapter Fifteen.

It wouldn't hurt to review a basic home-repair and maintenance manual beforehand. These books are usually full of pictures showing how things like plumbing, wiring, and other important home elements ought to look.

There are a few key things you should make sure you look at in your amateur home inspection. You don't necessarily have to nix the deal just because you find these red flags. (However, if you suspect structural problems, *do not even consider* buying the home without a contingency calling for an inspection by a structural engineer. If you lose the bidding war, so be it. You don't want to be saddled with a problem that's a nightmare to fix.) Most other problems simply translate into dollars. Of course, you may be stretching your budget to the breaking point already, and even $500 more for a new *anything* is $500 too much. But if your budget allows, you can take a lot of the emotion out of the homebuying decision by translating property flaws to dollars. In a balanced market, you'd be able to negotiate with the seller to pay for the flaws; in a raging seller's market, you'll bear them alone. Do your best, however, to translate home repair problems to dollars, and then let the bottom line be your guide to deciding whether to buy. A new roof can cost you tens of thousands of dollars, depending on how complicated the roof is. Upgrading the electrical system costs a few thousand. A new furnace or hot water heater is a phone call (and a credit card number) away. If you really want the home, and the price (plus likely repairs) falls within your top-dollar limit, go ahead and make an offer. If they don't, keep looking.

## Electricity

Go outdoors and look at the electric meter. You don't have to touch anything! If it's an older home, you may see that the metal box on which the meter is mounted is old and small (only about one foot square). If so, then the electric supply to that home is probably not more than 100 amps. That home's electrical service has not been upgraded, and you'll have to foot the bill should you decide to install a central air conditioning system or add an extra room. Updated, 200-amp boxes are rectangular, roughly two feet tall by fifteen inches wide.

Inside, look at the circuit box or, in an older home, the fuse box. Does it *look* as if any electrical work was done in a tidy, professional manner? Sloppy work may be the sign of do-it-yourself jobs, which might not have been inspected by local building officials. Does it look as if the owners keep a jumbled supply of fuses on hand near the fuse box? If so, you can reasonably suspect that they tend to blow fuses frequently, and you'll want to upgrade if you like the luxury of using a hair dryer or clothes iron wherever and whenever you wish.

Do the current owners use a lot of extension cords? That's a sign that there aren't enough conveniently placed outlets (a common problem in older homes). It could also indicate a possible problem with one or more of the outlets that they haven't had fixed.

Aluminum wiring? Look at any exposed electrical wires you can find in an unfinished basement or utility room. If you see "Al" or "Aluminum" marked on the electric wire, you need to call in a licensed electrician. That's a sign that the home contains aluminum wiring, a cheap alternative that was used on some homes between 1965 and 1973. Aluminum wiring poses a greater risk of fire than the traditional copper wiring. (Copper wires are sometimes marked "CU.") Many of these homes have been rewired with copper already, but some homeowners have chosen to retrofit their aluminum wiring with special copper connections at switches, wall outlets, and other connections. You need the help of a licensed electrician to make sure the system is safe—and you *still* might want to budget for a big rewiring project after buying the home.

Are there GFI (ground fault circuit interrupter) electric outlets in the kitchen and bathrooms? They're required by the National Electrical Code nationwide for outlets near water or outdoors. These extra-sensitive, extra-fast circuit breakers should be used in the kitchen and bath. They are designed to break a circuit immediately and could save you or a family member from electrocution if, say, an old radio fell into the bathtub. Look for the square outlet with two tiny "test" buttons somewhere in the kitchen and bath. Absence of GFI outlets doesn't necessarily mean you will be electrocuted, but it is a sign that the home's wiring has not been updated.

## Foundation

Look at the foundation, indoors and out. If the home has a basement, go downstairs and examine any unfinished concrete floor or wall areas. The presence of cracks is not necessarily a sign of trouble. It's normal for concrete to shrink, causing hairline cracks. (I once looked at Hoover Dam in Nevada with binoculars, while waiting for a tour to begin. It's loaded with cracks! So far, no dam breaks.) But some cracks are a warning of serious trouble. Something is moving, whether it's the home or the soil beneath or around it, and that's not good at all.

If you spot any of the following signs, you need to get an evaluation by a licensed structural engineer before you buy the home: gaping cracks, big enough for you to insert the tip of a pencil; cracks in which one side is not even with the plane of the wall; bulges in the concrete floor; bulging or bowing in a foundation wall; and cracks radiating in from the corners of the floor, walls or ceilings.

## Termites and Other Pests

Termites and carpenter ants leave telltale signs of their damage. Your mortgage lender will require a termite inspection before approving your loan (lenders won't agree to drop *their* contingencies no matter what) but you should keep an eye out for damage from a current or an old infestation. Look at the inside and outside of exterior walls for mud tubes, about one-quarter to one-half inch in diameter. Termites use these as sun-sheltered highways from soil to wood. Little piles of what looks like sawdust are signs that termites or ants have been eating their way through wood. If you see wood, say a floor joist, with tiny ruts drilled into it along the grain, that's termite damage (though it could be decades old, for all you know). Poking into suspect wood with a screwdriver may reveal that it's mush.

## Roof and Chimney

Look at the roof. No, you can't climb up on the roof during an ordinary home tour, but you can use a pair of binoculars and take a cursory look at the roof's condition from the ground. You can see if tiles are cracked or missing, or if the edges of asphalt shingles are curling or crumbling. If so, you can count on investing in a new roof soon after closing day. If it looks really shabby, you could find water damage in the attic.

While you have your binoculars out, try to get a look at the chimney. You can't judge whether the flue inside will be safe for building a fire next Thanksgiving, but you can at least try to see if bricks are loose or the chimney is pulling away from the home.

241

## Water Damage and Basement

Pay special attention to spongy floor or wall surfaces near (and downstairs from!) bathtubs, showers, toilets, dishwashers, and washing machines. Sponginess is a sign of water damage and rot— and of repair bills. If the floor/wall joints in the shower look as if they've been caulked with a fire hose, take that as a clue that there may be a leakage problem with that shower.

In the basement, is everything placed up off the floor? Are there rust stains on the floor? Strong moldy smells? All these are signs of water or flooding problems.

If there's a bedroom or nanny suite in the basement, make sure there's a door or window that's big enough and low enough (generally, that means no more than 42 inches off the ground, but local codes can vary) for someone to climb out in case of fire. It's dangerous—and a violation of fire codes—to allow someone to sleep in a room that has no fire exit. The previous owner may have finished the room without obtaining necessary building permits.

## Asbestos

Is there stuff around the home that might contain asbestos? In homes built before 1978, you might find asbestos used as insulation around the furnace or heating ducts. Look for a white, plaster-like coating and evidence of any crumbling. The danger with asbestos is that these hardy fibers can break off and enter your lungs, where they can cause cancer and other lung diseases, so the material needs to be removed or encapsulated if it's in a broken, crumbly state. Asbestos also was used in floor and ceiling tiles and in some exterior siding. If it's intact and doing its job, you might be able to leave it alone. But if you decide to remove it, you'll need to hire a pro to do the job correctly without releasing dangerous fibers into the air and then to dispose of the hazardous waste legally. Of course, you'll pay extra for these services.

## Temperature Control: Heat and Air Conditioning

With heating and air-conditioning units, there's little way to tell if they're really up to the job just by looks alone. But, you can at least look to see whether they're new and shiny or old and beaten up. Is the hot water heater big enough to accommodate your family? (Here's a very rough rule of thumb. Two people with two bathrooms might get by with a forty-gallon tank. Four people with three bathrooms might need sixty gallons. Put five people in the same three-bathroom home, and you might need a seventy-five-gallon tank.) Does the water heater make rumbling percolator noises? That's a sign you may have to replace it soon.

## The Appraisal Comes in Low

In a balanced market, buyers have the luxury of adding an appraisal contingency to their offers. In other words, the deal is off if the property doesn't appraise for at least the contracted price. In a fierce seller's market, however, you may not be able to add this important contingency.

Just because you make a purchase offer without an appraisal contingency (which ordinarily says that you'll buy the home at the specified price *if* the appraiser values the property at that price or greater) doesn't mean there won't be an appraisal. The mortgage lender will insist on it. And if a bidding war has inflated the selling price, there's a very good chance the appraiser's estimate won't be as high as the price you've agreed to pay. So what are you going to do? You may find yourself hunting for extra cash to put into the deal.

Let's look at some numbers to see how the scenario might play out. Suppose your $800,000 offer made you the winning bidder in a hotly contested price war. You have $300,000 profit from the sale of your old home that you intend to use as a downpayment, and you plan to take out a mortgage for $500,000. With such a hefty downpayment, your mortgage would be for only 63 percent of the new home's value, and you will easily qualify for a mortgage. But the appraiser says the house is worth only $750,000. The lender will still approve the $500,000 mortgage, because it represents only 67 percent of the home's appraised value. You're in the clear because of your hefty downpayment, made possible by the profitable sale of your old home.

But, take a look at another variation on this scenario. Suppose a job relocation has taken you from a moderately priced midwestern community to a superheated California market where prices are much higher than where you were selling a home. You've agreed to pay $800,000 for a surprisingly modest home, but the sale of your old home gave you only $80,000 in cash, enough for a 10 percent downpayment on the California home. You need a mortgage for 90 percent of the home's value, or $720,000. But the appraiser says the house is worth only $700,000. Even if the lender approves a loan for 100 percent of the property's value, that gives you a mortgage for only $700,000. You're still under contract to pay $800,000. So, you have a downpayment of $80,000, a mortgage for $700,000, and . . . a gap of $20,000. You'll have to find $20,000 in cash *somewhere*, perhaps by tapping other investments, or even by selling your car or borrowing from a relative.

What happens if you simply can't come up with more cash? Almost certainly, you'll have to back out of the deal. The seller will be very unhappy—and you may not get your earnest money back.

These are the risks you take on when you agree to strip your purchase offer of all the standard contingencies that protect buyers! The only way to protect yourself is to play out the worst-case scenarios in your mind *before* you make the offer. Think it through: If you agree to pay $10,000 or $20,000—or more— above the asking price, can you come up with extra cash if it appraises at a lower amount? Would you be able to pay for thousands of dollars in unexpected repairs in the first year or two to cover flaws that might have been uncovered by a home inspector? If the answers are yes, then go ahead and buy naked.

Steel yourself, though, against the notion that rising prices will bail you out of a bad homebuying decision after only a year or two. Despite the boom of the early 2000s, when some people made tens of thousands of dollars in profit by buying and flipping properties over a short time, real estate remains a long-term investment. Owning a home for five to ten years or longer remains a safe, solid investment, even if you have to pay top dollar to get it. However, short-term investments in real estate are as risky as buying hog bellies or foreign currencies and reselling them for profit.

# Razzi's Rules to Live By

### 🏠 Hunt like a predator.
You have to stalk homes as they come on the market, then act swiftly and present the seller with a killer contract.

### 🏠 Give the seller what the seller wants.
Money always counts—but other terms could seal the deal. Delay your closing, rush your closing, rent back to them after closing—do whatever it takes.

## 🏠 Be ready to buy naked.

You may have to strip your purchase contract of common buyer protections. Your only protection will come from the extra preparation and scrutiny you apply up-front.

## 🏠 Know your real top dollar.

Your *real* top dollar is somewhere between the price at which you would kick yourself for losing out to another bidder and the price where you'd walk away with no remorse at all. Then put an escalation clause into your purchase offer that would raise your bid to that secret top dollar, should it be necessary.

## 🏠 Dump the flake.

If your agent has a reputation for bringing offers that fall apart before closing, you'll lose bidding wars . . . and may never know that the real reason was other agents' distaste for working with yours.

## 🏠 The listings king has the edge.

This agent is most likely to learn about homes *before* they come on the market, and can get you in fast.

## 🏠 Keep an eye out for fresh prey.

Watch for signs that homes are about to come on the market. It never hurts to knock on the door or to write a lovely, hand-written letter to the owners, asking if they plan to sell.

## 🏠 Be ready for love at first sight.

In a raging seller's market, be prepared to buy the very first day you see the home, without even a professional inspection. Pore over the home and its innards, doing as much of a mini-inspection as possible.

## 🏠 Flaws equal dollars.

Most flaws simply translate to repair dollars. But major structural flaws should be a deal-killer. If you see any red flags of structural flaws, pass on the home unless you get it cleared by an engineer first.

## 🏠 Do a worst-case scenario.

Do a worst-case scenario before writing a big check for earnest money. If the appraisal comes in low and the repair bills come in high, can you still swing the deal?

# How to Wrap up the Deal

"The kitchen at Green Gables was a cheerful apartment—or would have been cheerful if it had not been so painfully clean as to give it something of the appearance of an unused parlor."

L.M. MONTGOMERY, *Anne of Green Gables*

CONTRACT PENDING! (Or, in Californian, "You're in escrow!") Your deal is *almost* done. But you—and your buyer's agent—need to stay on top of the details to make sure the deal goes through to closing without a hitch. Depending on the desires of the buyer and the seller, you can have a couple of months between acceptance of your purchase offer and closing day, or perhaps just a couple of weeks. This is the time when great real estate agents (both the buyer's agent and the seller's agent) really earn their commission. The best agents have the experience that allows them to avoid problems *before* they come up. They've covered all your bases in the purchase contract, and they know how important it is to tend to all the details in that contract promptly and proactively.

Both you and the seller will want to satisfy—and then remove—all of the contingencies in your contract. You want to proceed quickly and methodically through your list of chores. And you have plenty of chores on your list! You also have chores that aren't detailed in your purchase contract but that are crucial for a smooth transition from one home to another. Arrange for movers to look at your belongings and give you written quotes. Insist on in-person,

## CHECKLIST

- ☐ Finalize your mortgage application.
- ☐ Give the lender any extra documents necessary to process your loan. (If the lender calls requesting a document, jump!)
- ☐ Lock in your interest rate and points, and get a written confirmation of the lock and its expiration date.
- ☐ Schedule the home inspection as quickly as possible so you have time to arrange for any pre-closing repairs that you and the seller agree upon.
- ☐ Line up a new homeowners' insurance policy.
- ☐ Decide who you will use to handle the closing.

written quotes! Nonbinding telephone quotes are a hallmark of scam artists. Avoid Internet referral services for movers; they have a bad reputation for links to disreputable moving companies. (If ever there is a time when you need to pay more heed to a company's reputation than to its low price, it's when you hire a moving service to load all your precious belongings onto a truck and drive off into the sunset. While you're at it, pay the moving company extra to fully insure your load. The standard insurance coverage included in movers' base price pays a pittance for anything that's lost, stolen or broken.)

Arrange for utilities to be turned off at your old home and turned on at the new one. Have the post office forward your mail to the new address. (The U.S. Postal Service allows you to arrange for forwarding to start at a later date through its Web site, *https://moversguide.usps.com.*) File a change-of-address form for all your bank, brokerage and credit card accounts, magazine subscriptions, and even with the Internal Revenue Service. (Use IRS Form 8822, Change of Address, which you can download at *www.irs.gov.* You can't afford to miss an audit notice—or a refund.) You have a lot to do!

## The Professional Home Inspection

Your first task is to find a thorough, professional home inspector, and that can require a bit of investigation. Most buyers ask their real estate agents for a referral. Your agent is likely to offer the names of two or three inspectors and resist recommending one as being the best. That helps the agent avoid liability in case you're dissatisfied with the performance of the inspector. But there's also good reason for you to do this search on your own.

Home inspectors often complain that if they're too rigorous in their examinations and too frequently point out flaws, they'll be tagged "deal-killers" by real estate agents—who then will stop referring buyers to them. You, of course, want the inspector's best, unadulterated judgment on the condition of that home. You're quite capable of deciding whether any particular flaws are severe enough to kill the deal. Above all, you want to be sure of getting an inspector who does *not* make repairs him- or herself. That's a blatant conflict of interest—all you want is an unbiased, objective professional opinion of the property's condition.

## Finding a Qualified Inspector

Home inspectors are licensed or regulated by state authorities in twenty-eight states. You can find a review of those laws and regulations at a Web site maintained by the American Society of Home Inspectors (ASHI), at *www.ashi.org*. You also can search for ASHI-certified inspectors near you through the Web site. Even if your state is among those that regulate home inspectors, you want to be sure to look for an inspector that is certified by either ASHI or by the National Institute of Building Inspectors (NIBI). NIBI originally developed as the training arm for the HouseMaster franchise of home inspectors, but the organization now trains other inspectors as well. You can look up NIBI-certified inspectors at *www.nibi.com*.

## Getting the Most out of Your Inspection

You'll get the most out of your inspection if you go along with the inspector. Of course, this allows you to see for yourself that the inspector actually exerted a little effort (and, for instance, climbed up into the attic to check it out firsthand), but it also allows you to ask questions as you go. Does the electric service coming into the house look sufficient? Is the deck attached to the house correctly? Discipline yourself to focus only on the nuts and bolts of the house; this isn't the time to be measuring windows for new draperies.

Once you get the inspector's report, try to get that contingency removed as quickly as possible. If you're satisfied with the property conditions—and keep in mind *no* house will be perfect—go ahead and sign off on the form saying that contingency has been removed. If you and the seller need to talk about repairs, as in who will arrange for them and who will pay the bill, deal with it quickly. Home inspection costs vary from $150 to $600 or more, depending on your market, the size and age of your home, and any special inspections you want to include. As always, shop around.

Your mortgage lender will insist that you have a qualified pest-control company perform an inspection for termites and other wood-damaging insects. (Extra inspections you might consider are covered in Chapter Fourteen.) Your real estate agent ought to be able to arrange for this and can tell you whether the buyer or seller customarily pays this expense in your market.

## Homeowners' Insurance

You will need to show proof of a homeowners' insurance policy, paid up for one year, when you go to closing. And you need to start shopping for it right away. Hurricanes Andrew in 1992 through Katrina and Rita in 2005 have led insurance companies to make sure they're not overly exposed to massive losses anywhere in the country. Insurers have grown much more picky about which homeowners and which properties they will cover.

## Potential Policy Problems

Before agreeing to give you a policy, insurers will check the CLUE database for the claims background of your new home and for your own history of filing claims. (You'll find more on getting a CLUE report in Chapter Twelve.) If either you or a previous owner of the home you're buying has filed two or more claims in the past few years, you could have trouble getting a policy, especially one at a reasonable price. Homeowners with low credit scores also can have trouble getting policies. (Insurers say that statistics show that people with low scores tend to file more claims.) You also might face trouble getting a policy if you live in an area that's prone to natural disasters. These include hurricanes and tropical storms along the Atlantic and Gulf Coasts, hail storms in Texas and the south-central states, and wildfires in California.

## Policy-Shopping

When shopping for a new policy on a home, ask for a quote from the company that now insures your home (or rental apartment) and from the company that insures your vehicle. Companies often extend discounts to long-time, claim-free customers and to people who insure both their home and auto with them. Be sure to tell the insurance companies if your new home will have an electronic security or sprinkler system. Basic safety equipment, such as window locks or simple burglar alarms, can qualify for discounts of 5 percent or more, while elaborate systems that report directly to fire or police departments may qualify for discounts as large as 15 to 20 percent.

Make sure the dollar amount of your insurance coverage will pay for a complete reconstruction if your home were destroyed by fire or some other misfortune. That's going to be an amount *less* than your purchase price and most likely less than your mortgage amount because you're only insuring the structure, not the land. Land, in most communities, is worth far more than the home built upon it.

If you're buying a home with an unusually high rebuilding cost, say it's a historic home or a masterpiece of modern architecture, you may need to go to an insurer such as The Chubb Group of Insurance Companies, which specializes in such properties. You can find them at *www.chubb.com*. Military families and veterans often find good insurance deals through USAA, a company that specializes in selling financial services to people associated with the military. You can reach them at *www.usaa.com*.

## Title Insurance: Take It

Title insurance guarantees that the title is clear from ownership claims by others. Title insurance is sold by the same company that researches the history of the home's title and verifies that the sellers have undisputed legal ownership and can sell you title to the home without problem.

You have to buy the title insurance from a company that is acceptable to your lender, but you have some opportunity to shop around.

Lenders insist that buyers purchase a title insurance policy that covers *the lenders* in case someone comes forward and claims that they have an ownership right to that home. The insurance pays for legal fees to defend against such a claim, and it would cover the lender's losses in the rare case that someone else did have a legitimate claim to the property. Shortly before your closing, the person handling the close will ask if you would also like to purchase coverage for yourself. Go ahead and spend the money. You deserve the same protection that the lender gets. For a one-time fee of a couple of hundred dollars, paid at closing, you can get coverage against any claims to the title for as long as you own the home. These situations are rare, but they can happen. And a loss would be devastating to your finances. Perhaps a long-lost divorced spouse of the seller comes forward saying he or she still has a right to the home. Perhaps someone comes forward saying the home is actually part of their inheritance. Or a neighbor claims that the back third of your lot is actually part of his or her property. Title insurance would pay your legal fees to defend against such a claim and would compensate you if the long-lost owner prevailed. The best policies also protect you if, in the past, an unpaid contractor registered a "mechanic's lien" against the property. Bite the bullet and buy the coverage.

If the home has changed hands in recent years, talk with the title insurance company the sellers used and ask if they will offer you a cheaper "reissue" rate on the title insurance. Similarly, if the lender or title company requires a survey of the property's legal boundaries, you might be able to save money by requesting an updated survey from the company that last performed that service. Make sure that would be acceptable to your lender.

## Flood Insurance

Before giving final approval to your loan, the lender will check flood survey maps to see if your new home lies within a flood zone. If it does, the lender will require that you buy a federal flood insurance policy. Standard homeowners' policies do not cover flood losses; the only coverage you can get is through the federal flood insurance program. While the federal government is the insurer, the policies are sold through regular homeowners' insurance companies. The lender, of course, is not acting out of kindly concern that you be covered in case there is a flood. The lender wants to make sure its collateral (and, incidentally, your home equity) is not eaten up by flood losses.

Even if your lender does not require a flood insurance policy, you should evaluate your flood risk and consider buying coverage. Your homeowners' insurance agent can help you evaluate your flood risk, based on the government's flood maps, and give you a quote for flood coverage. You can get more information from the National Flood Insurance Program's Web site, at *www.floodsmart.gov*. The site explains flood insurance and allows you to get a ballpark idea of what coverage might cost. (The government says the average premium is $400 per year, but that cost can rise dramatically in a high-risk area.) Keep in mind that there is always a thirty-day lag before flood insurance coverage goes into effect—*except* when your lender requires coverage for a new mortgage loan and you buy the coverage when you take out the loan. The program is designed that way to discourage people from buying only when they see that water levels are starting to rise.

Similarly, ordinary homeowners' insurance policies do not cover earthquake damage. If you live in an earthquake-prone area, particularly California, talk with your insurance agent about buying supplemental earthquake coverage. These plans tend to be expensive and have high deductibles (10 to 15 percent of your insurance coverage amount in the plan run by the California

Earthquake Authority), but they're the only way to get coverage. For information on what the California plan covers and an online premium calculator, go to *www.earthquakeauthority.com*.

## Getting a Pro to Handle the Close

The closing process (also called "settlement") varies a bit from one part of the country to another, but the purpose of closing remains essentially the same. It's a paper-laden, gun-free reenactment of all the hostage exchange scenes you've seen in the movies. The seller has the hostage (the deed to your new home). You have the ransom (a huge amount of money, usually being borrowed through a mortgage loan). You meet at a neutral place (the closing office) and demonstrate to each other that you've got the goods (the home and the money) and aren't up to any funny stuff. It can be done with buyer and seller (and their real estate agents) meeting around a conference table or it can be done in their absence—as long as everyone has signed all the necessary papers.

What you need is to find a trustworthy hostage negotiator to manage the swap. That's the closing agent, title attorney, or escrow officer, depending on where you live. (In some parts of the country, lawyers handle closings. In other areas, including California, independent escrow companies and title insurance companies do the job, typically without the buyer and seller present.) Local custom (or your negotiation) will dictate whether the seller or buyer chooses the person or company that will handle your close. Real estate agents and lenders may offer recommendations about closing agents, but you definitely should *not* feel under any obligation to follow their recommendation. Unfortunately, there have been allegations of illegal kickbacks of fees from title companies back to home builders and real estate agents who referred business to them. Always remember you're the one buying these services, and you're the one whose business should be courted. Feel free to call several closing agents and ask about their fees. Also ask friends, neighbors, and relatives for recommendations of title companies that handled proceedings smoothly and economically.

# Different Ways to Hold Title

Before closing, your closing agent will ask you how you would like to hold title to the property. You have to choose among several different legal forms of ownership, each of which provides slightly different legal benefits. Laws vary from state to state, and your title company or lawyer can advise you on the specifics that apply where you live. These, however, are the common forms of ownership:

## Ownership in Severalty

This option is designed for individuals buying property all by themselves. Focus on the word "sever" rather than "several," for this form of ownership means you are severing ties to other owners.

## Tenancy by the Entirety

Only married couples may own a home in this fashion. Each spouse has an equal, undivided interest in the property. That is, each one owns 100 percent of the home and neither can sell, mortgage, or transfer their interest to someone else unless both agree to it. If one spouse dies, complete ownership of the home transfers to the other spouse without going through probate proceedings. Also, although the courts have been nibbling away at this protection, creditors (except for the mighty IRS) seeking payment for the debt incurred by only one of the spouses cannot seize a home owned this way.

Tenancy by the entirety is available in fewer than half the states. According to tax and accounting publisher CCH, Inc., those include Delaware, the District of Columbia, Florida, Hawaii, Illinois, Indiana, Maryland, Massachusetts, Michigan, New Jersey, North Carolina, Ohio, Pennsylvania, Rhode Island, Tennessee, Vermont, Virginia, and Wyoming.

## Joint Tenancy with Right of Survivorship

This is the other common format used by married couples, but it also is available to owners who are not married. It can be used for properties with more than two owners. Each owner must have an equal interest in the property. (Two people would own it fifty/fifty; three owners would each own a third, and so on.) You cannot divvy up the home, say with one partner owning the downstairs and the other owning upstairs. If one owner dies, ownership passes to the other(s) without probate. One owner may sell, mortgage, or transfer his or her interest in the property without the approval of the other owner(s).

## Tenancy in Common

Two or more people may own a property in this way. Owners can have unequal shares of ownership (say a sixty/forty split), but they may not divvy up parts of the home into the part one owns and the part the other owns. One owner can sell, mortgage, or transfer his or her ownership without the consent of the other owners. If one owner dies, his or her share of ownership passes on to heirs through a probate proceeding, according to the terms of the owner's will.

## Community Property

In community property states (Arizona, California, Idaho, Louisiana, Nevada, New Mexico, Texas, Washington, and Wisconsin, according to CCH, Inc.), couples who buy a home while married own it equally. Neither can sell, mortgage, or transfer his or her interest in the property without the signature of the other. By writing it in their will, either spouse can pass down their interest in the home to anyone they wish, but if a spouse dies without a will, ownership automatically transfers to the other spouse. Couples can choose to own through "community property with right of survivorship" which means that, after one spouse's death, full ownership transfers to the other spouse without probate.

# What If You Change Your Mind About Buying?

Ohhh boy! This isn't going to be pleasant. You're bound by a contract, after all. But you may be able to find some escape hatches. You might even be able to get out of the deal without forfeiting your earnest money.

If you're in a roaring seller's market, your seller *might* not mind letting you go, at least if you aren't too close to the closing date. They may be able to get a higher offer, or they could have one or more other buyers already lined up with backup contracts. Your real estate agent may be able to size up the situation and advise you — but you can't expect your agent to be happy at the news of your change of heart, either.

Contingencies are your first line of escape. The home-inspection contingency sometimes is used for just this purpose. (And that's one very good reason why sellers want you to get your inspection and remove that contingency pronto.) You seize upon a

260

defect revealed by the inspection report and declare it as the reason you no longer want to buy. Sellers, understandably, try to guard against this by insisting on contract language that allows them the opportunity to repair defects.

If you have a mortgage contingency, you could try to sabotage your loan approval, perhaps by opening several very large lines of credit that will scare mortgage lenders away. However, it would take months for you to recover from such a scorched-earth strategy and be able to qualify for a mortgage on a different home.

You may have to walk away from your earnest money deposit. The sellers could try to sue you for "specific performance," trying to force you to go through with the purchase. But that carries its own expense in terms of money, time, and hassle. They may agree to just keep your money and let you go. However, they also might take that earnest money of yours and put it into constructing a good voodoo doll made in your image!

## Buyer's Remorse

I haven't met anyone, first-time buyer or repeat offender, who managed to buy a new home without going through a bout of buyer's remorse. It usually hits around two or three in the morning, that combination of worry, dread, and doom that has you convinced you're making a mistake. "What am I doing?" "We're buying the wrong home." "We're getting robbed!" "It's not really as nice as this place!" "We'll never have money again." I don't know how you can avoid your dose of buyer's remorse, but I know you can coach yourself through it.

First, recall the steps outlined in the first three chapters of this book. Review those chapters at 2:00 A.M., if it helps. When you first started planning your purchase, you went through all the numbers and even tried your after-purchase budget on for size. Unless you've gone wild with your purchase offer, you know you *can* afford this deal. Just remind yourself by looking at the hard numbers.

Second, understand that much of your angst stems from the fact that you really like the home you're in right now, and you probably feel sad about leaving it. Even if this move is going to offer a big jump in your standard of living, you're giving up *something*. We form intimate attachments to our homes. They shelter us; they reflect our personalities. We can walk through them barefoot in the dark because we know the feel of the floor and the way the wood squeaks when we reach the bottom step. We like our neighbors, or the way the morning sun shines in the bedroom window, or the spot under the tree where the kids used to play when they were small. There will be subtle things that grow on you as you become familiar with your new home, but you don't yet know what they'll be. You *do* know what you're giving up.

It may help ease your anxiety by acknowledging how much you've loved this home. Give it a send-off! Even though you have a huge chore list to master before closing day, take the time to invite your family and friends over for a goodbye party—*at your home,* even if it's a studio apartment. Before you start packing up and moving on, celebrate this place that has sheltered you so well. Your friends may enjoy one last visit, themselves.

Third, focus on the future. Dwell on the excitement of your new life in your new home. Flip through decorating books. Look at paint colors. Plan the garden. Make a visit to your new grocery store and other shops, if they're reasonably close. The flip side of fear is excitement, and if you focus on the excitement, at least some of the fear will be crowded out.

Your children are probably going through similar anxiety, though they may have a hard time expressing it. (They may just get unusually cranky as their way of coping!) Involve your children in planning your send-off party and your new-home planning. Can you manage one last sleepover before you move? Be sure to collect all their friends' telephone numbers, e-mail addresses, and instant message names so they can stay in touch.

You and the kids can plant a sapling in the back yard of your old home, just to leave a little bit of yourselves behind. (Don't forget to take a photo marking the event!) Write your names and birth dates in an out-of-the way spot in the basement or garage. Let them choose paint colors and window coverings for their new bedrooms. Visit their new schools, and spend a Saturday on the playground. Investigate new baseball and soccer teams and Scout troops, and let them help you find out where they can take ballet lessons—or whatever their hobby is at the moment. And be sure to take photographs of *every* room in your old home before you start dismantling and packing for your move!!

## Razzi's Rules to Live By

### 🏠 Inspect the home inspector.
You want one who has credentials and doesn't kowtow to the local real estate agents. Run away from an inspector who offers to make repairs him- or herself. Then put on your old jeans and go along for the tour.

### 🏠 Shop for an insurance policy ASAP.
You could have trouble getting a decently priced policy if you or the home you're buying has a history of claims. Buy a policy big

enough to pay for complete rebuilding, *not* for the price of the home or the size of your mortgage.

### 🏠 You can shop for closing agents.

All you want is efficient competence at a fair price. That's not too much to ask—so ask for it.

### 🏠 Give buyer's remorse its due.

And then give it the boot. Review the logic of your decision, and focus on the excitement ahead.

### 🏠 Say goodbye.

Give your dear old home a proper send-off. It's the decent thing to do for the place that has served you well up until now.

# CHAPTER SIXTEEN

# Closing Day!

"I think of this house clamped to the side of Tinker Creek as an anchor-hold. It holds me at anchor to the rock bottom of the creek itself and it keeps me steadied in the current, as a sea anchor does, facing the stream of light pouring down. It's a good place to live; there's a lot to think about."

ANNIE DILLARD, *Pilgrim at Tinker Creek*

NERVES ARE NORMAL! You have a big piece of business at hand. In truth, however, closing day should be an easy few hours of signing papers and shaking hands. By now all your decisions should have been made; all the details should have been addressed. Still, it can take your breath away as you see splayed out before you all the details of just how many fees and taxes and commissions are being paid out of this deal. And you have to sign a shocking number of legal documents.

It will take some pressure off you (and everyone else) if you can schedule your closing at least several days before your interest-rate lock is scheduled to expire. If something should be amiss in your closing documents, at least you would have time to address the problem. Also, you'll reduce your stress by scheduling your moving van to arrive at least a day or two *after* closing. Encountering a problem with the closing—and then having movers show up on the new doorstep you don't yet own—definitely would be worse than spending a night or two at the EconoLodge.

## Scheduling the Close: End-of-Month Savings?

You may have heard that you can save money by closing at the end of the month. The truth is there is some short-term benefit in terms of the amount of cash you have to bring to the closing table, but the benefit to your budget is temporary, and you shouldn't let it drive the decision. Let's say you're closing during April. At closing, you will be expected to pay interest on your new mortgage to cover the period from the closing date through the end of the month. If you're closing on April 10, your closing costs would include your interest payment for April 10 through April 30. If you were to close on April 25, on the other hand, you would owe for only five days. Five days' worth of interest costs a whole lot less than twenty days, so it appears obvious that you ought to close late in the month. The amount of cash you have to bring to closing is lower.

But here's why the benefit is only temporary. Mortgage loans are a bit unusual in that you pay the interest *in arrears*. (And your early mortgage payments are largely for interest.) That is, your May 1 mortgage payment actually pays your April bill. You would have covered April's payment at closing, so you don't have a payment due that May 1. Your first payment will be due June 1, to cover May's bill.

So, by closing on April 10, you would have to produce a larger amount of money at closing, but you also would enjoy a longer time, fifty-one days, before your first regular monthly payment was due. If you closed on April 25, you would have only thirty-six days respite before your first payment. Of course, with the earlier closing date, you actually own the home for more days as well.

In sum, you can minimize your closing costs by scheduling your closing date late in the month. But the benefit is fleeting. Other considerations may be more important in setting your closing date, including the expiration date for your interest-rate lock and your (or the seller's) need to get the deal finalized as early as possible.

## The Important Final Look

You should arrange to have one final walk-through of the home you're buying either the day before closing or early in the big day itself. After all, you deserve to see that the home is still in good shape and that the sellers have left in place all the things that you expect to convey with the home. Ideally, they will have loaded their belongings onto the moving truck and you can get a good look at any damage that might have been done by less-than-delicate movers.

You probably shouldn't make a fuss if you find a few dings in the drywall; it will be easier to buy a can of spackle and fix the flaws yourself than to make it an issue at closing. More serious problems, however, such as missing items or abandoned furniture that you will have to pay to haul out of the home, need to be addressed. Will the buyers take care of it before closing, or will they compensate you in cash? Are you concerned enough about the problem to refuse to close until it has been dealt with? Are you willing (or even able) to delay closing until the problem is resolved? These are things you have to discuss right away with your agent and the seller's agent.

# What to Take to the Closing Table

You should take several things along to the closing table. Your closing agent or real estate agent will phone you, most likely the day before, to tell you how much cash you need. They will expect this money in a cashier's check or certified check. (Ask the closing agent for the name to whom the check should be payable. If in doubt, simply have it made out to yourself, and sign it over to the closing agent at the closing table.) You also should take along your regular checkbook just in case there are small discrepancies that you need to cover. The rest of your closing-day paraphernalia should include:

☐ a photo ID

☐ proof of your paid-up homeowners' insurance policy

☐ accordion file containing all the documents involved in the home purchase and mortgage transactions.

Be sure your file contains the good faith estimate of closing costs that your lender gave you when you applied for the loan. You should compare the actual closing statement with the estimate and question any significant discrepancies.

## The HUD-1 and the Good-Faith Estimate

There's one important document you have the right to see on the day before closing, but you have to ask the closing agent to let you see it. (Phone the closing agent a few days ahead of time to warn them that you intend to review the document early.) That document is the U.S. Department of Housing and Urban Development Settlement Statement, commonly known as the HUD-1 form. It's a line-by-line accounting of who is paying what to whom at closing. Compare it with your good faith estimate of closing costs, looking for big changes in dollar amounts and for new items. Ask your closing agent to explain anything that doesn't make sense. It's their job to help you understand the proceedings.

By necessity, some things *will* be different on your actual closing statement compared to what is shown on the good-faith estimate. Your payments for prorated mortgage interest and property taxes will vary according to how early or late your closing date falls in the month, for example. Your lender also will set up an escrow account to handle your ongoing payments for homeowners' insurance, property taxes, and homeowners' association fees and will charge you several hundred dollars to start funding that new account. Each month, along with your mortgage payment, you will pay an extra amount into the escrow account, and the lender that services your mortgage loan will pay those bills as they come due. (Lenders do this to make sure their equity isn't threatened because you allowed a homeowners' insurance policy to lapse or because you failed to pay your property taxes and the government placed a lien against the property.)

## Keep an Eye out for Junk Fees

You also need to be on the lookout for numbers that are significantly bigger than the estimate and for "junk fees" that amount to nothing more than a grab for your wallet. Of course they're not labeled "junk fees"; they sound official. If, on either the good-faith estimate or on the HUD-1 closing statement, you see charges for things like a processing fee, document preparation fee, document review fee, messenger fee, funding fee, shipping fee, or appraisal review fee, question it. After all, you're already paying a loan fee (through points or a marked-up interest rate), and you're paying for the services of your title company and the closing agent. Additional fees, ostensibly to cover their office procedures, are nothing more than a money grab.

Unfortunately, consumer protection laws are weak in this area, and there's little to stop a lender or title company from tacking on new fees or inflating legitimate fees. But you at least can squawk if they do it. And you might as well squawk loudly while you're at it!

If you're surprised by such fees at the closing table, your cell phone will be a good weapon. Let's say your title insurance fee is far higher than what was quoted in the good-faith estimate. Ask if there has been a mistake. Or go ahead and phone the title insurance company, just to verify that the number is correct. You could try phoning your loan officer to ask about unexpected lending fees. (I did just that during the closing of a recent mortgage refinancing. The "mistake" was corrected, and we went through with the closing.) If the appraisal fee looks high, phone the appraisal company and verify it. Ditto for the pest inspection fee.

Some lenders and title companies will mark up these fees. At least don't go along with it quietly. This is one reason why you want to review the HUD-1 statement the day before closing! You'll find a list of average amounts for closing costs, based on a survey of lenders nationwide, in Appendix Five and a sample of the HUD-1 Form in Appendix Four.

# Home-Buying and Taking out a Mortgage: Two Simultaneous Processes

Your closing actually involves two distinct processes. You're buying a home, *and* you're taking out a mortgage loan. Each process is accomplished through its own very important legal document. You should review each one carefully, making sure all the names, addresses, dollar amounts, interest rates, and other terms are correct. If you find an error, get it fixed before you sign! Do not allow yourself to feel rushed. These are the key instruments of a real estate transaction:

- The deed. The seller conveys ownership of the property to you by signing a deed and delivering that deed to you, the buyer, at closing. Once you sign the deed, title (another word for ownership) to the property transfers to you, and your deed can be recorded in the county government's land records. Your closing agent or title company typically will handle these details for you.

- The promissory note. Basically, this is an IOU saying you promise to repay the money you are borrowing over a specific number of years and at a specific interest rate.

- The mortgage. By signing this document, you place a lien against the property giving your lender the right to foreclose (that is, seize the property) if you fail to pay back the loan under the terms of the promissory note. In some places, lenders use a deed of trust instead of a mortgage. It accomplishes the same thing but makes the foreclosure process easier for the lender.

Those are the most important of the documents you will review and sign at closing. But there's more paperwork coming your way!

271

You will be asked to sign a variety of documents, such as a document verifying that the name on your documents truly is your legal name, and a document from the lender explaining that your mortgage loan may be resold to another institution at any time, without your consent. Look each one over, front and back, and then sign away.

## Finally, the Handshake!

At last, you have your stack of signed documents (which you will file away in a fireproof box or safe). At closing, the sellers are supposed to give you all the keys, lock combinations, and garage-door openers to your new home. It's time to shake hands all around the table and race over to your new home to try out those new keys and have your first look-around as owners! Congratulations! Pop open a bottle of champagne and celebrate right there in your new, unfurnished living room!

## Razzi's Rules to Live By

### 🏠 Don't crowd your lock-in.

Schedule closing for at least several days before your interest-rate lock-in is set to expire. Leave yourself time to deal with problems that might delay your closing.

### 🏠 Assert your rights.

You have a right to review the main closing document, the HUD-1 Uniform Settlement Statement, a day before closing. But you have to ask for it!

## 🏠 Take a last look-around.

Take a final walk-through of the property shortly before closing to make sure it's in acceptable condition.

## 🏠 Fight junk fees.

You're not in a very strong bargaining position to fight dubious last-minute fees, but you at least can question them and ask to have them removed. Call them "errors" to help save face—and increase the odds that they'll be "corrected."

## 🏠 Celebrate!

Is there any place better for dancing than the big, empty floor of your new home?

# PART FOUR

# home
# at
# last

# CHAPTER SEVENTEEN

# Home At Last

"Though I get home
How late, how late!
Better will be the ecstasy
That they have done expecting me."

EMILY DICKINSON, *Life XLVIII*

HOME SALES ARE A REMARKABLY PUBLIC TRANSACTION. You might prefer to stay mum about exactly how much you agreed to pay for your new home, but within a short time, the exact dollar amount will be recorded in your local government's property records. The new neighbors, of course, are keenly interested in finding out how much the newcomer paid to get into their neighborhood. Either through gossip or public-records sleuthing, the sales price soon will be common knowledge. There are plenty of businesses keen on spotting you as a new homeowner, as well.

As noted in Chapter One, buyers of newly built homes spend an average of $8,905 on their homes during the first twelve months of ownership. Buyers of existing homes spend $3,766. Lots of businesses know your wallet is open, and they want a share of that spending. You can expect to receive more than your share of fliers for lawn services, decorators, and remodelers.

# Pitches You Should Ditch

You also will receive a flurry of financial pitches. Most of them can safely be thrown in the trash — or into the shredder if they contain any personal information about you. (Always open mail from your mortgage lender. Much of it will be junk, such as offers for home equity loans and credit cards, but there will be the occasional extremely important notice shipped your way that you can't afford to miss.) The following sections describe some of the pitches likely to be coming through your mailbox.

## Mortgage Life Insurance

Most people do need some life insurance, especially if they have families. But you don't need this variety. Mortgage life insurance policies will pay off your outstanding mortgage balance if either of the homeowners dies. They're aimed particularly at couples, offering assurance that the surviving spouse (and any children) wouldn't have to worry about paying for the roof over head in a time of mourning — and beyond.

Surely that's a sound financial goal, but you can achieve it better with an ordinary term life-insurance policy payable to the surviving spouse. In fact, you may need an insurance policy for an amount quite a bit greater than your outstanding mortgage balance. And the surviving spouse might not even want to pay off a tax-deductible low-interest rate mortgage. Having the proceeds of an ordinary term life-insurance policy would free the survivor to pay off other, more expensive debts, pay college tuition, or invest the money to provide long-term financial security. It's easy to get quotes on term life-insurance policies at *www.insweb.com*.

## Biweekly Payment Plans

At first glance, these plans seem to make money materialize out of the clouds. Here's the pitch: If you take your regular monthly mortgage payment (let's say it's $1,000) and simply break it into two payments ($500, payable every two weeks) you will pay off your mortgage early and save tens of thousands of dollars in mortgage interest over the life of the loan. For a fee of about $200 (or more) these oh-so-helpful intermediaries will set you up with a plan that automatically debits your checking account for half your mortgage payment every two weeks. They'll pass the money on to your lender, and you can painlessly cut years off your loan term and save tens of thousands of dollars over the life of the loan.

Actually, the mechanics of these plans are quite transparent and not magical at all. You pay off the loan early because you're *paying more money* each year. By making payments every two weeks, you end up making thirteen months' worth of payments each year instead of twelve. (Fifty-two weeks of the year divided by two equals twenty-six half-payments. Divide that by two to arrive at the number of monthly payments . . . and abracadabra, you have thirteen months of payments.) And, yes, prepaying your loan balance by applying an extra month's worth of payments *will* reduce your loan term and thereby reduce your overall interest payment.

But there are several reasons why you should say "No, thank you" to this offer. First, there's no good reason to trust an unknown intermediary with your precious mortgage payment (what if they run off with your cash?). Moreover, you certainly don't want to pay them a couple of hundred dollars for the privilege. Second, don't underestimate how hard it might be on your budget to squeeze out an extra month's payment each year. Third, if you do wish to retire your loan early and cut down on interest expenses, most loans allow you to make prepayments of principal at any time. They'll even set up your payment schedule so it includes an extra couple of bucks (or couple of hundred bucks) each month, to be applied toward principal. And they'll do this for free. All you have to do is ask. Fourth, before prepaying principal, you should look at the investment options that you might take advantage of with that money. If you can earn a better return investing in stocks, bonds, mutual funds, or other investments, you may be considerably better off with those investments rather than tying your money up in a mortgage.

The calculators at *www.hsh.com* can help you figure out how much you might save by prepaying on your mortgage, either through regular monthly or annual payments or by plunking one big pot of cash down against your outstanding balance.

## Surprise, Your Loan Has Been Sold!

The Bailey Bros. Building and Loan Association (of Frank Capra's *It's a Wonderful Life*) may have held on to mortgage loans for the duration, but these days, mortgages are financial instruments that usually are chopped up and sold for parts. Big financial companies like Fannie Mae and Freddie Mac, among others, buy mortgage loans and slice and dice them for resale on the investment markets. All the interest you pay each month might be lumped in with the interest payments of other homeowners and sold on Wall Street as one type of bond. Investors on the other side of the world might actually receive your interest payments through such a bond. All your principal payments might be part of another bond—sold to a completely different investor in a different part of the world. All of this happens invisibly from the perspective of the borrower.

But there's one valuable part of your mortgage that, when sold, is very noticeable to a homeowner: the job of servicing your mortgage. Typically, a mortgage company (such as Wells Fargo or Washington Mutual, Inc.) buys from other lenders the rights to service some of mortgages those lenders have made. Servicing includes collecting your payments each month, managing your escrow account for property taxes and homeowners' insurance premiums, answering questions, and reporting your annual interest payments to you and the IRS each year.

It's very likely your servicing will be sold shortly after you take out your mortgage. You'll receive a notice from your lender notifying you that your loan has been sold and telling you to expect to receive new payment information (a new payment-coupon book or automatic debiting information) from the new lender. This can even happen repeatedly, as the job of servicing your mortgage gets sold and sold again. Unfortunately, borrowers have absolutely no say in this deal. If you don't think the new company is as responsive to your questions as the old one, or if the new company doesn't pay your property taxes as promptly as you'd like, you can't take your servicing business elsewhere without refinancing your whole mortgage. (And there's no guarantee the new lender wouldn't sell your servicing to the same company you're trying to escape!)

This hand-off to a new servicing company is completely routine, but you still need to verify that the switch is legitimate. Don't ever start sending your payments to a new company without first verifying with the old company that it has indeed sold your servicing to the new one. Federal law requires that your old mortgage company must mail you *written* (not e-mail!) notice at least fifteen days before your servicing change goes into effect. That notice must give you the name of the new servicing company and its toll-free phone number that you can call for more information. The terms of your mortgage, including the loan amount, payment schedule, and interest rate, will not change with the switch to a new servicer.

Federal law also says a homeowner cannot be penalized with a late fee if, within sixty days of the effective date of the switch to a new servicer, he or she sends a mortgage payment to the old servicer instead of the new one. For more information, including instructions on how you should address complaints to your loan servicer, go to the U.S. Department of Housing and Urban Development Web site, at *www.hud.gov*.

## As You Settle In

### Support your local locksmith

Don't delay in calling in a locksmith to change *all* the locks in your new home. There's no telling how many copies of your keys may be floating around. The previous owners might have lost track of how many they distributed over the years. Real estate agents have had at least one key. A few neighbors may have them. Former spouses or boyfriends or girlfriends could have copies. The pet-sitter might have one. Even contractors who've worked on the home over the years may have made copies—or hidden a spare somewhere around the grounds—without the previous owners even knowing about it.

You'll sleep better knowing that you've taken the extra step to secure your family. While you're at it, change the combinations to garage-door keypads and the electronic security system, if you have one.

These precautions are especially important if you're moving into a brand-new home development that is not yet completely built-out. Theft is incredibly common from construction sites, and, face it, part of your neighborhood is still a construction site. There's a steady stream of strangers coming through the area, and residents have little reason to question them.

## Meet the Neighbors

Some neighborhoods are great about welcoming newcomers with invitations and freshly baked cookies, but other neighborhoods don't quite have their welcome wagons tuned up. Take the initiative yourself, and invite your new neighbors in for a casual get-together. They're probably dying to meet you, even if they haven't had time to stop by and say hello. Settling in becomes much easier if you can ask a neighbor or two for references to lawn services, contractors, and neighborhood restaurants, so go ahead and break the ice yourself.

Don't delay in inviting your old friends over for a look-round, either. I've known people who waited *years* to invite friends over to see their "new" home because they didn't want to show it off until they'd finished rehabbing this or that. Go ahead and break in your new home as soon as you've unpacked most of the boxes. There's nothing better than having loved ones visit to make a place feel like home.

# Razzi's Rules to Live By

### 🏠 Buy insurance on your own terms.

Most people need life insurance, but you don't need specialized mortgage life policies that automatically pay the loan if one spouse dies. The remaining spouse may be better off with an affordable term life insurance policy that pays cash. They then have the choice of paying off the mortgage—or investing the money to provide ongoing income.

### 🏠 Abracadabra, blah, blah, blah.

There's no magic involved in a biweekly mortgage plan. You simply make an extra payment each year.

### 🏠 Skip the middleman.

You don't need to pay an intermediary to switch to a biweekly mortgage payment plan. If you would like to prepay your mortgage, most loan servicers will arrange it for you—for free.

### 🏠 Expect to be jilted.

Your lender very likely will sell the job of servicing your mortgage to another company. But don't send your payment off to a new address until you've received a letter from the original lender informing you of the switch in advance.

### 🏠 Mayberry doesn't exist.

Change the locks and keypad combinations—even if you've moved into a friendly subdivision. Give yourself a fresh start in securing your home.

## ⌂ Reach out to your new neighbors.

*Everybody* is busy these days, maybe too busy to welcome a newcomer to the neighborhood. Break in your new home the right way by inviting new neighbors and old friends over as soon as you can manage.

# CHAPTER EIGHTEEN

# Home Rituals

"From then on, people in China knew Kitchen God was watching them. From his corner in every house and every shop, he saw all kinds of good and bad habits spill out: generosity or greediness, a harmonious nature or a complaining one. And once a year, seven days before the new year, Kitchen God flew back up the fireplace to report whose fate deserved to be changed, better for worse, or worse for better."

AMY TAN, *The Kitchen God's Wife*

A HOME IS A SACRED PLACE. It is our refuge, a place where the soul is nurtured and where we let our defenses down and allow ourselves to be vulnerable, knowing we are safe. Across cultures, it's common for people to develop rituals for blessing their new home. It's a wonderful idea to participate in such rites and traditions; if your own religious or ethnic group doesn't follow a practice such as those described here, you might wish to build your own, perhaps borrowing from the rituals others have used through the years.

# Christian House Blessings

House blessings are particularly popular in the Roman Catholic, Episcopalian, and Orthodox churches. In Catholic homes, a priest may be invited to bless the house—specifically, to bless those who dwell in it. The priest may join the family and some friends in reading scripture. Here's one typical prayer that might be said in addition to scripture readings:

> When Christ took flesh through the Blessed Virgin Mary, he made his home with us. Let us now pray that he will enter this home and bless it with His presence. May He always be here among us; may He nurture our love for each other, share in our joys, comfort us in our sorrows. Inspired by His teachings and example, let us seek to make our home before all else a dwelling place of love, diffusing far and wide the goodness of Christ.

At any time, Catholic households may sprinkle holy water, blessed at the church at Easter time, as a form of prayer asking God to sanctify their home.

In Episcopal households, the "Celebration for a Home" ritual includes scripture readings and may include a procession through the rooms of the home with specific prayers for each one. After returning to the living room, members of the household may present the priest offerings of bread and wine to be shared as communion. Incense and holy water may be used to symbolize the purification and blessing of the home.

In the Orthodox tradition, homes are blessed on January 6, Theophany (or Epiphany, commemorating Christ's baptism and the revelation of the Holy Trinity, the belief that one God consists of Father, Son, and Holy Spirit). Shortly after the holy day, a priest visits the home and sprinkles it with holy water that was blessed at the church on Theophany. Among the prayers is this one:

> Grant, O Lord, a prosperous and peaceful life, health and salvation and the furtherance of all good things to all Your servants who dwell herein, and preserve them for many years.

## Jewish Home Blessings

The home is central to many Jewish religious traditions, and observant Jews will affix a mezuzah to their door frames. Encased in a small elongated box, a mezuzah is a handwritten parchment with passages from the Book of Deuteronomy (6:4-9 and 11:13-21):

> Hear, Israel, the Lord is our God, the Lord is One. Blessed be the Name of His glorious kingdom for ever and ever and you shall love the Lord your God with all your heart and with all your soul and with all your might. And these words that I command you today shall be in your heart. And you shall teach them diligently to your children, and you shall speak of them when you sit at home, and when you walk along the way, and when you lie down and when you rise up. And you shall bind them as a sign on your hand, and they shall be for frontlets between your eyes. And you shall write them on the doorposts of your house and on your gates.

And it shall come to pass if you surely listen to the commandments that I command you today, to love the Lord your God, and to serve him with all your heart and all your soul, that I will give rain to your land, the early and the late rains, that you may gather in your grain, your wine and your oil. And I will give grass in your fields for your cattle and you will eat and you will be satisfied. Beware, lest your heart be deceived, and you turn and serve other gods, and worship them. And anger of the Lord will blaze against you, and he will close the heavens and there will not be rain, and the earth will not give you its fullness, and you will perish quickly from the good land that the Lord gives you.

## Islamic Home Blessing Customs

Many Muslim families, after moving into a new home, will invite family and friends in to speak of God and to bless the home. They may read from the Quran, possibly asking each person present to read from its thirty sections. By these readings, the household asks for angels of mercy and protection to come to the family. After the readings, everyone present shares some food and may present housewarming gifts to the household.

## Hindu Home Blessings

Hindu families moving into a newly built house may perform a housewarming ceremony known as Griha Pravesh when they first enter. It's important that they choose an auspicious time for the first entry, based on astrological charts.

A priest first performs a ceremony outside the home. Participants fill a copper pot with water, grains, and a coin. They place a coconut on top of the pot and cover it with red cloth. The husband and wife then take the pot inside and place it near a ceremonial fire (or *havan*), which is intended to prevent harmful influences, remove negative vibrations and create a peaceful environment. After the deities have been worshipped and the priests have been offered a feast, the family may move in. Doing so earlier could subject the household to trouble and misery.

## Buddhist Home Rituals

Buddhists typically hold a blessing ceremony in their new home. Followers build a shrine with an image of Buddha and invite monks in for a ceremony to bless the home and its inhabitants. In Thailand, for example, this ceremony is called Keun Baan Mai. Before the ceremony, the family members drape a white, sacred thread completely around the outside of their home. The thread carries the vibrations of the prayers around the home to protect it and its inhabitants. The monks will sit on cushions and chant for about an hour, after which the homeowners will offer them food. The monks sprinkle holy water on the home and on all those present and, before leaving, mark the door with a blessed white paste in a special pattern of nine spots.

## Sikh Home Blessing

Upon moving into a new home, Sikhs celebrate with a continuous reading of scripture, the Sri Guru Granth Sahib. This reading by family and friends takes about forty-eight hours to complete, which is followed by further readings and hymns and sharing of a sacred pudding called Karah Prashad made of wheat flour, sugar, and ghee (clarified butter).

## Hawaiian Home Blessings

In Hawaii, it's customary to bless a new home, a new place of business, or any new venture. In a traditional Hawaiian house blessing, a *kahu* (guardian or minister) will ask for blessings from *Akua* (God) and clear any *kapu* (curses or negative energy) that remain with a place. The *kahu* cleanses the home and the participants by sprinkling salt water about and unties a special *maile lei* that earlier had been draped across the threshold. (The *maile lei* is an open-ended lei of green leaves, made from a fragrant native vine that's part of the periwinkle family and which is traditionally associated with the goddess of Hula.) After the untying of the *maile lei*, members of the household may take up residence in their new home.

## Native American Traditions

Native American tribes have different ceremonies for blessing or purifying a home. In the Navajo Nation, for example, owners of a traditional dwelling, or hogan, will ask a medicine man to perform a house blessing ceremony or *hooghan da ashdlisigil*. (A blessing ceremony may be used for a contemporary home as well as for a traditional hogan.) The medicine man will bless the east (believed to be the direction from which all good things come), south, west, and finally the north points of the hogan, saying a prayer for each and marking the points with corn meal. Afterward, the participants share a meal.

Many Native Americans also conduct smudging ceremonies to purify a home, a person, or another place or object. The practice has been adopted by New Age followers. A traditional smudging ceremony uses special aromatic herbs such as sage, sweetgrass, cedar, and tobacco, alone or in combination. The herbs are burned in an abalone shell and wafted around the home, covering all the compass points, starting with the east and moving clockwise. Sometimes an eagle feather is used to fan the smoke about the home and its inhabitants, purifying the home and driving out negative energy.

## Plain Old Good Luck

Who can't use a little luck around the house? The superstitious among us have no lack of talismans and habits that we hope might imbue a bit of luck on our homes (and thereby, ourselves). I still follow an old superstition my Irish grandmother handed down, namely, that luck will be brought upon the household if the first person to enter the front door at the start of the new year is a dark-haired man. Right after a stroke-of-midnight kiss, I shoo my dark-haired husband out the back door and let him in the front, ensuring good luck for the year. (In truth, I realize my good luck is in having a husband who's willing to humor me with this little tradition.)

A horseshoe nailed over the door is an ancient lucky talisman. Tradition dictates that it's lucky *only* if it's nailed in the "u" position, with the open end toward the ceiling, so as to catch the good luck. Of course nailing it in that position requires two nails, versus the single nail that could hold it up in the opposite direction. Using two nails to hold up a piece of iron over your head certainly sounds luckier than nailing that deadly missile up with just one.

In countries that surround the Mediterranean Sea, there are different versions of a talisman posted in the house to ward off the evil eye. Long ago, people believed the evil eye was a form of bad luck borne of covetousness. A jealous look upon a baby, for example, could take away a family's fertility or the production of fruit trees or milk cows. Italians might guard against the evil eye by wearing hand- or horn-shaped amulets around their necks; in Turkey, the equivalent protection is a piece of blue glass with the image of an eye painted in the center. In other areas, those seeking luck place a hand symbol somewhere in their home to ward off the evil effects.

Among Jews, for example, a *hamsa* symbol representing a protective hand may be hung on the wall to bring good luck and ward off the evil eye. The rough shape of a hand, fingers down, may be adorned with Hebrew letters, images of Israel, or other symbols. Among Muslims, a similar symbol is called a Hand of Fatima, and has the fingers pointing upward.

## Blessings and Good Fortune in Your New Home

I believe that building a life in a new home is luck all by itself. I wish you luck, wisdom, and fearlessness in choosing a new home for yourself and your family. May you find shelter, comfort, and serenity there for years to come.

# APPENDICES

# Razzi's Rules

### 🏠 Six months' inventory is key.

That's the dividing line that separates a balanced market from those favoring buyers or sellers. If it would take about six months to sell every home that's currently for sale, that's a balanced market. If it would take less time, the conditions favor sellers, creating a seller's market. If it would take more time, conditions favor buyers, which means it's a buyer's market. Ask your agent what kind of market you're in.

### 🏠 Take advantage of leverage.

A mortgage allows you to take a down payment of 20 percent or less and parlay that to earn much bigger profits based on the full value of the home. Such leverage allows a small investment to grow into large net worth.

### 🏠 The government wants you to own.

The government offers wonderful tax breaks to encourage ownership—so take Uncle Sam up on them!

### 🏠 Budget without shame.

You and your spouse or partner should dive into a detailed budgeting exercise *together*. If you make it a no-blame, no-shame look at where your money really goes, you can identify where the money really will come from for your new home purchase.

## 🏠 Lenders don't care where your kids go to school.

Loan officers don't count as debts some big expenses that you might consider to be set in stone. They figure you might find a cheaper alternative if you needed the money for a mortgage payment. Keep this in mind when figuring out how much *you* can afford, not what the lender says you can qualify to borrow.

## 🏠 Time beats risk.

You only have to worry about slow housing markets or soft prices if you actually have to *sell* while the market is tough. Most owners ride out tough markets without any problem. A home that can accommodate changing needs over a decade or so is a very safe bet.

## 🏠 Test-drive your new budget.

If you think you can devote an extra $100 or $200 or whatever amount to the cost of living in a new home, make believe you've bought the home already. Adopt your new budget now and put the extra cash into the bank each month. Prove to yourself that you really can afford the move. You'll sleep better for it.

## 🏠 Adjust your tax withholding right away.

Go ahead—it's legal! Reduce the amount of money withheld from your paycheck for payroll taxes when you buy your new home. You don't have to wait until you file your taxes to benefit from the tax breaks.

## 🏠 You might be a first-time buyer, again.

Even if you have owned before, you still might qualify as a first-timer. Government programs typically define "first-time" as not having owned within the last two or three years.

## 🏠 Tap retirement funds gingerly.

Be aware of the tax penalties you might trigger—*and* remember that you're spending not only today's retirement dollar, but all the earnings that dollar would garner between today and retirement day.

## 🏠 Beware the stock market.

The stock market is no place to keep your down payment savings. Stock prices swing too wildly to be a safe place for money that you will need soon. Stick to money-market funds, bank money-market accounts, and short-term certificates of deposit while you build your down payment fund.

## 🏠 Get some help.

Look for local programs that help first-time buyers come up with a down payment. You just may be eligible for a little grant!

## 🏠 Think twice about paying in cash for a retirement home.

You might do better if some of that cash goes into an investment that continues to grow during the early years of what everyone hopes will be a long retirement.

## 🏠 Match your mortgage to your time frame.

The traditional 30-year fixed-rate mortgage is a favorite because it offers unbeatable predictability. But if you expect to move or refinance within the next ten years, you can save with an adjustable or hybrid loan.

## 🏠 It's the margin that counts.

Interest rates on ARMs are determined by your index plus the *margin*, or markup. Pay close attention—that margin reveals the true cost of your loan.

### 🏠 Save big by paying off early.

You can save hundreds of thousands of dollars of interest by paying off your loan in fifteen years instead of thirty. The bigger your loan amount and the higher your interest rate, the greater are the savings you get from prepayment.

### 🏠 Money costs what money costs.

When interest rates rise or fall, the indexes used to determine ARM rates will follow, all in step. There's nothing special about COFI or LIBOR indexes compared to the more common Treasury security index.

### 🏠 Watch for these mortgage menaces.

These three mortgage features could threaten your long-term financial health: balloon payments, negative amortization, and prepayment penalties. Always check your loan documents for them.

### 🏠 Just say no to interest-only ARMs and option ARMs.

Your payments are certain to rise, but your ability to profit from homeownership is anything but certain.

### 🏠 Shopping is shopping.

The process of finding the right home, the right mortgage, the right insurance policy is fundamentally the same as finding the right business suit or new car. Figure out what you need; zero in on what you really want; scour the marketplace to find out what's available; brace yourself for sales pitches; choose the most appropriate, comfortable option; hold out for the best price.

### 🏠 There are many lenders competing for your business.

It's true even if you have a weak credit history. Shop aggressively.

297

### ⌂ Never forget the loan officer is a salesperson.

He or she wants to sell you a mortgage, the larger the better.

### ⌂ A mortgage broker is not necessarily searching for the best loan for you.

He or she may point you toward the loan that earns him or her the biggest fee.

### ⌂ Get your FICO credit scores and your credit reports.

Do it at least six months before you shop for a mortgage, so you have time to fix mistakes.

### ⌂ Resist being pushed into a loan for high-risk borrowers.

You're most at risk of being taken advantage of if your credit scores are between 600 and 640. Unscrupulous lenders may push you into a loan for high-risk borrowers because it earns them more profit.

### ⌂ Ask which of your three FICO scores the lender will use.

Do they routinely use the highest, middle, or lowest score (based on reports from the three different credit bureaus)? If your credit is questionable, obviously you will want to avoid those that go with the lowest score.

### ⌂ Track interest rates every day for a week.

You'll learn to recognize a good deal when you see it.

### ⌂ Don't pay points if you expect to move in a few years.

You won't benefit from the lower payments long enough to recover the upfront cost.

## 🏠 Get preapproved for a mortgage.

Get your loan lined up before you even start shopping for a home.

## 🏠 Compare lenders' fees as well as the points and interest rates they quote.

Later, at closing, compare the actual fees they charge with their good-faith estimate and question anything that's unexpected. Go ahead, be a pest—at least until lenders display a little more good faith in their good-faith estimates!

## 🏠 Never click on an e-mail link to a financial-services company.

Con artists can whisk you off to a fake Web site that looks very convincing, complete with familiar logos, brand names, and slogans. *Always* type in the Web address yourself before you disclose any sensitive financial information over the Internet.

## 🏠 If it isn't in writing, it doesn't exist.

Make sure to get your loan preapproval in writing, along with any other assurances from lenders and sales people.

## 🏠 Guard your interest-rate lock.

Make sure your lock lasts long enough for you to close, get the commitment in writing, and push everybody to close before it expires.

## 🏠 A bridge will take you there.

If you're truly determined not to give up your current home unless you find the perfect replacement, you may have to buy first. A bridge loan (often simply a home-equity line of credit) can help you make the jump.

299

### 🏠 It's tough to get out of a townhouse.

Townhouses offer a lot of house for the money (because you own so little land), and it can be difficult to find a detached house that offers a comparable lifestyle. You may have to settle for less house, a longer commute, or a very high price.

### 🏠 Kids see the darndest things.

Children can spot things about a new home or neighborhood that you might miss. Listen to their opinions—but don't let them drive the decision.

### 🏠 You might not believe what's "verboten" at your own home.

Check to see if a homeowners' association or local zoning laws prohibit something important to your family, like a fenced yard or basketball hoops.

### 🏠 You can keep your cash.

Forget the old "rollover" rules. Old tax laws that required you to buy ever-more-expensive homes to shelter your profit are dead, dead, dead. You can now pocket up to $500,000 as a married couple or $250,000 as a single as often as every two years without paying tax on that home-sale profit.

### 🏠 Soundproofing is the key to happiness.

At least it is in condo/co-op apartments and townhouses. Be careful buying older condos; many that went condo in the 1970s and 80s were originally built as rentals, with scant attention to insulation for sound and heat-retention. Visit close to dinner time, when residents are likely to be at their noisiest.

## 🏠 Beware of renters.

If the share of renters in a condo or townhouse development hits 30 percent or more, subsequent buyers can have difficulty getting a mortgage, making it more difficult to sell units.

## 🏠 If it doesn't perc, take a pass.

With a rural or near-rural lot, you will not be allowed to build unless the land drains well enough to support a septic system. Pay for your own evaluation, to be sure.

## 🏠 Test the waters.

If you plan to dock a boat along your own shoreline, measure the water depth yourself. Don't rely simply on the word of the seller or real estate agent.

## 🏠 Read the dreary documents.

You must read the association documents—the financial statements and the Codes, Covenants, and Restrictions—when you buy a condo, co-op, or a detached house in a neighborhood association. You want to see that they've been setting aside money for predictable repairs and replacements to common areas.

## 🏠 Love the rules you're with.

If you're going to chafe at restrictions on your ability to keep a boat, play basketball in the driveway, or paint your front door blue, make sure those activities aren't prohibited *before* you buy. Those dreary documents sometimes spark fights.

## 🏠 Technology makes crazy things possible.

We can have giant windows facing the wind and rain. Air conditioning allows us to build homes without good natural ventilation. Just make sure your home's features really do have technology that's up to the job.

### 🏠 All homes have trade-offs.
Quaint, old homes may lack closets. An attached garage is convenient, but it may thwart the efficient traffic flow of a traditionally styled home.

### 🏠 Porches distort your perception.
Often, a large porch will make a home look much bigger from the outside than it really is on the inside.

### 🏠 Wide, open spaces have limits.
They can be gorgeous to look at and wonderful to live in. But wide-open floor plans can be noisy and hard to decorate and may lack privacy.

### 🏠 Location really is the most important thing.
Never allow yourself to be seduced by a lovely house in a neighborhood that doesn't feel right.

### 🏠 Get out of the car.
Walk or bicycle the neighborhood to get a true flavor of what it would be like to live there.

### 🏠 See what creeps out after dark.
Visit in the evening, especially if you're buying in the city. Do you feel safe? Is there enough parking? Are streetlights harsh?

### 🏠 Be wary of the woods.
Unless you own them, those lovely woods backing up to a home may be developed someday. Once you buy the house, those woods could

transform into someone else's back yard—or even a commercial building, depending on how strict local zoning rules are.

### 🏠 Try the commute on a Monday morning, and hope for rain.

Yes, indeed, you need to set the alarm early, hop in the car, and drive to the neighborhood you're sizing up. Then get yourself to work from there, by car or public transit, however you'd probably do it if you owned a home there. Reverse the commute in the evening, and then drive back home.

### 🏠 Trust only what you see.

Don't count on the proposed schools, shops, and places of worship marked on the developer's map. They might never get built—at least, not in your lifetime.

### 🏠 You have the luxury of renting.

You no longer have to buy a home to protect your home-sale profits from tax. Renting for a year or longer could help if you're not completely convinced the relocation is wise, or if you simply want to learn more about the area before buying a home.

### 🏠 Get a relocation specialist to help.

They're better tuned to the needs of people moving from out of town. Get a referral from your local real estate agent, or from *www.relo.com*.

### 🏠 Tune in to local news.

Tiny community newspapers and local chat boards, such as those listed on *www.craigslist.org*, are great ways to get inside info on a new community. The Web site *www.relocationessentials.com* also provides good information on local schools and neighborhoods.

## 🏠 Go beyond the agent's tour.

It's good salesmanship to drive you to a new neighborhood via the scenic route. Drive around and get your own feel for areas not included on the agent's tour. You deserve the whole picture.

## 🏠 If they can't help negotiate, they're not much help.

If you do line up a top-notch negotiator as your buyer's agent, keep your personal info close to the vest—and don't abdicate your negotiating role completely to the agent.

## 🏠 No one likes a tattletale.

Ask a simple question of prospective agents: How will you make sure my information stays private and that I have someone who can negotiate on my behalf?

## 🏠 Ask the magic question.

"Would you choose this agent again?" is the question to ask when interviewing an agent's previous clients. Then be quiet and listen. If they hesitate or make excuses, move on to another agent.

## 🏠 Two agents are better than one.

At least they are if you're considering two very different markets. But make sure you're not under obligation to pay both of them on the same deal!

## 🏠 Why pay top dollar to a rookie?

New agents and seasoned agents usually charge the same commission. Do you want to pay to be a new agent's learning experience?

## 🏠 If you want out, get out.

If things aren't working out with your buyer's agent, talk to the broker about being transferred to another agent in that same brokerage.

## 🏠 Who cares if your agent hates FSBOs?

If it's the home you want, it's the home you want, and your buyer's agent should help you buy it. Tell your agent you want to see homes being sold by limited-service agents and FSBO sellers.

## 🏠 Search FSBO Web sites.

Some sites worth monitoring include *www.forsalebyowner.com*, *www.homesbyowner.com*, and *www.fsbo.com*.

## 🏠 Ask a lawyer for help.

If a FSBO seller hands you a contract and suggests you use it as your purchase contract, be sure to have it reviewed by your own real estate lawyer *before* you sign.

## 🏠 It never hurts to ask.

If you admire a home, and especially if you suspect it's being gussied up for sale, go ahead and ask the owners if they'd consider selling it to you. It's not an intrusion, it's a compliment!

## 🏠 The early bird catches the new birdhouse.

Move fast when you find a home you like, whether it's being sold FSBO or with an agent's help. Someone else may be falling in love with it too.

## 🏠 Be picky, but practical.

Do a self-check to make sure that the neighborhoods you're aiming for are realistic, given your budget, and that you *and* your spouse really have your heart in making this move. Go through your list of nice-to-haves and must-haves to see if there's any more room for compromise. Then hold on to your money until you find the right house.

## 🏠 Forget about the appliances.

Sure, they usually come with the house (though this varies according to local custom). But as you size up a home, keep in mind that for a couple of thousand dollars you could buy yourself some first-rate machines to cool, cook, and wash. Don't let the presence or absence of a chic cooktop sway your judgment on a house that costs *hundreds* of thousands of dollars.

## 🏠 Give your poor memory a break.

Take photos of houses as you tour. And prepare your own customized cheat sheet to help make sure you pay attention to all the things that matter most to you—and aren't sidetracked by the owner's lovely antiques and art work.

## 🏠 Beware of baby furniture.

Undersized furniture and wall-sized mirrors are tip-offs that a room is unusually small. Fresh paint (especially in odd places) can be a sign that the seller is hiding something. Bad smells never lie; they could be a sign of mold or other problems.

## 🏠 Get a CLUE.

Especially if you're buying a home in an area prone to hail, tropical storms, or hurricanes, you want to find out if the home has a history of insurance claims. If it does, you could have trouble getting an insurance policy at a decent price.

## 🏠 Judge the book by its cover.

Go outside and examine the materials and craftsmanship used for the home's exterior. Give bonus points to materials that resist water, rot, and termites.

### 🏠 Don't ask the Ouija board.

If you're spooked by the idea that someone has died in a home, that a crime has been committed there, or that it has a reputation for ghosts in the attic, speak up! Ask the seller or the seller's agent if any such things happened in the home. They're under no obligation to volunteer it. If there was a notorious event, it could actually stigmatize the property, limiting your ability to resell it later.

### 🏠 Forget the asking price.

The *real* price of that home—the price you should pay—is set by the market. It may be lower (or occasionally higher) than the asking price.

### 🏠 Look for haggle potential.

Watch for signs that your buyer may be willing to settle for a lower price. These include a home that's been on the market longer than usual, bad winter weather, signs that an owner already has moved out, and estate sales.

### 🏠 Treat earnest money carefully.

This chunk of cash that you present with your purchase offer, signifying your seriousness about buying, is at risk if you decide to back out of the deal. Don't make any bigger an earnest money payment than is necessary in your market.

### 🏠 When in doubt, spell it out.

With a swipe of the seller's pen, your purchase offer magically becomes a binding contract. Get everything you want written into that purchase offer right from the start. Include a list of all the things you expect to convey with the house, including light fixtures, window coverings, play sets and appliances.

### 🏠 Protect yourself with contingencies.

If the home turns out not to be as good a deal as it first appeared to be, or if your ability to get a decent mortgage is not as certain as you thought it was, you need an escape hatch from your contract to buy that home. Contingencies are your escape hatch. Include contingencies for home inspection, appraisal, and financing. Other contingencies can be used for special needs.

### 🏠 You can haggle with builders.

They'll try to dictate the terms of the contract, and it's tough to get them to budge from their asking price. But builders may be willing to throw in a few free upgrades if that's what it takes to seal your deal.

### 🏠 It's easy to say no to a fax machine.

Proactive real estate agents like to present their offers in person whenever possible. It allows them to cast the offer in its best light and even sell it a bit. Urge your agent not to simply fax your offer in to the seller's agent if it can be avoided.

### 🏠 Make it a limited-time offer.

Sellers may try to shop your offer around, hoping to drum up a better offer from someone else. Talk with your agent about putting an expiration date on your offer, to limit their ability to shop it— and to create a bit of urgency. Remember, you can revoke your offer at any point before the sellers sign it.

## 🏠 Counteroffers pave the way to a deal.

Don't be surprised if you have to go through a round or two of counteroffers that tailor the deal to meet the needs of both buyer and seller.

## 🏠 Agents have their own interests.

Agents can get fretful about the back-and-forth of counteroffers. Remember, they have a keen interest in seeing you finally sign off on the deal (a deal whose terms *they* don't have to live with). An agent's commission check rests on getting a signed deal moving along swiftly toward the closing table.

## 🏠 Get as good as you give.

When negotiating, ask for a little something for every concession you make. Not only will that strategy net more for you, but it may limit the number of requests the sellers make, once they know each one carries a price.

## 🏠 Don't go in for the kill.

Even if you're in a position to wring the last drop out of negotiations, remember that the most successful negotiations leave *both* parties feeling they got what they needed and are being treated fairly. You still have several weeks of interaction ahead with those sellers, and you might need their cooperation later. Don't leave them feeling burned.

## 🏠 Paper is your friend; time is your enemy.

Document everything and keep all your papers in an accordion file for easy reference. Jump on all the little tasks you have to perform before closing; you literally cannot afford to waste any time.

## 🏠 Get it in writing.

Make it your policy, your mantra, your dogma: Get it in writing. Every single agreement between you and the seller, you and your lender, you and *everyone else* must be in writing or it doesn't exist.

## 🏠 Hunt like a predator.

You have to stalk homes as they come on the market, then act swiftly and present the seller with a killer contract.

## 🏠 Give the seller what the seller wants.

Money always counts—but other terms could seal the deal. Delay your closing, rush your closing, rent back to them after closing—do whatever it takes.

## 🏠 Be ready to buy naked.

You may have to strip your purchase contract of common buyer protections. Your only protection will come from the extra preparation and scrutiny you apply up-front.

## 🏠 Know your real top dollar.

Your *real* top dollar is somewhere between the price at which you would kick yourself for losing out to another bidder and the price where you'd walk away with no remorse at all. Then put an escalation clause into your purchase offer that would raise your bid to that secret top dollar, should it be necessary.

## 🏠 Dump the flake.

If your agent has a reputation for bringing offers that fall apart before closing, you'll lose bidding wars . . . and may never know that the real reason was other agents' distaste for working with yours.

### 🏠 The listings king has the edge.

This agent is most likely to learn about homes *before* they come on the market, and can get you in fast.

### 🏠 Keep an eye out for fresh prey.

Watch for signs that homes are about to come on the market. It never hurts to knock on the door or to write a lovely, handwritten letter to the owners, asking if they plan to sell.

### 🏠 Be ready for love at first sight.

In a raging seller's market, be prepared to buy the very first day you see the home, without even a professional inspection. Pore over the home and its innards, doing as much of a mini-inspection as possible.

### 🏠 Flaws equal dollars.

Most flaws simply translate to repair dollars. But major structural flaws should be a deal-killer. If you see any red flags of structural flaws, pass on the home unless you get it cleared by an engineer first.

### 🏠 Do a worst-case scenario.

Do a worst-case scenario before writing a big check for earnest money. If the appraisal comes in low and the repair bills come in high, can you still swing the deal?

### 🏠 Inspect the home inspector.

You want one who has credentials and doesn't kowtow to the local real estate agents. Run away from an inspector who offers to make repairs him- or herself. Then put on your old jeans and go along for the tour.

### 🏠 Shop for an insurance policy ASAP.

You could have trouble getting a decently priced policy if you or the home you're buying has a history of claims. Buy a policy big enough to pay for complete rebuilding, *not* for the price of the home or the size of your mortgage.

### 🏠 You can shop for closing agents.

All you want is efficient competence at a fair price. That's not too much to ask—so ask for it.

### 🏠 Give buyer's remorse its due.

And then give it the boot. Review the logic of your decision, and focus on the excitement ahead.

### 🏠 Say goodbye.

Give your dear old home a proper send-off. It's the decent thing to do for the place that has served you well up until now.

### 🏠 Don't crowd your lock-in.

Schedule closing for at least several days before your interest-rate lock-in is set to expire. Leave yourself time to deal with problems that might delay your closing.

### 🏠 Assert your rights.

You have a right to review the main closing document, the HUD-1 Uniform Settlement Statement, a day before closing. But you have to ask for it!

### 🏠 Take a last look-around.

Take a final walk-through of the property shortly before closing to make sure it's in acceptable condition.

## 🏠 Fight junk fees.

You're not in a very strong bargaining position to fight dubious last-minute fees, but you at least can question them and ask to have them removed. Call them "errors" to help save face—and increase the odds that they'll be "corrected."

## 🏠 Celebrate!

Is there any place better for dancing than the big, empty floor of your new home?

## 🏠 Buy insurance on your own terms.

Most people need life insurance, but you don't need specialized mortgage life policies that automatically pay the loan if one spouse dies. The remaining spouse may be better off with an affordable term life insurance policy that pays cash. They then have the choice of paying off the mortgage—or investing the money to provide ongoing income.

## 🏠 Abracadabra, blah, blah, blah.

There's no magic involved in a biweekly mortgage plan. You simply make an extra payment each year.

## 🏠 Skip the middleman.

You don't need to pay an intermediary to switch to a biweekly mortgage payment plan. If you would like to prepay your mortgage, most loan servicers will arrange it for you—for free.

## 🏠 Expect to be jilted.

Your lender very likely will sell the job of servicing your mortgage to another company. But don't send your payment off to a new address until you've received a letter from the original lender informing you of the switch in advance.

### ⌂ Mayberry doesn't exist.

Change the locks and keypad combinations—even if you've moved into a friendly subdivision. Give yourself a fresh start in securing your home.

### ⌂ Reach out to your new neighbors.

*Everybody* is busy these days, maybe too busy to welcome a newcomer to the neighborhood. Break in your new home the right way by inviting new neighbors and old friends over as soon as you can manage.

# Cheat Sheet for Touring a Home

This cheat sheet is a tool for your first look at a home. Make a copy for each home you see, and customize it to reflect your own wants and needs. But don't make it so detailed that filling it out interferes with fully discovering the home and soaking up some of its ambiance. Don't make it the equivalent of a home inspection; that can wait until later, after you've decided whether you'd really like to live there.

### ADDRESS:

Notable feature: (Something like "yellow house with porch swing.") _____

Any dark, gloomy rooms? _____

### WINDOWS:

Enough in each room?_____

General condition? Metal, wood, or vinyl frames? _____

Double-hung, sliding, casement (which crank out) or other type? _____

Skylights?_____

### STORAGE:

Enough closets?_____

Long-term storage space in basement, garage or attic?_____

315

## BATHROOMS:

Tubs or showers? _____

Whirlpools? _____

Sprays? _____

Well-kept? _____

## KITCHEN:

Microwave location? _____

Enough refrigerator space? _____

Cabinet material? _____

Enough cabinets? _____

Pantry? _____

Countertop material? _____

General appliance condition? _____

## FLOOR MATERIAL AND CONDITION:

In the kitchen? _____

Elsewhere? _____

## OBVIOUS CONSTRUCTION FLAWS OR OBSOLESCENCE:

Cracked walls? _____

Uneven floors or stairs? _____

Lots of extension cords in use? _____

Moldy smells? _____

## AIR CONDITIONING:

Central, window units or none at all? _____

## SPACE FOR SPECIAL THINGS:

Computer, piano, big-screen TV? _____

## SPACE FOR GREETING GUESTS:

Is the foyer or hallway cramped? _____

Roomy? _____

Coat closet? _____

## HOUSEKEEPING TRAPS:

Plant ledges? _____

Oversize windows in two-story foyers? _____

Ultra-high recessed lights? _____

## GARAGE SPACE:

Can it fit your car or the SUV? _____

Secure storage space? _____

If separate from the home, condition of outer walls and roof? _____

## LAUNDRY:

In basement? _____

Kitchen? _____

Near bedrooms?_____

## TRAFFIC FLOW THROUGH THE HOME:

Bottlenecks that may interfere with getting everybody out of the home each morning? _____

Bedrooms too close to living areas? _____

Bathrooms placed conveniently?_____

Stairways located conveniently? _____

## LANDSCAPING:

Lush?_____

Needs work? _____

Patio? _____

Deck? _____

Too sunny? _____

Too shaded?_____

Flat?_____

Hilly? _____

# Handy Web Sites

## Mortgage and credit information:

**www.annualcreditreport.com**

This site, sponsored by the three major credit-report bureaus, Equifax, TransUnion, and Experian, is the place to go once a year to request the free credit report to which you are entitled by federal law.

**www.myfico.com**

The myfico Web site is run by the credit score giant FairIsaac Corp., which takes information from your credit reports maintained by Equifax, TransUnion, and Experian and distills that information into three numbers—your credit scores for each company. You can buy a report with a single version of your FICO score for $14.95. More expensive packages give you all three scores and personal finance advice. There are lots of free features available on the Web site that will help you learn how to improve your scores and to predict the interest rates you should be offered by lenders based on your scores.

**www.equifax.com**
**www.experian.com**
**www.transunion.com**
These are the Web sites of the three big companies that maintain credit histories. Start first by requesting your free annual report from *www.annualcreditreport.com*. If you find problems with the individual reports, move on to the individual credit reporting companies.

**www.hsh.com**
You'll find a weekly survey of average interest rates across the country on this site, owned by HSH Associates, a financial publishing company based in New Jersey. You can download a free package of mortgage calculators that will allow you to play "what-if" scenarios, and for $11 you can buy a recent survey of the rate and point combinations being offered by lenders in your metro area. The local surveys are available for California, New Jersey, New York and many of the larger cities elsewhere around the country.

**www.homeloans.va.gov/veteran.htm**
This Web site, maintained by U.S. Department of Veterans Affairs, has a wealth of information about no-downpayment mortgage loans available to veterans and active-duty military personnel. It links to a site that allows you to search for lenders making VA mortgages in your community.

**www.hud.gov/offices/hsg/sfh/res/rightsmtgesrvcr.cfm**
The U.S. Department of Housing and Urban Development outlines its rules for how lenders must notify you that they've sold your loan

to another company and that you should begin sending payments to a different address. It includes a sample of a written complaint letter that you can send to the lender in case problems come up.

**www.debtadvice.com**
The National Foundation for Credit Counseling offers reasonably priced help in getting out from under troublesome debt as well as managing lesser debt loads. They also provide counseling for people who plan to become homeowners.

**www.countrywide.com**
**www.eloan.com**
**www.gmacmortgage.com**
**www.lendingtree.com**
**www.wamumortgage.com**
**www.wellsfargo.com/mortgage/**
These are among the biggest companies offering mortgages over the Internet. You might also look for the Web site of banks and other financial institutions you already do business with when you start mortgage shopping.

**www.hud.gov**
Some of the best resources available through the U.S. Department of Housing and Urban Development's Web site are found through its "Information by State" link. It connects you to local homebuying programs and downpayment assistance resources.

## Condos and co-ops

**www.ncb.coop/**
It offers a range of financial services, but the National Cooperative Bank and its subsidiaries, based in Washington, D.C., specialize in providing mortgages to people buying condos and co-ops.

**www.coophousing.org**
The National Association of Housing Cooperatives is a great source of information for co-op owners and board members. The site links to several lenders that are comfortable writing mortgage loans for these homes.

## Insurance information:

**www.choicetrust.com**
Before an insurance company agrees to offer you a homeowners insurance policy, it will check for a claim history on the CLUE report maintained by ChoiceTrust. You can get a copy of your own report for free at the site. Sellers may want to give buyers a copy of the special sellers' version for $19.50, which omits personal information such as the homeowner's name, Social Security number and date of birth.

**www.floodsmart.gov**
Although you buy flood insurance through the same agents that sell ordinary homeowners' insurance policies, the federal government actually provides the flood insurance. This site, run by the National Flood Insurance Program, has explanations about judging your flood risk, details about the insurance coverage, and an estimator

that helps you calculate what the premium might be for your home. You also can search for agents serving your community.

## www.earthquakeauthority.com

Homeowners and renters in California can obtain earthquake insurance through the California Earthquake Authority, a privately funded organization founded by the state legislature. This site explains coverage (which is limited) and deductibles (which are high) and allows you to estimate the premium for your home. You also can search for an insurance company that participates in the program.

## www.insweb.com

You'll be asked to enter specific information about your address and the home you'd like to insure before you can get rates from several companies quoted to you by e-mail.

## www.chubb.com

Owners of historic homes or very expensive homes may want to look for homeowners insurance with Chubb, which has special policies tailored for that market.

## www.lc.usaa.com

Members of the military are eligible to join USAA, a Texas-based company that offers auto and homeowners insurance and other financial services. Their policies consistently win high marks based on price and customer satisfaction. Go to the Web site to confirm whether you're eligible.

## Change of address:

https://moversguide.usps.com
The U.S. Postal Service Web site allows you to enter information for mail forwarding.

www.irs.gov/taxtopics/tc157.html
At this Internal Revenue Service site you can download a copy of Form 8822, Address Change Request, which you should send to the IRS to make sure you receive notices about tax audits (or refunds!) without delay.

## Home inspections:

www.ashi.org/customers/state.asp
With more than 6,000 members, the American Society of Home Inspectors, Inc. is the nation's largest association of home inspectors. You can search for members according to ZIP code or by metro area.

www.nibi.com
You can search for inspectors certified by the National Institute of Building Inspectors, a training organization affiliated with the House Master franchise of home inspectors.

www.epa.gov/lead/index.html
If you buy a home built before 1978, the seller is required to give you a form disclosing anything he or she knows about the presence of lead-based paint in the home. You can find more information about reducing the risks of lead at this site run by the U.S. Environmental Protection Agency.

www.epa.gov/radon
The federal government recommends that everyone test their home for the presence of radon gas, the second-leading cause of lung cancer. You can learn about testing and removing radon from your home at this site.

## To find For-Sale-By-Owner homes:

www.forsalebyowner.com
www.homesbyowner.com
www.fsbo.com
You never know where a home being sold directly by the owner might turn up. It pays to search all these sites—and to check local newspaper classified ads—to see if there's a gem in your target neighborhood.

www.craigslist.org
For the many metro areas that have a spot on Craigslist, you'll find homes being sold with the help of real estate brokers mixed in with those being sold directly by the owner.

## Illegal discrimination:

www.hud.gov/complaints/housediscrim.cfm
If you suspect you have been discriminated against on account of race, color, national origin, religion, sex, family status, or disability when trying to buy or rent a home this is the place to register a complaint. There's a link for making complaints online, plus info on filing a complaint by mail or phone, if you prefer.

## Relocation to another city:

**www.relo.com**

Usually corporations contract with a company like Relo Direct to manage moves for executives or groups of employees, but individuals can purchase some services directly from the company—and get free online help in researching communities and managing your home purchase and sale.

**www.relocationessentials.com**

You can search for communities with the income, education, and age profiles you desire, research schools, and compare local living costs for free with this site.

**www.craigslist.org**

So, you're moving to a new city and wondering if the neighborhoods on the west side of town get a little rough after dark. Post a question on the Craigslist message board, and there's a good chance you'll get lots of opinions from locals.

## Miscellaneous:

**www.realtor.com**

You can search more than two million home listings across the country on this site, maintained by the National Association of Realtors. You also can use it to search for real estate brokers and agents.

**www.jdpower.com/cc/index.jsp**

You can review consumer satisfaction rankings for mortgage providers, homeowners insurers, and home builders according to surveys by J.D. Power and Associates.

# HUD-1 Statement of Settlement Costs

A. **Settlement Statement**

U.S. Department of Housing
and Urban Development

OMB Approval No. 2502-0265
(expires 9/30/2006)

**B. Type of Loan**

| | | |
|---|---|---|
| 1. ☐ FHA 2. ☐ FmHA 3. ☐ Conv. Unins. 4. ☐ VA 5. ☐ Conv. Ins. | 6. File Number: | 7. Loan Number: | 8. Mortgage Insurance Case Number: |

**C. Note:** This form is furnished to give you a statement of actual settlement costs. Amounts paid to and by the settlement agent are shown. Items marked "(p.o.c.)" were paid outside the closing; they are shown here for informational purposes and are not included in the totals.

| D. Name & Address of Borrower: | E. Name & Address of Seller: | F. Name & Address of Lender: |
|---|---|---|
| | | |

| G. Property Location: | H. Settlement Agent: | |
|---|---|---|
| | Place of Settlement: | I. Settlement Date: |

| J. Summary of Borrower's Transaction | | K. Summary of Seller's Transaction | |
|---|---|---|---|
| **100. Gross Amount Due From Borrower** | | **400. Gross Amount Due To Seller** | |
| 101. Contract sales price | | 401. Contract sales price | |
| 102. Personal property | | 402. Personal property | |
| 103. Settlement charges to borrower (line 1400) | | 403. | |
| 104. | | 404. | |
| 105. | | 405. | |
| **Adjustments for items paid by seller in advance** | | **Adjustments for items paid by seller in advance** | |
| 106. City/town taxes          to | | 406. City/town taxes          to | |
| 107. County taxes          to | | 407. County taxes          to | |
| 108. Assessments          to | | 408. Assessments          to | |
| 109. | | 409. | |
| 110. | | 410. | |
| 111. | | 411. | |
| 112. | | 412. | |

326

| 120. Gross Amount Due From Borrower | | 420. Gross Amount Due To Seller | |
|---|---|---|---|
| **200. Amounts Paid By Or In Behalf Of Borrower** | | **500. Reductions In Amount Due To Seller** | |
| 201. Deposit or earnest money | | 501. Excess deposit (see instructions) | |
| 202. Principal amount of new loan(s) | | 502. Settlement charges to seller (line 1400) | |
| 203. Existing loan(s) taken subject to | | 503. Existing loan(s) taken subject to | |
| 204. | | 504. Payoff of first mortgage loan | |
| 205. | | 505. Payoff of second mortgage loan | |
| 206. | | 506. | |
| 207. | | 507. | |
| 208. | | 508. | |
| 209. | | 509. | |
| **Adjustments for items unpaid by seller** | | **Adjustments for items unpaid by seller** | |
| 210. City/town taxes          to | | 510. City/town taxes          to | |
| 211. County taxes          to | | 511. County taxes          to | |
| 212. Assessments          to | | 512. Assessments          to | |
| 213. | | 513. | |
| 214. | | 514. | |
| 215. | | 515. | |
| 216. | | 516. | |
| 217. | | 517. | |
| 218. | | 518. | |
| 219. | | 519. | |
| **220. Total Paid By/For Borrower** | | **520. Total Reduction Amount Due Seller** | |
| **300. Cash At Settlement From/To Borrower** | | **600. Cash At Settlement To/From Seller** | |
| 301. Gross Amount due from borrower (line 120) | | 601. Gross amount due to seller (line 420) | |
| 302. Less amounts paid by/for borrower (line 220) | ( ) | 602. Less reductions in amt. due seller (line 520) | ( ) |
| **303. Cash** ☐ From  ☐ To Borrower | | **603. Cash** ☐ To  ☐ From Seller | |

**L. Settlement Charges**

| | | Paid From Borrowers Funds at Settlement | Paid From Seller's Funds at Settlement |
|---|---|---|---|
| **700. Total Sales/Broker's Commission based on price $** @ % = | | | |
| Division of Commission (line 700) as follows: | | | |
| 701. $                    to | | | |
| 702. $                    to | | | |
| 703. Commission paid at Settlement | | | |
| 704. | | | |
| **800. Items Payable In Connection With Loan** | | | |
| 801. Loan Origination Fee          % | | | |
| 802. Loan Discount          % | | | |
| 803. Appraisal Fee          to | | | |
| 804. Credit Report          to | | | |
| 805. Lender's Inspection Fee | | | |
| 806. Mortgage Insurance Application Fee to | | | |
| 807. Assumption Fee | | | |
| 808. | | | |
| 809. | | | |
| 810. | | | |
| 811. | | | |
| **900. Items Required By Lender To Be Paid In Advance** | | | |
| 901. Interest from          to          @$ /day | | | |
| 902. Mortgage Insurance Premium for          months to | | | |
| 903. Hazard Insurance Premium for          years to | | | |
| 904.          years to | | | |
| 905. | | | |
| **1000. Reserves Deposited With Lender** | | | |
| 1001. Hazard insurance          months@$ per month | | | |
| 1002. Mortgage insurance          months@$ per month | | | |
| 1003. City property taxes          months@$ per month | | | |
| 1004. County property taxes          months@$ per month | | | |
| 1005. Annual assessments          months@$ per month | | | |
| 1006.          months@$ per month | | | |
| 1007.          months@$ per month | | | |

# Appendices

| 1008. | | | months @ $ | | per month | | | |
|---|---|---|---|---|---|---|---|---|
| **1100. Title Charges** | | | | | | | | |
| 1101. Settlement or closing fee | to | | | | | | | |
| 1102. Abstract or title search | to | | | | | | | |
| 1103. Title examination | to | | | | | | | |
| 1104. Title insurance binder | to | | | | | | | |
| 1105. Document preparation | to | | | | | | | |
| 1106. Notary fees | to | | | | | | | |
| 1107. Attorney's fees | to | | | | | | | |
| (includes above items numbers: | | | | | ) | | | |
| 1108. Title insurance | to | | | | | | | |
| (includes above items numbers: | | | | | ) | | | |
| 1109. Lender's coverage | $ | | | | | | | |
| 1110. Owner's coverage | $ | | | | | | | |
| 1111. | | | | | | | | |
| 1112. | | | | | | | | |
| 1113. | | | | | | | | |
| **1200. Government Recording and Transfer Charges** | | | | | | | | |
| 1201. Recording fees: Deed $ | ; Mortgage $ | | ; Releases $ | | | | | |
| 1202. City/county tax/stamps: Deed $ | ; Mortgage $ | | | | | | | |
| 1203. State tax/stamps: Deed $ | ; Mortgage $ | | | | | | | |
| 1204. | | | | | | | | |
| 1205. | | | | | | | | |
| **1300. Additional Settlement Charges** | | | | | | | | |
| 1301. Survey          to | | | | | | | | |
| 1302. Pest inspection to | | | | | | | | |
| 1303. | | | | | | | | |
| 1304. | | | | | | | | |
| 1305. | | | | | | | | |
| **1400. Total Settlement Charges (enter on lines 103, Section J and 502, Section K)** | | | | | | | | |

Section 5 of the Real Estate Settlement Procedures Act (RESPA) requires the following: • HUD must develop a Special Information Booklet to help persons borrowing money to finance the purchase of residential real estate to better understand the nature and costs of real estate settlement services; • Each lender must provide the booklet to all applicants from whom it receives or for whom it prepares a written application to borrow money to finance the purchase of residential real estate; • Lenders must prepare and distribute with the Booklet a Good Faith Estimate of the settlement costs that the borrower is likely to incur in connection with the settlement. These disclosures are manadatory.

Section 4(a) of RESPA mandates that HUD develop and prescribe this standard form to be used at the time of loan settlement to provide full disclosure of all charges imposed upon the borrower and seller. These are third party disclosures that are designed to provide the borrower with pertinent information during the settlement process in order to be a better shopper.

The Public Reporting Burden for this collection of information is estimated to average one hour per response, including the time for reviewing instructions, searching existing data sources, gathering and maintaining the data needed, and completing and reviewing the collection of information.

This agency may not collect this information, and you are not required to complete this form, unless it displays a currently valid OMB control number.

The information requested does not lend itself to confidentiality.

# Some Typical Closing Fees

These common loan fees are based on a national survey of more than 150 lenders in December 2004, by HSH Associates, a financial publishing company in Pompton Plains, N.J. The survey is conducted twice a year; updated results can be found at *www.hsh.com*.

## Appraisal Fee

78 percent of lenders surveyed charged an appraisal fee. The average amount charged was $315.

## Credit Report

72 percent of lenders charged a credit report fee, with the average reported amount of $26.

## Loan Application

The vast majority of lenders charge a fee at the time of application. In some areas it may consist of the credit report and appraisal fees, but in the survey, 41 percent of mortgage lenders specifically charged an application fee that was NOT for the credit report and appraisal. The average amount charged was $275.

## Document Preparation

57 percent of the lenders surveyed charged a document preparation fee, at an average of $204.

## Flood Certification

93 percent of lenders charged this fee, and it costs an average of $18.

# State Real Estate Commissions

## ALABAMA

Alabama Real Estate
  Commission
1201 Carmichael Way
Montgomery, AL 36106
Phone: 334-242-5544

*www.arec.state.al.us/*

## ALASKA

Real Estate Commission
550 W. 7th Ave., Suite 1500
Anchorage, AK 99501-3567
Phone: 907-269-8197

*www.dced.state.ak.us/occ/prec
  .htm*

## ARIZONA

Department of Real Estate
2910 N. 44th St., Suite 100
Phoenix, AZ 85018
Phone: 602-468-1414

*www.re.state.az.us/*

## ARKANSAS

Real Estate Commission
612 S. Summit St.
Little Rock, AR 72201-4740
Phone: 501-683-8010

*www.state.ar.us/arec/arecweb
  .html*

## CALIFORNIA

State of California
Department of Real Estate
P.O. Box 187000
Sacramento, CA 95818-7000

Phone: 916-227-0864

*www.dre.ca.gov/*

## COLORADO

Division of Real Estate
1900 Grant St., Suite 600
Denver, CO 80203
Phone: 303-894-2166 or -2185

*www.dora.state.co.us/real-estate/*

## CONNECTICUT

Department of Consumer
    Protection
165 Capitol Ave.
Hartford, CT 06106
Phone: 860-713-6050

*www.ct.gov/dcp/site/default.asp*

## DELAWARE

Real Estate Commission
861 Silver Lake Blvd., Suite 203
Dover, DE 19904
Phone: 302-744-4519

*www.professionallicensing.state.d
    e.us/boards/realestate*

## DISTRICT OF COLUMBIA

Board of Real Estate
941 North Capitol St., NE
Washington, DC 20002
Phone: 202-442-4400

*www.dcra.dc.gov/dcra/site/
    default.asp*

## FLORIDA

Dept. of Business and
    Professional Regulation
    Customer Contact Ctr.
1940 N. Monroe St.
Tallahassee, FL 32399-1027
Phone: 850-487-1395

*www.state.fl.us/dbpr/re/index
    .shtml*

## GEORGIA

Real Estate Commission
229 Peachtree St. NE, Suite
    1000 - International Tower
Atlanta, GA 30303-1605
Phone: 404-656-3916

*www.grec.state.ga.us/*

## HAWAII

Real Estate Branch
335 Merchant St., Room 333
Honolulu, HI 96813
Phone: 808-586-2643

*www.hawaii.gov/hirec*

## IDAHO

Real Estate Commission
P.O. Box 83720
Boise, ID 83720-0077
Phone: 208-334-3285; toll-free
    in Idaho, 866-447-5411

*www.idahorealestatecommission.
    com*

## ILLINOIS

Division of Banks and Real
    Estate
500 East Monroe St.
Springfield, IL 62701
Phone: 217-782-3000

*www.idfpr.com/default.asp*

## INDIANA

Professional Licensing Agency
Attn: Indiana Real Estate
    Commission
402 W. Washington St., Room
    W072
Indianapolis, IN 46204
Phone: 317-234-3009

*www.in.gov/pla/bandc/estate/*

## IOWA

Professional Licensing Division
1920 S.E. Hulsizer Rd.
Ankeny, IA 50021-3941
Phone: 515-281-7393 or -5910

*www.state.ia.us/government
    /com/prof/sales/home.html*

## KANSAS

Real Estate Commission
Three Townsite Plaza, Suite 200
120 SE 6th Ave.
Topeka, KS 66603
Phone: 785-296-3411

*www.accesskansas.org/krec/*

## KENTUCKY

Real Estate Commission
10200 Linn Station Rd., Suite
    201
Louisville, KY 40223
Phone: 502-429-7250

*www.krec.ky.gov/*

## LOUISIANA

Real Estate Commission
P.O Box 14785
Baton Rouge, LA 70898-4785
Phone: 225-765-0191; toll-free
    in Louisiana, 800-821-4529

*www.lrec.state.la.us/*

## MAINE

Dept. of Professional and
    Financial Regulation
Office of Licensing and
    Registration
35 State House Station
Augusta, ME 04333-0035
Phone: 207-624-8603

*www.state.me.us/pfr/olr/*

## MARYLAND

Real Estate Commission
500 N. Calvert St.
Baltimore, MD 21202-3651
Phone: 410-230-6200 or -6201

*www.dllr.state.md.us/license/
    real_est/reintro.html*

## MASSACHUSETTS

Division of Professional
    Licensure
239 Causeway St.
Boston, MA 02114
Phone: 617-727-3074

*www.mass.gov/dpl/*

## MICHIGAN
Dept. of Labor & Economic
Growth, Licensing Div.
P.O. Box 30004
Lansing, MI 48909
Phone: 517-241-9265 or -9263
*www.michigan.gov/cis*

## MISSISSIPPI
Real Estate Commission
P.O. Box 12685
Jackson, MS 39236
Phone: 601-932-9191
*www.mrec.state.ms.us/*

## MISSOURI
Real Estate Commission
P.O. Box 1339
3605 Missouri Blvd.
Jefferson City, MO 65102
Phone: 573-751-2628
http://pr.mo.gov/realestate.asp

## MONTANA
Board of Realty Regulation
P.O. Box 200513
301 South Park
Helena, MT 59620-0513
Phone: 406-841-2300
*www.discoveringmontana.com/
dli/bsd/license/bsd_boards/
rre_board/board_page.asp*

## NEBRASKA
Real Estate Commission
P.O. Box 94667
1200 N St., Suite 402
Lincoln, NE 68509-4667
Phone: 402-471-2004
*www.nrec.state.ne.us/*

## NEVADA
Real Estate Division
2501 E. Sahara Ave., Suite 102
Las Vegas, NV 89104-4137
Phone: 702-486-4033
*www.red.state.nv.us/*

## NEW HAMPSHIRE
Real Estate Commission
State House Annex, Room 434
25 Capitol St.
Concord, NH 03301
Phone: 603-271-2701
*www.nh.gov/nhrec/*

## NEW JERSEY
Real Estate Commission
240 W. State St.
P.O. Box 328
Trenton, NJ 08625-0328
Phone: 609-292-8280
*www.state.nj.us/dobi/remnu
.shtml*

## NEW MEXICO

Real Estate Commission
5200 Oakland Ave., N.E.
Albuquerque, NM 87113
Phone: 505-222-9820; toll-free in
    New Mexico: 800-801-7505

*www.state.nm.us/clients/nmrec/*

## NEW YORK

Division of Licensing Services
84 Holland Ave.
Albany, NY 12208-3490
Phone: 518-474-4429

*www.dos.state.ny.us/lcns/
    realest.html*

## NORTH CAROLINA

Real Estate Commission
P.O. Box 17100
Raleigh, NC 27619-7100
Phone: 919-875-3700

*www.ncrec.state.nc.us/about/
    about.asp*

## NORTH DAKOTA

Real Estate Commission
P.O. Box 727
Bismark, ND 58502-0727
Phone: 701-328-9749

*www.governor.state.nd.us/boards/
    boards-query.asp?
    Board_ID=93*

## OHIO

Department of Commerce
Division of Real Estate &
    Professional Licensing
77 S. High St., 20th Floor
Columbus, OH 43215-6133
Phone: 614-466-4100

*www.com.state.oh.us/real/*

## OKLAHOMA

Real Estate Commission
Shepherd Mall
2401 N.W. 23rd St., Suite 18
Oklahoma City, OK 73107
Phone: 405-521-3387; toll-free
    in Oklahoma: 866-521-3389

*www.orec.state.ok.us/*

## OREGON

Real Estate Agency
1177 Center Street NE
Salem, OR 97301-2505
Phone: 503-378-4170

*www.rea.state.or.us/*

## PENNSYLVANIA

Real Estate Commission
P.O. Box 2649
Harrisburg, PA 17105-2649
Phone: 717-783-3658

*www.dos.state.pa.us/bpoa/cwp/
    view.asp?a=1104&Q=433107*

## RHODE ISLAND

Department of Business
    Regulation/Real Estate
233 Richmond St.
Providence, RI 02903
Phone: 401-222-2246

*www.dbr.state.ri.us/real_estate
    .html*

## SOUTH CAROLINA

Department of Labor, Licensing
    & Regulation
P.O Box 11847
Columbia, SC 29211-1847
Phone: 803-896-4400

*www.llr.state.sc.us/POL/
    RealEstateCommission/
    INDEX.ASP*

## SOUTH DAKOTA

Real Estate Commission
221 W. Capitol, Suite 101
Pierre, SD 57501
Phone: 605-773-3600

*www.state.sd.us/sdrec/*

## TENNESSEE

Real Estate Commission
500 James Robertson Pkwy.
Nashville, TN 37243-1151
Phone: 615-741-2273; toll-free
    in Tennessee: 800-342-4031

*www.state.tn.us/commerce/
    boards/trec/*

## TEXAS

Real Estate Commission
P.O. Box 12188
Austin, TX 78711-2188
Phone: 512-459-6544; toll-free
    in Texas: 800-250-8732

*www.trec.state.tx.us/*

## UTAH

Division of Real Estate
P.O. Box 146711
Salt Lake City, UT 84114-6711
Phone: 801-530-6747

*www.commerce.utah.gov/dre/*

## VERMONT

Office of Professional
    Regulation
Real Estate Commission
81 River St.
Montpelier, VT 05609-1101
Phone: 802-828-3228

*http://vtprofessionals.org/oprl/
    real_estate/*

## VIRGINIA

Department of Professional and
    Occupational Regulation
3600 W. Broad St.
Richmond, VA 23230
Phone: 804-367-8500

*www.state.va.us/dpor*

## WASHINGTON

Department of Licensing
Business and Professions
  Division, Real Estate
P.O. Box 9015
Olympia, WA 98507-9015
Phone: 360-664-6500 or -6488

*www.dol.wa.gov/realestate/*
  *refront.htm*

## WEST VIRGINIA

Real Estate Commission
300 Capitol St., Suite 400
Charleston, WV 25301
Phone: 304-558-3555

*www.wvrec.org/*

## WYOMING

Real Estate Commission
2020 Carey Ave., Suite 100
Cheyenne, WY 82002
Phone: 307-777-71415

*http://realestate.state.wy.us/*

# Typical Flaws and Repair Costs

| Deficiencies | 0–12 years old | 13–29 years old |
|---|---|---|
| Roofing problems | 19% | 49% |
| Electrical system problems | 14% | 30% |
| Aluminum wiring | <1% | 6% |
| Plumbing system problems | 9% | 20% |
| Old or mixed piping | <1% | 18% |
| Poor water pressure | 2% | 4% |
| Central air conditioning | 14% | 29% |
| Central heating | 15% | 60% |
| Inadequate insulation | 12% | 31% |
| Structural problems | 9% | 14% |
| Water seepage | 23% | 26% |

Reprinted with permission. Any reprinting, reproduction or transmission is prohibited without written permission. HouseMaster ® is a registered trademark of HMA Franchise Systems, Inc.

A survey of more than 2,000 resale homes by the HouseMaster home inspection franchise system revealed the typical incidence of flaws, based on the home's age, and cost estimates for suggested repairs.

| 30 years or older | Suggested repairs | Cost estimates |
|---|---|---|
| 55% | New wooden shingles<br>New asphalt shingles | $3,200–$5,000<br>$1,600–$2,600 |
| 49% | New service panel | $800–$1,500 |
| 5% | Upgrade connections | $20–$30 per outlet |
| 40% | Replace sections<br>Replace shower pan<br>Replace water heater | $300–$800<br>$900–$1,600<br>$350–$600 |
| 9% | Replace piping system | $3,000–$5,000 |
| 21% | Replace condenser unit<br>New compressor | $1,800–$2,500<br>$800–$1,200 |
| 54% | New water boiler<br>New warm–air furnace | $2,000–$3,000<br>$1,500–$2,200 |
| 49% | Improve/add insulation | $800–$1,500 |
| 32% | Major repair/rebuild<br>Underpin (support) | $6,000–$15,000<br>$3,000–$8,000 |
| 47% | Drainage system<br>Sump pump/pit | $3,500–$5,000<br>$600–$800 |

# Examples of Real Estate Contracts

In the following pages you will find the contracts and disclosure forms used during a home sale in California. While each state has its own laws governing the sale of real estate and will require specific forms tailored to those laws, reviewing the California documents can help you get a feel for what you can expect to encounter.

Buyer broker Agreement

CALIFORNIA
ASSOCIATION
OF REALTORS®

**BUYER BROKER AGREEMENT - EXCLUSIVE**
**Right to Represent**
(C.A.R. Form BBE, Revised 10/04)

1. **EXCLUSIVE RIGHT TO REPRESENT:** _____ ("Buyer")
grants _____ ("Broker")
beginning on (date) _____ and ending at: **(i)** 11:59 p.m. on (date) _____, or **(ii)** completion of
a resulting transaction, whichever occurs first ("Representation Period"), the exclusive and irrevocable right, on the terms
specified in this Agreement, to represent Buyer in acquiring real property or a manufactured home. Broker agrees to exercise
due diligence and reasonable efforts to fulfill the following authorizations and obligations. Broker will perform its obligations
under this Agreement through the individual signing for Broker below, who is either Broker individually or an associate-licensee
(an individual licensed as a real estate salesperson or broker who works under Broker's real estate license). Buyer agrees that
Broker's duties are limited by the terms of this Agreement, including those limitations set forth in paragraphs 5 and 6.
2. **AGENCY RELATIONSHIPS:**
   **A. DISCLOSURE:** If the property described in paragraph 4 includes residential property with one-to-four dwelling units,
   Buyer acknowledges receipt of the "Disclosure Regarding Real Estate Agency Relationships" form prior to entering into
   this Agreement.
   **B. BUYER REPRESENTATION:** Broker will represent, as described in this Agreement, Buyer in any resulting transaction.
   **C. (1) POSSIBLE DUAL AGENCY WITH SELLER:** (C(1) APPLIES UNLESS C(2)(i) or (ii) is checked below.)
   Depending on the circumstances, it may be necessary or appropriate for Broker to act as an agent for both Buyer and a seller,
   exchange party, or one or more additional parties ("Seller"). Broker shall, as soon as practicable, disclose to Buyer any
   election to act as a dual agent representing both Buyer and Seller. If Buyer is shown property listed with Broker, Buyer
   consents to Broker becoming a dual agent representing both Buyer and Seller with respect to those properties. In event of
   dual agency, Buyer agrees that: **(a)** Broker, without the prior written consent of Buyer, will not disclose to Seller that the Buyer
   is willing to pay a price greater than the price offered; **(b)** Broker, without the prior written consent of Seller, will not disclose
   to Buyer that Seller is willing to sell property at a price less than the listing price; and **(c)** other than as set forth in (a) and
   (b) above, a dual agent is obligated to disclose known facts materially affecting the value or desirability of the Property to
   both parties.
   **OR (2) SINGLE AGENCY ONLY:** (APPLIES ONLY IF (i) or (ii) is checked below.)
   ☐ **(i) Broker's firm lists properties for sale:** Buyer understands that this election will prevent Broker from showing Buyer
   those properties that are listed with Broker's firm or from representing Buyer in connection with those properties. Buyer's
   acquisition of a property listed with Broker's firm shall not affect Broker's right to be compensated under paragraph 3. In any
   resulting transaction in which Seller's property is not listed with Broker's firm, Broker will be the exclusive agent of Buyer and not
   a dual agent also representing Seller.
   **OR** ☐ **(ii) Broker's firm DOES NOT list property:** Entire brokerage firm only represents buyers and does not list property. In any
   resulting transaction, Broker will be the exclusive agent of Buyer and not a dual agent also representing Seller.
   **D. OTHER POTENTIAL BUYERS:** Buyer understands that other potential buyers may, through Broker, consider, make offers
   on or acquire the same or similar properties as those Buyer is seeking to acquire. Buyer consents to Broker's representation
   of such other potential buyers before, during and after the Representation Period, or any extension thereof.
   **E. CONFIRMATION:** If the Property includes residential property with one-to-four dwelling units, Broker shall confirm the agency
   relationship described above, or as modified, in writing, prior to or coincident with Buyer's execution of a Property Contract.
3. **COMPENSATION TO BROKER:**
   **NOTICE: The amount or rate of real estate commissions is not fixed by law. They are set by each Broker
   individually and may be negotiable between Buyer and Broker (real estate commissions include all
   compensation and fees to Broker).**
   Buyer agrees to pay to Broker, irrespective of agency relationship(s), as follows:
   **A. AMOUNT OF COMPENSATION:** (Check (1), (2) or (3). Check only one.)
   ☐ **(1)** _____ percent of the acquisition price AND (if checked ☐) $ _____ .
   **OR** ☐ **(2)** $ _____ .
   **OR** ☐ **(3)** Pursuant to the compensation schedule attached as an addendum _____ .
   **B. BROKER RIGHT TO COMPENSATION:** Broker shall be entitled to the compensation provided for in paragraph 3A:
   **(1)** If Buyer enters into an agreement to acquire property described in paragraph 4, on those terms or any other terms
   acceptable to Buyer during the Representation Period, or any extension thereof.
   **(2)** If, within ___ **calendar days** after expiration of the Representation Period or any extension thereof, Buyer enters into an
   agreement to acquire property described in paragraph 4, which property Broker introduced to Buyer, or for which Broker
   acted on Buyer's behalf. The obligation to pay compensation pursuant to this paragraph shall arise only if, prior to or within
   **3 (or ☐ _____) calendar days** after expiration of this Agreement or any extension thereof, Broker gives Buyer a written
   notice of those properties which Broker introduced to Buyer, or for which Broker acted on Buyer's behalf.

The copyright laws of the United States (Title 17 U.S. Code) forbid the
unauthorized reproduction of this form, or any portion thereof, by photocopy
machine or any other means, including facsimile or computerized formats.
Copyright © 1991-2004, CALIFORNIA ASSOCIATION OF REALTORS®,
INC. ALL RIGHTS RESERVED.

Buyer and Broker acknowledge receipt of a copy of this page.
Buyer's Initials (_____)(_____)
Broker's Initials (_____)(_____)

**BBE REVISED 10/04 (PAGE 1 OF 4)**

| Reviewed by | Date |
| --- | --- |

EQUAL HOUSING
OPPORTUNITY

Reprinted with permission, CALIFORNIA ASSOCIATION OF REALTORS. Endorsement not implied.

# Appendices

## Buyer broker Agreement

Buyer: _____ Date: _____

   **C. PAYMENT OF COMPENSATION:** Compensation is payable:
     **(1)** Upon completion of any resulting transaction, and if an escrow is used, through escrow.
     **(2)** If acquisition is prevented by default of Buyer, upon Buyer's default.
     **(3)** If acquisition is prevented by a party to the transaction other than Buyer, when Buyer collects damages by suit, settlement or otherwise. Compensation shall equal one-half of the damages recovered, not to exceed the compensation provided for in paragraph 3A, after first deducting the unreimbursed expenses of collection, if any.
   **D. BUYER OBLIGATION TO PAY COMPENSATION:** Buyer is responsible for payment of compensation provided for in this Agreement. **However, if anyone other than Buyer compensates Broker for services covered by this Agreement, that amount shall be credited toward Buyer's obligation to pay compensation.** If the amount of compensation Broker receives from anyone other than Buyer exceeds Buyer's obligation, the excess amount shall be disclosed to Buyer and if allowed by law paid to Broker, or (if checked) ☐ credited to Buyer, or ☐ other _____.
   **E.** Buyer hereby irrevocably assigns to Broker the compensation provided for in paragraph 3A from Buyer's funds and proceeds in escrow. Buyer agrees to submit to escrow any funds needed to compensate Broker under this Agreement. Broker may submit this Agreement, as instructions to compensate Broker, to any escrow regarding property involving Buyer and a seller or other transferor.
   **F.** **"BUYER"** includes any person or entity, other than Broker, related to Buyer or who in any manner acts on Buyer's behalf to acquire property described in paragraph 4.
   **G. (1)** Buyer has not previously entered into a representation agreement with another broker regarding property described in paragraph 4, unless specified as follows (name other broker here): _____
     **(2)** Buyer warrants that Buyer has no obligation to pay compensation to any other broker regarding property described in paragraph 4, unless Buyer acquires the following property(ies): _____.
     **(3)** If Buyer acquires a property specified in G(2) above during the time Buyer is obligated to compensate another broker, Broker is neither: **(i)** entitled to compensation under this Agreement, nor **(ii)** obligated to represent Buyer in such transaction.
**4. PROPERTY TO BE ACQUIRED:**
   Any purchase, lease or other acquisition of any real property or manufactured home described as follows:
_____
_____
_____
   Price range: $_____ to $_____
**5. BROKER AUTHORIZATIONS AND OBLIGATIONS:**
   **A.** Buyer authorizes Broker to: **(i)** locate and present selected properties to Buyer, present offers authorized by Buyer, and assist Buyer in negotiating for acceptance of such offers; **(ii)** assist Buyer with the financing process, including obtaining loan pre-qualification; **(iii)** upon request, provide Buyer with a list of professionals or vendors who perform the services described in the attached Buyer's Inspection Advisory; **(iv)** order reports, and schedule and attend meetings and appointments with professionals chosen by Buyer; **(v)** provide guidance to help Buyer with the acquisition of property; and **(vi)** obtain a credit report on Buyer.
   **B.** For property transactions of which Broker is aware and not precluded from participating in by Buyer, Broker shall provide and review forms to create a property contract ("Property Contract") for the acquisition of a specific property ("Property"). With respect to such Property, Broker shall: **(i)** if the Property contains residential property with one-to-four dwelling units, conduct a reasonably competent and diligent on-site visual inspection of the accessible areas of the Property (excluding any common areas), and disclose to Buyer all facts materially affecting the value or desirability of such Property that are revealed by this inspection; **(ii)** deliver or communicate to Buyer any disclosures, materials or information received by, in the personal possession of or personally known to the individual signing for Broker below during the Representation Period; and **(iii)** facilitate the escrow process, including assisting Buyer in negotiating with Seller. Unless otherwise specified in writing, any information provided through Broker in the course of representing Buyer has not been and will not be verified by Broker. Broker's services are performed in compliance with federal, state and local anti-discrimination laws.
**6. SCOPE OF BROKER DUTY:**
   **A.** While Broker will perform the duties described in paragraph 5B, Broker recommends that Buyer select other professionals, as described in the attached Buyer's Inspection Advisory, to investigate the Property through inspections, investigations, tests, surveys, reports, studies and other available information ("Inspections") during the transaction. Buyer agrees that these Inspections, to the extent they exceed the obligations described in paragraph 5B, are not within the scope of Broker's agency duties. Broker informs Buyer that it is in Buyer's best interest to obtain such Inspections.
   **B.** Buyer acknowledges and agrees that Broker: **(i)** Does not decide what price Buyer should pay or Seller should accept; **(ii)** Does not guarantee the condition of the Property; **(iii)** Does not guarantee the performance, adequacy or completeness of inspections, services, products or repairs provided or made by Seller or others; **(iv)** Does not have an obligation to conduct an inspection of common areas, or offsite areas of the Property; **(v)** Shall not be responsible for identifying defects on the Property, in common areas or offsite unless such defects are visually observable by an inspection of reasonably accessible areas of the Property or are known to Broker; **(vi)** Shall not be responsible for inspecting public records or permits concerning the title or use of Property; **(vii)** Shall not be responsible for identifying the location of boundary lines or other items affecting title; **(viii)** Shall not be responsible for verifying square footage, representations of others or information contained in Investigation reports, Multiple Listing Service, advertisements, flyers or other promotional material; **(ix)** Shall not be responsible for providing legal or tax advice regarding any aspect of a transaction entered into by Buyer or Seller; and **(x)** Shall not be responsible for providing other advice or information that exceeds the knowledge, education and experience required to perform real estate licensed activity. Buyer agrees to seek legal, tax, insurance, title and other desired assistance from appropriate professionals.

Buyer and Broker acknowledge receipt of a copy of this page.

Buyer's Initials (_____)(_____)
Broker's Initials (_____)(_____)

| Reviewed by _____ Date _____ |
| --- |

Copyright © 1991-2004, CALIFORNIA ASSOCIATION OF REALTORS®, INC.
**BBE REVISED 10/04 (PAGE 2 OF 4)**

EQUAL HOUSING OPPORTUNITY

Reprinted with permission, CALIFORNIA ASSOCIATION OF REALTORS. Endorsement not implied.

## Buyer broker Agreement

Buyer: _____ Date: _____

**C.** Broker owes no duty to inspect for common environmental hazards, earthquake weaknesses, or geologic and seismic hazards. If Buyer receives the booklets titled "Environmental Hazards: A Guide for Homeowners, Buyers, Landlords and Tenants," "The Homeowner's Guide to Earthquake Safety," or "The Commercial Property Owner's Guide to Earthquake Safety," the booklets are deemed adequate to inform Buyer regarding the information contained in the booklets and, other than as specified in 5B above, Broker is not required to provide Buyer with additional information about the matters described in the booklets.

**7. BUYER OBLIGATIONS:**

**A.** Buyer agrees to timely view and consider properties selected by Broker and to negotiate in good faith to acquire a property. Buyer further agrees to act in good faith toward the completion of any Property Contract entered into in furtherance of this Agreement. Within **5 (or** ☐ _____ **) calendar days** from the execution of this Agreement, Buyer shall provide relevant personal and financial information to Broker to assure Buyer's ability to acquire property described in paragraph 4. If Buyer fails to provide such information, or if Buyer does not qualify financially to acquire property described in paragraph 4, then Broker may cancel this Agreement in writing. Buyer has an affirmative duty to take steps to protect him/herself, including discovery of the legal, practical and technical implications of discovered or disclosed facts, and investigation of information and facts which are known to Buyer or are within the diligent attention and observation of Buyer. Buyer is obligated to and agrees to read all documents provided to Buyer. Buyer agrees to seek desired assistance from appropriate professionals, selected by Buyer, such as those referenced in the attached Buyer's Inspection Advisory.

**B.** Buyer shall notify Broker in writing (C.A.R. Form BMI) of any material issue to Buyer, such as, but not limited to, Buyer requests for information on, or concerns regarding, any particular area of interest or importance to Buyer ("Material Issues").

**C. Buyer agrees to: (i) indemnify, defend and hold Broker harmless from all claims, disputes, litigation, judgments, costs and attorney fees arising from any incorrect information supplied by Buyer, or from any Material Issues that Buyer fails to disclose in writing to Broker, and (ii) pay for reports, Inspections and meetings arranged by Broker on Buyer's behalf.**

**D.** Buyer is advised to read the attached Buyer's Inspection Advisory for a list of items and other concerns that typically warrant Inspections or investigation by Buyer or other professionals.

**8. DISPUTE RESOLUTION:**

**A. MEDIATION:** Buyer and Broker agree to mediate any dispute or claim arising between them out of this Agreement, or any resulting transaction, before resorting to arbitration or court action, subject to paragraph 8B(2) below. Paragraph 8B(2) below applies whether or not the arbitration provision is initialed. Mediation fees, if any, shall be divided equally among the parties involved. If, for any dispute or claim to which this paragraph applies, any party commences an action without first attempting to resolve the matter through mediation, or refuses to mediate after a request has been made, then that party shall not be entitled to recover attorney fees, even if they would otherwise be available to that party in any such action. THIS MEDIATION PROVISION APPLIES WHETHER OR NOT THE ARBITRATION PROVISION IS INITIALED.

**B. ARBITRATION OF DISPUTES: (1) Buyer and Broker agree that any dispute or claim in law or equity arising between them regarding the obligation to pay compensation under this Agreement, which is not settled through mediation, shall be decided by neutral, binding arbitration, including and subject to paragraph 8B(2) below. The arbitrator shall be a retired judge or justice, or an attorney with at least five years of residential real estate law experience, unless the parties mutually agree to a different arbitrator, who shall render an award in accordance with substantive California law. The parties shall have the right to discovery in accordance with Code of Civil Procedure §1283.05. In all other respects, the arbitration shall be conducted in accordance with Title 9 of Part III, of the California Code of Civil Procedure. Judgment upon the award of the arbitrator(s) may be entered in any court having jurisdiction. Interpretation of this agreement to arbitrate shall be governed by the Federal Arbitration Act.**

**(2) EXCLUSIONS FROM MEDIATION AND ARBITRATION:** The following matters are excluded from mediation and arbitration hereunder: **(i)** a judicial or non-judicial foreclosure or other action or proceeding to enforce a deed of trust, mortgage, or installment land sale contract as defined in Civil Code §2985; **(ii)** an unlawful detainer action; **(iii)** the filing or enforcement of a mechanic's lien; **(iv)** any matter that is within the jurisdiction of a probate, small claims, or bankruptcy court; and **(v)** an action for bodily injury or wrongful death, or for any right of action to which Code of Civil Procedure §337.1 or §337.15 applies. The filing of a court action to enable the recording of a notice of pending action, for order of attachment, receivership, injunction, or other provisional remedies, shall not constitute a waiver of the mediation and arbitration provisions.

**"NOTICE: BY INITIALING IN THE SPACE BELOW YOU ARE AGREEING TO HAVE ANY DISPUTE ARISING OUT OF THE MATTERS INCLUDED IN THE 'ARBITRATION OF DISPUTES' PROVISION DECIDED BY NEUTRAL ARBITRATION AS PROVIDED BY CALIFORNIA LAW AND YOU ARE GIVING UP ANY RIGHTS YOU MIGHT POSSESS TO HAVE THE DISPUTE LITIGATED IN A COURT OR JURY TRIAL. BY INITIALING IN THE SPACE BELOW YOU ARE GIVING UP YOUR JUDICIAL RIGHTS TO DISCOVERY AND APPEAL, UNLESS THOSE RIGHTS ARE SPECIFICALLY INCLUDED IN THE 'ARBITRATION OF DISPUTES' PROVISION. IF YOU REFUSE TO SUBMIT TO ARBITRATION AFTER AGREEING TO THIS PROVISION, YOU MAY BE COMPELLED TO ARBITRATE UNDER THE AUTHORITY OF THE CALIFORNIA CODE OF CIVIL PROCEDURE. YOUR AGREEMENT TO THIS ARBITRATION PROVISION IS VOLUNTARY."**

**"WE HAVE READ AND UNDERSTAND THE FOREGOING AND AGREE TO SUBMIT DISPUTES ARISING OUT OF THE MATTERS INCLUDED IN THE 'ARBITRATION OF DISPUTES' PROVISION TO NEUTRAL ARBITRATION."**

| | |
|---|---|
| Buyer's Initials _____ / _____ | Broker's Initials _____ / _____ |

Buyer and Broker acknowledge receipt of a copy of this page.

Buyer's Initials (_____)(_____)

Broker's Initials (_____)(_____)

Copyright © 1991-2004, CALIFORNIA ASSOCIATION OF REALTORS®, INC.
**BBE REVISED 10/04 (PAGE 3 OF 4)**

| |
|---|
| Reviewed by _____ Date _____ |

Reprinted with permission, CALIFORNIA ASSOCIATION OF REALTORS. Endorsement not implied.

# Appendices

## Buyer broker Agreement

Buyer: _____ Date: _____

9. **TIME TO BRING LEGAL ACTION:** Legal action for breach of this Agreement, or any obligation arising therefrom, shall be brought no more than two years from the expiration of the Representation Period or from the date such cause of action may arise, whichever occurs first.
10. **OTHER TERMS AND CONDITIONS,** including ATTACHED SUPPLEMENTS: ☐ Buyer's Inspection Advisory (C.A.R. Form BIA)
_____
_____
_____
_____
_____
_____

11. **ATTORNEY FEES:** In any action, proceeding or arbitration between Buyer and Broker regarding the obligation to pay compensation under this Agreement, the prevailing Buyer or Broker shall be entitled to reasonable attorney fees and costs, except as provided in paragraph 8A.
12. **ENTIRE AGREEMENT:** All understandings between the parties are incorporated in this Agreement. Its terms are intended by the parties as a final, complete and exclusive expression of their agreement with respect to its subject matter, and may not be contradicted by evidence of any prior agreement or contemporaneous oral agreement. This Agreement may not be extended, amended, modified, altered or changed, except in writing signed by Buyer and Broker. In the event that any provision of this Agreement is held to be ineffective or invalid, the remaining provisions will nevertheless be given full force and effect. This Agreement and any supplement, addendum or modification, including any copy, whether by copier, facsimile, NCR or electronic, may be signed in two or more counterparts, all of which shall constitute one and the same writing.

Buyer acknowledges that Buyer has read, understands, accepts and has received a copy of this Agreement.

Buyer _____ Date _____
Address _____ City _____ State _____ Zip _____
Telephone _____ Fax _____ E-mail _____

Buyer _____ Date _____
Address _____ City _____ State _____ Zip _____
Telephone _____ Fax _____ E-mail _____

Real Estate Broker (Firm) _____
By (Agent) _____ Date _____
Address _____ City _____ State _____ Zip _____
Telephone _____ Fax _____ E-mail _____

THIS FORM HAS BEEN APPROVED BY THE CALIFORNIA ASSOCIATION OF REALTORS® (C.A.R.). NO REPRESENTATION IS MADE AS TO THE LEGAL VALIDITY OR ADEQUACY OF ANY PROVISION IN ANY SPECIFIC TRANSACTION. A REAL ESTATE BROKER IS THE PERSON QUALIFIED TO ADVISE ON REAL ESTATE TRANSACTIONS. IF YOU DESIRE LEGAL OR TAX ADVICE, CONSULT AN APPROPRIATE PROFESSIONAL.

This form is available for use by the entire real estate industry. It is not intended to identify the user as a REALTOR®. REALTOR® is a registered collective membership mark which may be used only by members of the NATIONAL ASSOCIATION OF REALTORS® who subscribe to its Code of Ethics.

Published and Distributed by:
REAL ESTATE BUSINESS SERVICES, INC.
a subsidiary of the California Association of REALTORS®
525 South Virgil Avenue, Los Angeles, California 90020

**BBE REVISED 10/04 (PAGE 4 OF 4)**

Reviewed by _____ Date _____

Reprinted with permission, CALIFORNIA ASSOCIATION OF REALTORS. Endorsement not implied.

344

Real Estate Transfer Disclosure Statement

**CALIFORNIA ASSOCIATION OF REALTORS®**

**REAL ESTATE TRANSFER DISCLOSURE STATEMENT**
(CALIFORNIA CIVIL CODE §1102, ET SEQ.)
(C.A.R. Form TDS, Revised 10/03)

THIS DISCLOSURE STATEMENT CONCERNS THE REAL PROPERTY SITUATED IN THE CITY OF _____
_____, COUNTY OF _____, STATE OF CALIFORNIA,
DESCRIBED AS _____.

THIS STATEMENT IS A DISCLOSURE OF THE CONDITION OF THE ABOVE DESCRIBED PROPERTY IN COMPLIANCE
WITH SECTION 1102 OF THE CIVIL CODE AS OF (date) _____. IT IS NOT A WARRANTY OF ANY
KIND BY THE SELLER(S) OR ANY AGENT(S) REPRESENTING ANY PRINCIPAL(S) IN THIS TRANSACTION, AND IS
NOT A SUBSTITUTE FOR ANY INSPECTIONS OR WARRANTIES THE PRINCIPAL(S) MAY WISH TO OBTAIN.

### I. COORDINATION WITH OTHER DISCLOSURE FORMS

This Real Estate Transfer Disclosure Statement is made pursuant to Section 1102 of the Civil Code. Other statutes require disclosures, depending upon the details of the particular real estate transaction (for example: special study zone and purchase-money liens on residential property).

**Substituted Disclosures:** The following disclosures and other disclosures required by law, including the Natural Hazard Disclosure Report/Statement that may include airport annoyances, earthquake, fire, flood, or special assessment information, have or will be made in connection with this real estate transfer, and are intended to satisfy the disclosure obligations on this form, where the subject matter is the same:

☐ Inspection reports completed pursuant to the contract of sale or receipt for deposit.
☐ Additional inspection reports or disclosures: _____
_____

### II. SELLER'S INFORMATION

The Seller discloses the following information with the knowledge that even though this is not a warranty, prospective Buyers may rely on this information in deciding whether and on what terms to purchase the subject property. Seller hereby authorizes any agent(s) representing any principal(s) in this transaction to provide a copy of this statement to any person or entity in connection with any actual or anticipated sale of the property.

THE FOLLOWING ARE REPRESENTATIONS MADE BY THE SELLER(S) AND ARE NOT THE
REPRESENTATIONS OF THE AGENT(S), IF ANY. THIS INFORMATION IS A DISCLOSURE AND IS NOT
INTENDED TO BE PART OF ANY CONTRACT BETWEEN THE BUYER AND SELLER.

Seller ☐ is ☐ is not occupying the property.

**A. The subject property has the items checked below (read across):**

| | | |
|---|---|---|
| ☐ Range | ☐ Oven | ☐ Microwave |
| ☐ Dishwasher | ☐ Trash Compactor | ☐ Garbage Disposal |
| ☐ Washer/Dryer Hookups | | ☐ Rain Gutters |
| ☐ Burglar Alarms | ☐ Smoke Detector(s) | ☐ Fire Alarm |
| ☐ TV Antenna | ☐ Satellite Dish | ☐ Intercom |
| ☐ Central Heating | ☐ Central Air Conditioning | ☐ Evaporator Cooler(s) |
| ☐ Wall/Window Air Conditioning | ☐ Sprinklers | ☐ Public Sewer System |
| ☐ Septic Tank | ☐ Sump Pump | ☐ Water Softener |
| ☐ Patio/Decking | ☐ Built-in Barbecue | ☐ Gazebo |
| ☐ Sauna | | |
| ☐ Hot Tub | ☐ Pool | ☐ Spa |
| ☐ Locking Safety Cover* | ☐ Child Resistant Barrier* | ☐ Locking Safety Cover* |
| ☐ Security Gate(s) | ☐ Automatic Garage Door Opener(s)* | ☐ Number Remote Controls ____ |
| Garage: ☐ Attached | ☐ Not Attached | ☐ Carport |
| Pool/Spa Heater: ☐ Gas | ☐ Solar | ☐ Electric |
| Water Heater: ☐ Gas | ☐ Water Heater Anchored, Braced, or Strapped* | |
| Water Supply: ☐ City | ☐ Well | ☐ Private Utility or |
| Gas Supply: ☐ Utility | ☐ Bottled | Other_____ |
| ☐ Window Screens | ☐ Window Security Bars ☐ Quick Release Mechanism on Bedroom Windows* | |

Exhaust Fan(s) in _____ 220 Volt Wiring in _____ Fireplace(s) in _____
☐ Gas Starter _____ ☐ Roof(s): Type: _____ Age: _____ (approx.)
☐ Other: _____

Are there, to the best of your (Seller's) knowledge, any of the above that are not in operating condition? ☐ Yes ☐ No. If yes, then describe. (Attach additional sheets if necessary): _____
_____

**(\*see footnote on page 2)**

The copyright laws of the United States (Title 17 U.S. Code) forbid the unauthorized reproduction of this form, or any portion thereof, by photocopy machine or any other means, including facsimile or computerized formats. Copyright © 1991-2003, CALIFORNIA ASSOCIATION OF REALTORS®, INC. ALL RIGHTS RESERVED.
**TDS REVISED 10/03 (PAGE 1 OF 3) Print Date**

Buyer's Initials (_____)(_____)
Seller's Initials (_____)(_____)

Reviewed by _____ Date _____

EQUAL HOUSING OPPORTUNITY

Reprinted with permission, CALIFORNIA ASSOCIATION OF REALTORS. Endorsement not implied.

# Appendices

## Real Estate Transfer Disclosure Statement

Property Address: _____   Date: _____

**B.** Are you (Seller) aware of any significant defects/malfunctions in any of the following? ☐ Yes ☐ No. If yes, check appropriate space(s) below.

☐ Interior Walls ☐ Ceilings ☐ Floors ☐ Exterior Walls ☐ Insulation ☐ Roof(s) ☐ Windows ☐ Doors ☐ Foundation ☐ Slab(s)
☐ Driveways ☐ Sidewalks ☐ Walls/Fences ☐ Electrical Systems ☐ Plumbing/Sewers/Septics ☐ Other Structural Components
(Describe: _____
_____
_____
_____ )

If any of the above is checked, explain. (Attach additional sheets if necessary.): _____
_____
_____
_____

*This garage door opener or child resistant pool barrier may not be in compliance with the safety standards relating to automatic reversing devices as set forth in Chapter 12.5 (commencing with Section 19890) of Part 3 of Division 13 of, or with the pool safety standards of Article 2.5 (commencing with Section 115920) of Chapter 5 of Part 10 of Division 104 of, the Health and Safety Code. The water heater may not be anchored, braced, or strapped in accordance with Section 19211 of the Health and Safety Code. Window security bars may not have quick release mechanisms in compliance with the 1995 edition of the California Building Standards Code.

**C.** Are you (Seller) aware of any of the following:

1. Substances, materials, or products which may be an environmental hazard such as, but not limited to, asbestos, formaldehyde, radon gas, lead-based paint, mold, fuel or chemical storage tanks, and contaminated soil or water on the subject property . . . . . . . . . . . . . . . . . . . . . . . . . . . . . . . . . . . . . . . . . . . . . . ☐ Yes ☐ No
2. Features of the property shared in common with adjoining landowners, such as walls, fences, and driveways, whose use or responsibility for maintenance may have an effect on the subject property . . . . . . . . . . . . . . . . . . . . ☐ Yes ☐ No
3. Any encroachments, easements or similar matters that may affect your interest in the subject property . . . . . . . . ☐ Yes ☐ No
4. Room additions, structural modifications, or other alterations or repairs made without necessary permits . . . . . . . . ☐ Yes ☐ No
5. Room additions, structural modifications, or other alterations or repairs not in compliance with building codes . . . . ☐ Yes ☐ No
6. Fill (compacted or otherwise) on the property or any portion thereof . . . . . . . . . . . . . . . . . . . . . . . . . . . . . ☐ Yes ☐ No
7. Any settling from any cause, or slippage, sliding, or other soil problems . . . . . . . . . . . . . . . . . . . . . . . . . . ☐ Yes ☐ No
8. Flooding, drainage or grading problems . . . . . . . . . . . . . . . . . . . . . . . . . . . . . . . . . . . . . . . . . . . . . ☐ Yes ☐ No
9. Major damage to the property or any of the structures from fire, earthquake, floods, or landslides . . . . . . . . . . . . ☐ Yes ☐ No
10. Any zoning violations, nonconforming uses, violations of "setback" requirements . . . . . . . . . . . . . . . . . . . . . ☐ Yes ☐ No
11. Neighborhood noise problems or other nuisances . . . . . . . . . . . . . . . . . . . . . . . . . . . . . . . . . . . . . . . ☐ Yes ☐ No
12. CC&R's or other deed restrictions or obligations . . . . . . . . . . . . . . . . . . . . . . . . . . . . . . . . . . . . . . . ☐ Yes ☐ No
13. Homeowners' Association which has any authority over the subject property . . . . . . . . . . . . . . . . . . . . . . . . ☐ Yes ☐ No
14. Any "common area" (facilities such as pools, tennis courts, walkways, or other areas co-owned in undivided interest with others) . . . . . . . . . . . . . . . . . . . . . . . . . . . . . . . . . . . . . . . . . . . . . . . . . . . . . . . . ☐ Yes ☐ No
15. Any notices of abatement or citations against the property . . . . . . . . . . . . . . . . . . . . . . . . . . . . . . . . . ☐ Yes ☐ No
16. Any lawsuits by or against the Seller threatening to or affecting this real property, including any lawsuits alleging a defect or deficiency in this real property or "common areas" (facilities such as pools, tennis courts, walkways, or other areas co-owned in undivided interest with others) . . . . . . . . . . . . . . . . . . . . . . . . . . . . . . . . . ☐ Yes ☐ No

If the answer to any of these is yes, explain. (Attach additional sheets if necessary.): _____
_____
_____
_____

**Seller certifies that the information herein is true and correct to the best of the Seller's knowledge as of the date signed by the Seller.**

Seller_____   Date _____

Seller_____   Date _____

Buyer's Initials (_____)(_____)
Seller's Initials (_____)(_____)

Copyright © 1991-2003, CALIFORNIA ASSOCIATION OF REALTORS®, INC.
**TDS REVISED 10/03 (PAGE 2 OF 3)**

Reviewed by _____ Date _____

Reprinted with permission, CALIFORNIA ASSOCIATION OF REALTORS. Endorsement not implied.

Real Estate Transfer Disclosure Statement

Property Address: _____     Date: _____

### III. AGENT'S INSPECTION DISCLOSURE
(To be completed only if the Seller is represented by an agent in this transaction.)

**THE UNDERSIGNED, BASED ON THE ABOVE INQUIRY OF THE SELLER(S) AS TO THE CONDITION OF THE PROPERTY AND BASED ON A REASONABLY COMPETENT AND DILIGENT VISUAL INSPECTION OF THE ACCESSIBLE AREAS OF THE PROPERTY IN CONJUNCTION WITH THAT INQUIRY, STATES THE FOLLOWING:**

☐ Agent notes no items for disclosure.

☐ Agent notes the following items: _____

_____

_____

_____

Agent (Broker Representing Seller) _____ By _____ Date _____
    (Please Print)                                      (Associate Licensee or Broker Signature)

### IV. AGENT'S INSPECTION DISCLOSURE
(To be completed only if the agent who has obtained the offer is other than the agent above.)

**THE UNDERSIGNED, BASED ON A REASONABLY COMPETENT AND DILIGENT VISUAL INSPECTION OF THE ACCESSIBLE AREAS OF THE PROPERTY, STATES THE FOLLOWING:**

☐ Agent notes no items for disclosure.

☐ Agent notes the following items: _____

_____

_____

_____

Agent (Broker Obtaining the Offer) _____ By _____ Date _____
    (Please Print)                                      (Associate Licensee or Broker Signature)

**V. BUYER(S) AND SELLER(S) MAY WISH TO OBTAIN PROFESSIONAL ADVICE AND/OR INSPECTIONS OF THE PROPERTY AND TO PROVIDE FOR APPROPRIATE PROVISIONS IN A CONTRACT BETWEEN BUYER AND SELLER(S) WITH RESPECT TO ANY ADVICE/INSPECTIONS/DEFECTS.**

**I/WE ACKNOWLEDGE RECEIPT OF A COPY OF THIS STATEMENT.**

Seller _____ Date _____  Buyer _____ Date _____

Seller _____ Date _____  Buyer _____ Date _____

Agent (Broker Representing Seller) _____ By _____ Date _____
    (Please Print)                                      (Associate Licensee or Broker Signature)

Agent (Broker Obtaining the Offer) _____ By _____ Date _____
    (Please Print)                                      (Associate Licensee or Broker Signature)

**SECTION 1102.3 OF THE CIVIL CODE PROVIDES A BUYER WITH THE RIGHT TO RESCIND A PURCHASE CONTRACT FOR AT LEAST THREE DAYS AFTER THE DELIVERY OF THIS DISCLOSURE IF DELIVERY OCCURS AFTER THE SIGNING OF AN OFFER TO PURCHASE. IF YOU WISH TO RESCIND THE CONTRACT, YOU MUST ACT WITHIN THE PRESCRIBED PERIOD.**

**A REAL ESTATE BROKER IS QUALIFIED TO ADVISE ON REAL ESTATE. IF YOU DESIRE LEGAL ADVICE, CONSULT YOUR ATTORNEY.**

THIS FORM HAS BEEN APPROVED BY THE CALIFORNIA ASSOCIATION OF REALTORS® (C.A.R.). NO REPRESENTATION IS MADE AS TO THE LEGAL VALIDITY OR ADEQUACY OF ANY PROVISION IN ANY SPECIFIC TRANSACTION. A REAL ESTATE BROKER IS THE PERSON QUALIFIED TO ADVISE ON REAL ESTATE TRANSACTIONS. IF YOU DESIRE LEGAL OR TAX ADVICE, CONSULT AN APPROPRIATE PROFESSIONAL.
This form is available for use by the entire real estate industry. It is not intended to identify the user as a REALTOR®. REALTOR® is a registered collective membership mark which may be used only by members of the NATIONAL ASSOCIATION OF REALTORS® who subscribe to its Code of Ethics.

SURE TRAC
The System for Success®

Published and Distributed by:
REAL ESTATE BUSINESS SERVICES, INC.
a subsidiary of the California Association of REALTORS®
525 South Virgil Avenue, Los Angeles, California 90020

**TDS REVISED 10/03 (PAGE 3 OF 3)**

Reviewed by _____ Date _____

EQUAL HOUSING OPPORTUNITY

Reprinted with permission, CALIFORNIA ASSOCIATION OF REALTORS. Endorsement not implied.

# Appendices

Buyer's Inspection Advisory

CALIFORNIA
ASSOCIATION
OF REALTORS®

**BUYER'S INSPECTION ADVISORY**
(C.A.R. Form BIA, Revised 10/02)

Property Address: _____ ("Property").

**A. IMPORTANCE OF PROPERTY INVESTIGATION:** The physical condition of the land and improvements being purchased is not guaranteed by either Seller or Brokers. For this reason, you should conduct thorough investigations of the Property personally and with professionals who should provide written reports of their investigations. A general physical inspection typically does not cover all aspects of the Property nor items affecting the Property that are not physically located on the Property. If the professionals recommend further investigations, including a recommendation by a pest control operator to inspect inaccessible areas of the Property, you should contact qualified experts to conduct such additional investigations.

**B. BUYER RIGHTS AND DUTIES:** You have an affirmative duty to exercise reasonable care to protect yourself, including discovery of the legal, practical and technical implications of disclosed facts, and the investigation and verification of information and facts that you know or that are within your diligent attention and observation. The purchase agreement gives you the right to investigate the Property. If you exercise this right, and you should, you must do so in accordance with the terms of that agreement. This is the best way for you to protect yourself. It is extremely important for you to read all written reports provided by professionals and to discuss the results of inspections with the professional who conducted the inspection. You have the right to request that Seller make repairs, corrections or take other action based upon items discovered in your investigations or disclosed by Seller. If Seller is unwilling or unable to satisfy your requests, or you do not want to purchase the Property in its disclosed and discovered condition, you have the right to cancel the agreement if you act within specific time periods. If you do not cancel the agreement in a timely and proper manner, you may be in breach of contract.

**C. SELLER RIGHTS AND DUTIES:** Seller is required to disclose to you material facts known to him/her that affect the value or desirability of the Property. However, Seller may not be aware of some Property defects or conditions. Seller does not have an obligation to inspect the Property for your benefit nor is Seller obligated to repair, correct or otherwise cure known defects that are disclosed to you or previously unknown defects that are discovered by you or your inspectors during escrow. The purchase agreement obligates Seller to make the Property available to you for investigations.

**D. BROKER OBLIGATIONS:** Brokers do not have expertise in all areas and therefore cannot advise you on many items, such as soil stability, geologic or environmental conditions, hazardous or illegal controlled substances, structural conditions of the foundation or other improvements, or the condition of the roof, plumbing, heating, air conditioning, electrical, sewer, septic, waste disposal, or other system. The only way to accurately determine the condition of the Property is through an inspection by an appropriate professional selected by you. If Broker gives you referrals to such professionals, Broker does not guarantee their performance. You may select any professional of your choosing. In sales involving residential dwellings with no more than four units, Brokers have a duty to make a diligent visual inspection of the accessible areas of the Property and to disclose the results of that inspection. However, as some Property defects or conditions may not be discoverable from a visual inspection, it is possible Brokers are not aware of them. If you have entered into a written agreement with a Broker, the specific terms of that agreement will determine the nature and extent of that Broker's duty to you. **YOU ARE STRONGLY ADVISED TO INVESTIGATE THE CONDITION AND SUITABILITY OF ALL ASPECTS OF THE PROPERTY. IF YOU DO NOT DO SO, YOU ARE ACTING AGAINST THE ADVICE OF BROKERS.**

**E. YOU ARE ADVISED TO CONDUCT INVESTIGATIONS OF THE ENTIRE PROPERTY, INCLUDING, BUT NOT LIMITED TO THE FOLLOWING:**
1. **GENERAL CONDITION OF THE PROPERTY, ITS SYSTEMS AND COMPONENTS:** Foundation, roof, plumbing, heating, air conditioning, electrical, mechanical, security, pool/spa, other structural and non-structural systems and components, fixtures, built-in appliances, any personal property included in the sale, and energy efficiency of the Property. (Structural engineers are best suited to determine possible design or construction defects, and whether improvements are structurally sound.)
2. **SQUARE FOOTAGE, AGE, BOUNDARIES:** Square footage, room dimensions, lot size, age of improvements and boundaries. Any numerical statements regarding these items are APPROXIMATIONS ONLY and have not been verified by Seller and cannot be verified by Brokers. Fences, hedges, walls, retaining walls and other natural or constructed barriers or markers do not necessarily identify true Property boundaries. (Professionals such as appraisers, architects, surveyors and civil engineers are best suited to determine square footage, dimensions and boundaries of the Property.)
3. **WOOD DESTROYING PESTS:** Presence of, or conditions likely to lead to the presence of wood destroying pests and organisms and other infestation or infection. Inspection reports covering these items can be separated into two sections: Section 1 identifies areas where infestation or infection is evident. Section 2 identifies areas where there are conditions likely to lead to infestation or infection. A registered structural pest control company is best suited to perform these inspections.
4. **SOIL STABILITY:** Existence of fill or compacted soil, expansive or contracting soil, susceptibility to slippage, settling or movement, and the adequacy of drainage. (Geotechnical engineers are best suited to determine such conditions, causes and remedies.)

The copyright laws of the United States (Title 17 U.S. Code) forbid the unauthorized reproduction of this form, or any portion thereof, by photocopy machine or any other means, including facsimile or computerized formats. Copyright © 1991-2004, CALIFORNIA ASSOCIATION OF REALTORS®, INC. ALL RIGHTS RESERVED.

**BIA REVISED 10/02 (PAGE 1 OF 2)  Print Date**

Buyer's Initials (_____)(_____)
Seller's Initials (_____)(_____)

Reviewed by _____ Date _____

EQUAL HOUSING
OPPORTUNITY

---

Reprinted with permission, CALIFORNIA ASSOCIATION OF REALTORS. Endorsement not implied.

## Buyer's Inspection Advisory

Property Address: _____ Date: _____

5. **ROOF:** Present condition, age, leaks, and remaining useful life. (Roofing contractors are best suited to determine these conditions.)
6. **POOL/SPA:** Cracks, leaks or operational problems. (Pool contractors are best suited to determine these conditions.)
7. **WASTE DISPOSAL:** Type, size, adequacy, capacity and condition of sewer and septic systems and components, connection to sewer, and applicable fees.
8. **WATER AND UTILITIES; WELL SYSTEMS AND COMPONENTS:** Water and utility availability, use restrictions and costs. Water quality, adequacy, condition, and performance of well systems and components.
9. **ENVIRONMENTAL HAZARDS:** Potential environmental hazards, including, but not limited to, asbestos, lead-based paint and other lead contamination, radon, methane, other gases, fuel oil or chemical storage tanks, contaminated soil or water, hazardous waste, waste disposal sites, electromagnetic fields, nuclear sources, and other substances, materials, products, or conditions (including mold (airborne, toxic or otherwise), fungus or similar contaminants). (For more in formation on these items, you may consult an appropriate professional or read the booklets "Environmental Hazards: A Guide for Homeowners, Buyers, Landlords and Tenants," "Protect Your Family From Lead in Your Home" or both.)
10. **EARTHQUAKES AND FLOODING:** Susceptibility of the Property to earthquake/seismic hazards and propensity of the Property to flood. (A Geologist or Geotechnical Engineer is best suited to provide information on these conditions.)
11. **FIRE, HAZARD AND OTHER INSURANCE:** The availability and cost of necessary or desired insurance may vary. The location of the Property in a seismic, flood or fire hazard zone, and other conditions, such as the age of the Property and the claims history of the Property and Buyer, may affect the availability and need for certain types of insurance. Buyer should explore insurance options early as this information may affect other decisions, including the removal of loan and inspection contingencies. (An insurance agent is best suited to provide information on these conditions.)
12. **BUILDING PERMITS, ZONING AND GOVERNMENTAL REQUIREMENTS:** Permits, inspections, certificates, zoning, other governmental limitations, restrictions, and requirements affecting the current or future use of the Property, its development or size. (Such information is available from appropriate governmental agencies and private information providers. Brokers are not qualified to review or interpret any such information.)
13. **RENTAL PROPERTY RESTRICTIONS:** Some cities and counties impose restrictions that limit the amount of rent that can be charged, the maximum number of occupants, and the right of a landlord to terminate a tenancy. Deadbolt or other locks and security systems for doors and windows, including window bars, should be examined to determine whether they satisfy legal requirements. (Government agencies can provide information about these restrictions and other requirements.)
14. **SECURITY AND SAFETY:** State and local Law may require the installation of barriers, access alarms, self-latching mechanisms and/or other measures to decrease the risk to children and other persons of existing swimming pools and hot tubs, as well as various fire safety and other measures concerning other features of the Property. Compliance requirements differ from city to city and county to county. Unless specifically agreed, the Property may not be in compliance with these requirements. (Local government agencies can provide information about these restrictions and other requirements.)
15. **NEIGHBORHOOD, AREA, SUBDIVISION CONDITIONS; PERSONAL FACTORS:** Neighborhood or area conditions, including schools, proximity and adequacy of law enforcement, crime statistics, the proximity of registered felons or offenders, fire protection, other government services, availability, adequacy and cost of any speed-wired, wireless internet connections or other telecommunications or other technology services and installations, proximity to commercial, industrial or agricultural activities, existing and proposed transportation, construction and development that may affect noise, view, or traffic, airport noise, noise or odor from any source, wild and domestic animals, other nuisances, hazards, or circumstances, protected species, wetland properties, botanical diseases, historic or other governmentally protected sites or improvements, cemeteries, facilities and condition of common areas of common interest subdivisions, and possible lack of compliance with any governing documents or Homeowners' Association requirements, conditions and influences of significance to certain cultures and/or religions, and personal needs, requirements and preferences of Buyer.

Buyer and Seller acknowledge and agree that Broker: **(i)** Does not decide what price Buyer should pay or Seller should accept; **(ii)** Does not guarantee the condition of the Property; **(iii)** Does not guarantee the performance, adequacy or completeness of inspections, services, products or repairs provided or made by Seller or others; **(iv)** Does not have an obligation to conduct an inspection of common areas or areas off the site of the Property; **(v)** Shall not be responsible for identifying defects on the Property, in common areas, or offsite unless such defects are visually observable by an inspection of reasonably accessible areas of the Property or are known to Broker; **(vi)** Shall not be responsible for inspecting public records or permits concerning the title or use of Property; **(vii)** Shall not be responsible for identifying the location of boundary lines or other items affecting title; **(viii)** Shall not be responsible for verifying square footage, representations of others or information contained in Investigation reports, Multiple Listing Service, advertisements, flyers or other promotional material; **(ix)** Shall not be responsible for providing legal or tax advice regarding any aspect of a transaction entered into by Buyer or Seller; and **(x)** Shall not be responsible for providing other advice or information that exceeds the knowledge, education and experience required to perform real estate licensed activity. Buyer and Seller agree to seek legal, tax, insurance, title and other desired assistance from appropriate professionals.

**By signing below, Buyer and Seller each acknowledge that they have read, understand, accept and have received a Copy of this Advisory. Buyer is encouraged to read it carefully.**

_____ Date _____ _____ Date _____
Buyer Signature                Buyer Signature

_____ Date _____ _____ Date _____
Seller Signature               Seller Signature

THIS FORM HAS BEEN APPROVED BY THE CALIFORNIA ASSOCIATION OF REALTORS® (C.A.R.). NO REPRESENTATION IS MADE AS TO THE LEGAL VALIDITY OR ADEQUACY OF ANY PROVISION IN ANY SPECIFIC TRANSACTION. A REAL ESTATE BROKER IS THE PERSON QUALIFIED TO ADVISE ON REAL ESTATE TRANSACTIONS. IF YOU DESIRE LEGAL OR TAX ADVICE, CONSULT AN APPROPRIATE PROFESSIONAL.

This form is available for use by the entire real estate industry. It is not intended to identify the user as a REALTOR®. REALTOR® is a registered collective membership mark which may be used only by members of the NATIONAL ASSOCIATION OF REALTORS® who subscribe to its Code of Ethics.

Published and Distributed by:
REAL ESTATE BUSINESS SERVICES, INC.
a subsidiary of the California Association of REALTORS®
525 South Virgil Avenue, Los Angeles, California 90020

Reviewed by _____ Date _____

**BIA REVISED 10/02 (PAGE 2 OF 2)**

Reprinted with permission, CALIFORNIA ASSOCIATION OF REALTORS. Endorsement not implied.

# Appendices

California Residential Purchase Agreement

CALIFORNIA
ASSOCIATION
OF REALTORS®

**CALIFORNIA**
**RESIDENTIAL PURCHASE AGREEMENT**
**AND JOINT ESCROW INSTRUCTIONS**
For Use With Single Family Residential Property — Attached or Detached
(C.A.R. Form RPA-CA, Revised 10/02)

Date _____, at _____, California.
1. **OFFER:**
   A. **THIS IS AN OFFER FROM** _____ ("Buyer").
   B. **THE REAL PROPERTY TO BE ACQUIRED** is described as _____
      _____, Assessor's Parcel No. _____, situated in
      _____, County of _____, California, ("Property").
   C. **THE PURCHASE PRICE** offered is _____
      _____ Dollars $ _____.
   D. **CLOSE OF ESCROW** shall occur on _____ (date)(or ☐ _____ **Days** After Acceptance).
2. **FINANCE TERMS:** Obtaining the loans below **is a contingency** of this Agreement unless: **(i)** either 2K or 2L is checked below; or
   **(ii)** otherwise agreed in writing. Buyer shall act diligently and in good faith to obtain the designated loans. Obtaining deposit, down
   payment and closing costs **is not a contingency.** Buyer represents that funds will be good when deposited with Escrow Holder.
   A. **INITIAL DEPOSIT:** Buyer has given a deposit in the amount of . . . . . . . . . . . . . . . . . . . . . . . . . . . . . . . . . . . .$ _____
      to the agent submitting the offer (or to ☐ _____), by personal check
      (or ☐ _____), made payable to _____,
      which shall be held uncashed until Acceptance and then deposited within **3** business days after
      Acceptance (or ☐ _____), with
      Escrow Holder, (or ☐ into Broker's trust account).
   B. **INCREASED DEPOSIT:** Buyer shall deposit with Escrow Holder an increased deposit in the amount of . . . .$ _____
      within _____ **Days** After Acceptance, or ☐ _____
   C. **FIRST LOAN IN THE AMOUNT OF** . . . . . . . . . . . . . . . . . . . . . . . . . . . . . . . . . . . . . . . . . . . . . . .$ _____
      **(1)** NEW First Deed of Trust in favor of lender, encumbering the Property, securing a note payable at
      maximum interest of _____% fixed rate, or _____% initial adjustable rate with a maximum
      interest rate of _____%, balance due in _____ years, amortized over _____ years. Buyer
      shall pay loan fees/points not to exceed _____. (These terms apply whether the designated loan
      is conventional, FHA or VA.)
      **(2)** ☐ FHA ☐ VA: (The following terms only apply to the FHA or VA loan that is checked.)
      Seller shall pay _____% discount points. Seller shall pay other fees not allowed to be paid by
      Buyer, ☐ not to exceed $_____. Seller shall pay the cost of lender required Repairs
      (including those for wood destroying pest) not otherwise provided for in this Agreement, ☐ not to
      exceed $_____. (Actual loan amount may increase if mortgage insurance premiums,
      funding fees or closing costs are financed.)
   D. **ADDITIONAL FINANCING TERMS:** ☐ Seller financing, (C.A.R. Form SFA); ☐ secondary financing, . . . .$ _____
      (C.A.R. Form PAA, paragraph 4A); ☐ assumed financing (C.A.R. Form PAA, paragraph 4B)
      _____
      _____
   E. **BALANCE OF PURCHASE PRICE** (not including costs of obtaining loans and other closing costs) in the amount of . . .$ _____
      to be deposited with Escrow Holder within sufficient time to close escrow.
   F. **PURCHASE PRICE (TOTAL):** . . . . . . . . . . . . . . . . . . . . . . . . . . . . . . . . . . . . . . . . . . . . . . . . . . .$ _____
   G. **LOAN APPLICATIONS:** Within **7 (or** ☐ _____) **Days** After Acceptance, Buyer shall provide Seller a letter from lender or
      mortgage loan broker stating that, based on a review of Buyer's written application and credit report, Buyer is prequalified or
      preapproved for the NEW loan specified in 2C above.
   H. **VERIFICATION OF DOWN PAYMENT AND CLOSING COSTS:** Buyer (or Buyer's lender or loan broker pursuant to 2G) shall, within
      **7 (or** ☐ _____) **Days** After Acceptance, provide Seller written verification of Buyer's down payment and closing costs.
   I. **LOAN CONTINGENCY REMOVAL: (i)** Within **17 (or** ☐ _____) **Days** After Acceptance, Buyer shall, as specified in paragraph
      14, remove the loan contingency or cancel this Agreement; **OR (ii)** (if checked) ☐ the loan contingency shall remain in effect
      until the designated loans are funded.
   J. **APPRAISAL CONTINGENCY AND REMOVAL:** This Agreement is **(OR,** if checked, ☐ is NOT) contingent upon the Property
      appraising at no less than the specified purchase price. If there is a loan contingency, at the time the loan contingency is
      removed (or, if checked, ☐ within **17 (or** _____) **Days** After Acceptance), Buyer shall, as specified in paragraph 14B(3), remove
      the appraisal contingency or cancel this Agreement. If there is no loan contingency, Buyer shall, as specified in paragraph
      14B(3), remove the appraisal contingency within **17 (or** _____) **Days** After Acceptance.
   K. ☐ **NO LOAN CONTINGENCY** (If checked): Obtaining any loan in paragraphs 2C, 2D or elsewhere in this Agreement is NOT
      a contingency of this Agreement. If Buyer does not obtain the loan and as a result Buyer does not purchase the Property, Seller
      may be entitled to Buyer's deposit or other legal remedies.
   L. ☐ **ALL CASH OFFER** (If checked): No loan is needed to purchase the Property. Buyer shall, within **7 (or** ☐ _____) **Days** After Acceptance,
      provide Seller written verification of sufficient funds to close this transaction.
3. **CLOSING AND OCCUPANCY:**
   A. Buyer intends (or ☐ does not intend) to occupy the Property as Buyer's primary residence.
   B. **Seller-occupied or vacant property:** Occupancy shall be delivered to Buyer at _____ AM/PM, ☐ on the date of Close Of
      Escrow; ☐ on _____; or ☐ no later than _____ **Days** After Close Of Escrow. (C.A.R. Form PAA, paragraph 2.) If
      transfer of title and occupancy do not occur at the same time, Buyer and Seller are advised to: **(i)** enter into a written occupancy
      agreement; and **(ii)** consult with their insurance and legal advisors.

Buyer's Initials (_____)(_____)
Broker's Initials (_____)(_____)

The copyright laws of the United States (Title 17 U.S. Code) forbid the unauthorized
reproduction of this form, or any portion thereof, by photocopy machine or any other
means, including facsimile or computerized formats. Copyright © 1991-2004,
CALIFORNIA ASSOCIATION OF REALTORS®, INC. ALL RIGHTS RESERVED.
**RPA-CA REVISED 10/02 (PAGE 1 OF 8) Print Date**

Reviewed by _____ Date _____

EQUAL HOUSING
OPPORTUNITY

Reprinted with permission, CALIFORNIA ASSOCIATION OF REALTORS. Endorsement not implied.

## California Residential Purchase Agreement

Property Address: _____    Date: _____

    **C.** **Tenant-occupied property: (i) Property shall be vacant** at least 5 **(or** ☐ _____**) Days** Prior to Close Of Escrow, unless otherwise agreed in writing. **Note to Seller: If you are unable to deliver Property vacant in accordance with rent control and other applicable Law, you may be in breach of this Agreement.**
    **OR (ii)** (if checked) ☐ **Tenant to remain in possession.** The attached addendum is incorporated into this Agreement (C.A.R. Form PAA, paragraph 3.);
    **OR (iii)** (if checked) ☐ **This Agreement is contingent** upon Buyer and Seller entering into a written agreement regarding occupancy of the Property within the time specified in paragraph 14B(1). If no written agreement is reached within this time, either Buyer or Seller may cancel this Agreement in writing.
    **D.** At Close Of Escrow, Seller assigns to Buyer any assignable warranty rights for items included in the sale and shall provide any available Copies of such warranties. Brokers cannot and will not determine the assignability of any warranties.
    **E.** At Close Of Escrow, unless otherwise agreed in writing, Seller shall provide keys and/or means to operate all locks, mailboxes, security systems, alarms and garage door openers. If Property is a condominium or located in a common interest subdivision, Buyer may be required to pay a deposit to the Homeowners' Association ("HOA") to obtain keys to accessible HOA facilities.

**4.** **ALLOCATION OF COSTS** (If checked): Unless otherwise specified here, this paragraph only determines who is to pay for the report, inspection, test or service mentioned. If not specified here or elsewhere in this Agreement, the determination of who is to pay for any work recommended or identified by any such report, inspection, test or service shall be by the method specified in paragraph 14B(2).
    **A.** **WOOD DESTROYING PEST INSPECTION:**
        **(1)** ☐ Buyer ☐ Seller shall pay for an inspection and report for wood destroying pests and organisms ("Report") which shall be prepared by _____, a registered structural pest control company. The Report shall cover the accessible areas of the main building and attached structures and, if checked: ☐ detached garages and carports, ☐ detached decks, ☐ the following other structures or areas _____. The Report shall not include roof coverings. If Property is a condominium or located in a common interest subdivision, the Report shall include only the separate interest and any exclusive-use areas being transferred and shall not include common areas, unless otherwise agreed. Water tests of shower pans on upper level units may not be performed without consent of the owners of property below the shower.
        **OR (2)** ☐ **(If checked)** The attached addendum (C.A.R. Form WPA) regarding wood destroying pest inspection and allocation of cost is incorporated into this Agreement.
    **B.** **OTHER INSPECTIONS AND REPORTS:**
        **(1)** ☐ Buyer ☐ Seller shall pay to have septic or private sewage disposal systems inspected _____.
        **(2)** ☐ Buyer ☐ Seller shall pay to have domestic wells tested for water potability and productivity _____.
        **(3)** ☐ Buyer ☐ Seller shall pay for a natural hazard zone disclosure report prepared by _____.
        **(4)** ☐ Buyer ☐ Seller shall pay for the following inspection or report _____.
        **(5)** ☐ Buyer ☐ Seller shall pay for the following inspection or report _____.
    **C.** **GOVERNMENT REQUIREMENTS AND RETROFIT:**
        **(1)** ☐ Buyer ☐ Seller shall pay for smoke detector installation and/or water heater bracing, if required by Law. Prior to Close Of Escrow, Seller shall provide Buyer a written statement of compliance in accordance with state and local Law, unless exempt.
        **(2)** ☐ Buyer ☐ Seller shall pay the cost of compliance with any other minimum mandatory government retrofit standards, inspections and reports if required as a condition of closing escrow under any Law. _____.
    **D.** **ESCROW AND TITLE:**
        **(1)** ☐ Buyer ☐ Seller shall pay escrow fee _____.
        Escrow Holder shall be _____.
        **(2)** ☐ Buyer ☐ Seller shall pay for **owner's** title insurance policy specified in paragraph 12E _____.
        Owner's title policy to be issued by _____.
        (Buyer shall pay for any title insurance policy insuring Buyer's **lender**, unless otherwise agreed in writing.)
    **E.** **OTHER COSTS:**
        **(1)** ☐ Buyer ☐ Seller shall pay County transfer tax or transfer fee _____.
        **(2)** ☐ Buyer ☐ Seller shall pay City transfer tax or transfer fee _____.
        **(3)** ☐ Buyer ☐ Seller shall pay HOA transfer fee _____.
        **(4)** ☐ Buyer ☐ Seller shall pay HOA document preparation fees _____.
        **(5)** ☐ Buyer ☐ Seller shall pay the cost, not to exceed $ _____, of a one-year home warranty plan, issued by _____
        with the following optional coverage: _____.
        **(6)** ☐ Buyer ☐ Seller shall pay for _____.
        **(7)** ☐ Buyer ☐ Seller shall pay for _____.

**5.** **STATUTORY DISCLOSURES (INCLUDING LEAD-BASED PAINT HAZARD DISCLOSURES) AND CANCELLATION RIGHTS:**
    **A.** **(1)** Seller shall, within the time specified in paragraph 14A, deliver to Buyer, if required by Law: **(i)** Federal Lead-Based Paint Disclosures and pamphlet ("Lead Disclosures"); and **(ii)** disclosures or notices required by sections 1102 et. seq. and 1103 et. seq. of the California Civil Code ("Statutory Disclosures"). Statutory Disclosures include, but are not limited to, a Real Estate Transfer Disclosure Statement ("TDS"), Natural Hazard Disclosure Statement ("NHD"), notice or actual knowledge of release of illegal controlled substance, notice of special tax and/or assessments (or, if allowed, substantially equivalent notice regarding the Mello-Roos Community Facilities Act and Improvement Bond Act of 1915) and, if Seller has actual knowledge, an industrial use and military ordnance location disclosure (C.A.R. Form SSD).
        **(2)** Buyer shall, within the time specified in paragraph 14B(1), return Signed Copies of the Statutory and Lead Disclosures to Seller.
        **(3)** In the event Seller, prior to Close Of Escrow, becomes aware of adverse conditions materially affecting the Property, or any material inaccuracy in disclosures, information or representations previously provided to Buyer of which Buyer is otherwise unaware, Seller shall promptly provide a subsequent or amended disclosure or notice, in writing, covering those items. **However, a subsequent or amended disclosure shall not be required for conditions and material inaccuracies disclosed in reports ordered and paid for by Buyer.**

Buyer's Initials (_____)(_____)
Seller's Initials (_____)(_____)

Copyright © 1991-2004, CALIFORNIA ASSOCIATION OF REALTORS®, INC.
**RPA-CA REVISED 10/02 (PAGE 2 OF 8)**

Reviewed by _____ Date _____

EQUAL HOUSING OPPORTUNITY

Reprinted with permission, CALIFORNIA ASSOCIATION OF REALTORS. Endorsement not implied.

# Appendices

## California Residential Purchase Agreement

Property Address: _____ Date: _____

(4) If any disclosure or notice specified in 5A(1), or subsequent or amended disclosure or notice is delivered to Buyer after the offer is Signed, Buyer shall have the right to cancel this Agreement within **3 Days** After delivery in person, or **5 Days** After delivery by deposit in the mail, by giving written notice of cancellation to Seller or Seller's agent. (Lead Disclosures sent by mail must be sent certified mail or better.)

(5) **Note to Buyer and Seller: Waiver of Statutory and Lead Disclosures is prohibited by Law.**

**B. NATURAL AND ENVIRONMENTAL HAZARDS:** Within the time specified in paragraph 14A, Seller shall, if required by Law: **(i)** deliver to Buyer earthquake guides (and questionnaire) and environmental hazards booklet; **(ii)** even if exempt from the obligation to provide a NHD, disclose if the Property is located in a Special Flood Hazard Area; Potential Flooding (Inundation) Area; Very High Fire Hazard Zone; State Fire Responsibility Area; Earthquake Fault Zone; Seismic Hazard Zone; and **(iii)** disclose any other zone as required by Law and provide any other information required for those zones.

**C. DATA BASE DISCLOSURE:** NOTICE: The California Department of Justice, sheriff's departments, police departments serving jurisdictions of 200,000 or more and many other local law enforcement authorities maintain for public access a data base of the locations of persons required to register pursuant to paragraph (1) of subdivision (a) of Section 290.4 of the Penal Code. The data base is updated on a quarterly basis and a source of information about the presence of these individuals in any neighborhood. The Department of Justice also maintains a Sex Offender Identification Line through which inquiries about individuals may be made. This is a "900" telephone service. Callers must have specific information about individuals they are checking. Information regarding neighborhoods is not available through the "900" telephone service.

**6. CONDOMINIUM/PLANNED UNIT DEVELOPMENT DISCLOSURES:**

**A. SELLER HAS: 7 (or ☐ _____ ) Days** After Acceptance to disclose to Buyer whether the Property is a condominium, or is located in a planned unit development or other common interest subdivision (C.A.R. Form SSD).

**B.** If the Property is a condominium or is located in a planned unit development or other common interest subdivision, Seller has **3 (or ☐ _____ ) Days** After Acceptance to request from the HOA (C.A.R. Form HOA): **(i)** Copies of any documents required by Law; **(ii)** disclosure of any pending or anticipated claim or litigation by or against the HOA; **(iii)** a statement containing the location and number of designated parking and storage spaces; **(iv)** Copies of the most recent 12 months of HOA minutes for regular and special meetings; and **(v)** the names and contact information of all HOAs governing the Property (collectively, "CI Disclosures"). Seller shall itemize and deliver to Buyer all CI Disclosures received from the HOA and any CI Disclosures in Seller's possession. Buyer's approval of CI Disclosures is a contingency of this Agreement as specified in paragraph 14B(3).

**7. CONDITIONS AFFECTING PROPERTY:**

**A.** Unless otherwise agreed: **(i) the Property is sold (a) in its PRESENT physical condition as of the date of Acceptance and (b) subject to Buyer's Investigation rights; (ii)** the Property, including pool, spa, landscaping and grounds. is to be maintained in substantially the same condition as on the date of Acceptance; and **(iii)** all debris and personal property not included in the sale shall be removed by Close Of Escrow.

**B. SELLER SHALL,** within the time specified in paragraph 14A, **DISCLOSE KNOWN MATERIAL FACTS AND DEFECTS affecting the Property, including known insurance claims within the past five years, AND MAKE OTHER DISCLOSURES REQUIRED BY LAW** (C.A.R. Form SSD).

**C. NOTE TO BUYER:** You are strongly advised to conduct investigations of the entire Property in order to determine its present condition since Seller may not be aware of all defects affecting the Property or other factors that you consider important. Property improvements may not be built according to code, in compliance with current Law, or have had permits issued.

**D. NOTE TO SELLER:** Buyer has the right to inspect the Property and, as specified in paragraph 14B, based upon information discovered in those inspections: **(i)** cancel this Agreement; or **(ii)** request that you make Repairs or take other action.

**8. ITEMS INCLUDED AND EXCLUDED:**

**A. NOTE TO BUYER AND SELLER**: Items listed as included or excluded in the MLS, flyers or marketing materials are **not** included in the purchase price or excluded from the sale unless specified in 8B or C.

**B. ITEMS INCLUDED IN SALE:**

(1) All EXISTING fixtures and fittings that are attached to the Property;

(2) Existing electrical, mechanical, lighting, plumbing and heating fixtures, ceiling fans, fireplace inserts, gas logs and grates, solar systems, built-in appliances, window and door screens, awnings, shutters, window coverings, attached floor coverings, television antennas, satellite dishes, private integrated telephone systems, air coolers/conditioners, pool/spa equipment, garage door openers/remote controls, mailbox, in-ground landscaping, trees/shrubs, water softeners, water purifiers, security systems/alarms; and

(3) The following items: _____
_____.

(4) Seller represents that all items included in the purchase price, unless otherwise specified, are owned by Seller.

(5) All items included shall be transferred free of liens and without Seller warranty.

**C. ITEMS EXCLUDED FROM SALE:** _____
_____.

**9. BUYER'S INVESTIGATION OF PROPERTY AND MATTERS AFFECTING PROPERTY:**

**A.** Buyer's acceptance of the condition of, and any other matter affecting the Property, is a contingency of this Agreement as specified in this paragraph and paragraph 14B. Within the time specified in paragraph 14B(1), Buyer shall have the right, at Buyer's expense unless otherwise agreed, to conduct inspections, investigations, tests, surveys and other studies ("Buyer Investigations"), including, but not limited to, the right to: **(i)** inspect for lead-based paint and other lead-based paint hazards; **(ii)** inspect for wood destroying pests and organisms; **(iii)** review the registered sex offender database; **(iv)** confirm the insurability of Buyer and the Property; and **(v)** satisfy Buyer as to any matter specified in the attached Buyer's Inspection Advisory (C.A.R. Form BIA). Without Seller's prior written consent, Buyer shall neither make nor cause to be made: **(i)** invasive or destructive Buyer Investigations; or **(ii)** inspections by any governmental building or zoning inspector or government employee, unless required by Law.

**B.** Buyer shall complete Buyer Investigations and, as specified in paragraph 14B, remove the contingency or cancel this Agreement. Buyer shall give Seller, at no cost, complete Copies of all Buyer Investigation reports obtained by Buyer. Seller shall make the Property available for all Buyer Investigations. Seller shall have water, gas, electricity and all operable pilot lights on for Buyer's Investigations and through the date possession is made available to Buyer.

Buyer's Initials ( _____ )( _____ )
Seller's Initials ( _____ )( _____ )

Copyright © 1991-2004, CALIFORNIA ASSOCIATION OF REALTORS®, INC.
**RPA-CA REVISED 10/02 (PAGE 3 OF 8)**

Reviewed by _____ Date _____

EQUAL HOUSING OPPORTUNITY

Reprinted with permission, CALIFORNIA ASSOCIATION OF REALTORS. Endorsement not implied.

## California Residential Purchase Agreement

Property Address: _____ Date: _____

10. **REPAIRS:** Repairs shall be completed prior to final verification of condition unless otherwise agreed in writing. Repairs to be performed at Seller's expense may be performed by Seller or through others, provided that the work complies with applicable Law, including governmental permit, inspection and approval requirements. Repairs shall be performed in a good, skillful manner with materials of quality and appearance comparable to existing materials. It is understood that exact restoration of appearance or cosmetic items following all Repairs may not be possible. Seller shall: **(i)** obtain receipts for Repairs performed by others; **(ii)** prepare a written statement indicating the Repairs performed by Seller and the date of such Repairs; and **(iii)** provide Copies of receipts and statements to Buyer prior to final verification of condition.

11. **BUYER INDEMNITY AND SELLER PROTECTION FOR ENTRY UPON PROPERTY:** Buyer shall: **(i)** keep the Property free and clear of liens; **(ii)** Repair all damage arising from Buyer Investigations; and **(iii)** indemnify and hold Seller harmless from all resulting liability, claims, demands, damages and costs. Buyer shall carry, or Buyer shall require anyone acting on Buyer's behalf to carry, policies of liability, workers' compensation and other applicable insurance, defending and protecting Seller from liability for any injuries to persons or property occurring during any Buyer Investigations or work done on the Property at Buyer's direction prior to Close Of Escrow. Seller is advised that certain protections may be afforded Seller by recording a "Notice of Non-responsibility" (C.A.R. Form NNR) for Buyer Investigations and work done on the Property at Buyer's direction. Buyer's obligations under this paragraph shall survive the termination of this Agreement.

12. **TITLE AND VESTING:**
    A. Within the time specified in paragraph 14, Buyer shall be provided a current preliminary (title) report, which is only an offer by the title insurer to issue a policy of title insurance and may not contain every item affecting title. Buyer's review of the preliminary report and any other matters which may affect title are a contingency of this Agreement as specified in paragraph 14B.
    B. Title is taken in its present condition subject to all encumbrances, easements, covenants, conditions, restrictions, rights and other matters, whether of record or not, as of the date of Acceptance except: **(i)** monetary liens of record unless Buyer is assuming those obligations or taking the Property subject to those obligations; and **(ii)** those matters which Seller has agreed to remove in writing.
    C. Within the time specified in paragraph 14A, Seller has a duty to disclose to Buyer all matters known to Seller affecting title, whether of record or not.
    D. At Close Of Escrow, Buyer shall receive a grant deed conveying title (or, for stock cooperative or long-term lease, an assignment of stock certificate or of Seller's leasehold interest), including oil, mineral and water rights if currently owned by Seller. Title shall vest as designated in Buyer's supplemental escrow instructions. THE MANNER OF TAKING TITLE MAY HAVE SIGNIFICANT LEGAL AND TAX CONSEQUENCES. CONSULT AN APPROPRIATE PROFESSIONAL.
    E. Buyer shall receive a CLTA/ALTA Homeowner's Policy of Title Insurance. A title company, at Buyer's request, can provide information about the availability, desirability, coverage, and cost of various title insurance coverages and endorsements. If Buyer desires title coverage other than that required by this paragraph, Buyer shall instruct Escrow Holder in writing and pay any increase in cost.

13. **SALE OF BUYER'S PROPERTY:**
    A. This Agreement is NOT contingent upon the sale of any property owned by Buyer.
OR B. ☐ (If checked): The attached addendum (C.A.R. Form COP) regarding the contingency for the sale of property owned by Buyer is incorporated into this Agreement.

14. **TIME PERIODS; REMOVAL OF CONTINGENCIES; CANCELLATION RIGHTS: The following time periods may only be extended, altered, modified or changed by mutual written agreement. Any removal of contingencies or cancellation under this paragraph must be in writing (C.A.R. Form CR).**
    A. **SELLER HAS: 7 (or ☐ _____) Days** After Acceptance to deliver to Buyer all reports, disclosures and information for which Seller is responsible under paragraphs 4, 5A and B, 6A, 7B and 12.
    B. **(1) BUYER HAS: 17 (or ☐ _____) Days** After Acceptance, unless otherwise agreed in writing, to:
       **(i)** complete all Buyer Investigations; approve all disclosures, reports and other applicable information, which Buyer receives from Seller; and approve all matters affecting the Property (including lead-based paint and lead-based paint hazards as well as other information specified in paragraph 5 and insurability of Buyer and the Property); and
       **(ii)** return to Seller Signed Copies of Statutory and Lead Disclosures delivered by Seller in accordance with paragraph 5A.
       **(2)** Within the time specified in paragraph 14B(1), Buyer may request that Seller make repairs or take any other action regarding the Property (C.A.R. Form RR). Seller has no obligation to agree to or respond to Buyer's requests.
       **(3)** By the end of the time specified in 14B(1) (or 2I for loan contingency or 2J for appraisal contingency), Buyer shall, in writing, remove the applicable contingency (C.A.R. Form CR) or cancel this Agreement. However, if **(i)** government-mandated inspections/ reports required as a condition of closing; or **(ii)** Common Interest Disclosures pursuant to paragraph 6B are not made within the time specified in 14A, then Buyer has **5 (or ☐ _____) Days** After receipt of any such items, or the time specified in 14B(1), whichever is later, to remove the applicable contingency or cancel this Agreement in writing.
    C. **CONTINUATION OF CONTINGENCY OR CONTRACTUAL OBLIGATION; SELLER RIGHT TO CANCEL:**
       **(1) Seller right to Cancel; Buyer Contingencies:** Seller, after first giving Buyer a Notice to Buyer to Perform (as specified below), may cancel this Agreement in writing and authorize return of Buyer's deposit if, by the time specified in this Agreement, Buyer does not remove in writing the applicable contingency or cancel this Agreement. Once all contingencies have been removed, failure of either Buyer or Seller to close escrow on time may be a breach of this Agreement.
       **(2) Continuation of Contingency:** Even after the expiration of the time specified in 14B, Buyer retains the right to make requests to Seller, remove in writing the applicable contingency or cancel this Agreement until Seller cancels pursuant to 14C(1). Once Seller receives Buyer's written removal of all contingencies, Seller may not cancel this Agreement pursuant to 14C(1).
       **(3) Seller right to Cancel; Buyer Contract Obligations:** Seller, after first giving Buyer a Notice to Buyer to Perform (as specified below), may cancel this Agreement in writing and authorize return of Buyer's deposit for any of the following reasons: **(i)** if Buyer fails to deposit funds as required by 2A or 2B; **(ii)** if the funds deposited pursuant to 2A or 2B are not good when deposited; **(iii)** if Buyer fails to provide a letter as required by 2G; **(iv)** if Buyer fails to provide verification as required by 2H or 2L; **(v)** if Seller reasonably disapproves of the verification provided by 2H or 2L; **(vi)** if Buyer fails to return Statutory and Lead Disclosures as required by paragraph 5A(2); or **(vii)** if Buyer fails to sign or initial a separate liquidated damage form for an increased deposit as required by paragraph 16. **Seller is not required to give Buyer a Notice to Perform regarding Close of Escrow.**
       **(4) Notice To Buyer To Perform:** The Notice to Buyer to Perform (C.A.R. Form NBP) shall: **(i)** be in writing; **(ii)** be signed by Seller; and **(iii)** give Buyer at least **24 (or ☐ _____) hours** (or until the time specified in the applicable paragraph, whichever occurs last) to take the applicable action. A Notice to Buyer to Perform may not be given any earlier than **2 Days** Prior to the expiration of the applicable time for Buyer to remove a contingency or cancel this Agreement or meet a 14C(3) obligation.

Buyer's Initials (_____)(_____)
Seller's Initials (_____)(_____)

Copyright © 1991-2004, CALIFORNIA ASSOCIATION OF REALTORS®, INC.
**RPA-CA REVISED 10/02 (PAGE 4 OF 8)**

Reviewed by _____ Date _____

EQUAL HOUSING OPPORTUNITY

Reprinted with permission, CALIFORNIA ASSOCIATION OF REALTORS. Endorsement not implied.

# Appendices

## California Residential Purchase Agreement

Property Address: _____ Date: _____

**D. EFFECT OF BUYER'S REMOVAL OF CONTINGENCIES :** If Buyer removes, in writing, any contingency or cancellation rights, unless otherwise specified in a separate written agreement between Buyer and Seller, Buyer shall conclusively be deemed to have: **(i)** completed all Buyer Investigations, and review of reports and other applicable information and disclosures pertaining to that contingency or cancellation right; **(ii)** elected to proceed with the transaction; and **(iii)** assumed all liability, responsibility and expense for Repairs or corrections pertaining to that contingency or cancellation right, or for inability to obtain financing.

**E. EFFECT OF CANCELLATION ON DEPOSITS:** If Buyer or Seller gives written notice of cancellation pursuant to rights duly exercised under the terms of this Agreement, Buyer and Seller agree to Sign mutual instructions to cancel the sale and escrow and release deposits to the party entitled to the funds, less fees and costs incurred by that party. Fees and costs may be payable to service providers and vendors for services and products provided during escrow. **Release of funds will require mutual Signed release instructions from Buyer and Seller, judicial decision or arbitration award. A party may be subject to a civil penalty of up to $1,000 for refusal to sign such instructions if no good faith dispute exists as to who is entitled to the deposited funds (Civil Code §1057.3).**

**15. FINAL VERIFICATION OF CONDITION:** Buyer shall have the right to make a final inspection of the Property within **5 (or _____) Days** Prior to Close Of Escrow, NOT AS A CONTINGENCY OF THE SALE, but solely to confirm: **(i)** the Property is maintained pursuant to paragraph 7A; **(ii)** Repairs have been completed as agreed; and **(iii)** Seller has complied with Seller's other obligations under this Agreement.

**16. LIQUIDATED DAMAGES: If Buyer fails to complete this purchase because of Buyer's default, Seller shall retain, as liquidated damages, the deposit actually paid. If the Property is a dwelling with no more than four units, one of which Buyer intends to occupy, then the amount retained shall be no more than 3% of the purchase price. Any excess shall be returned to Buyer. Release of funds will require mutual, Signed release instructions from both Buyer and Seller, judicial decision or arbitration award.**
**BUYER AND SELLER SHALL SIGN A SEPARATE LIQUIDATED DAMAGES PROVISION FOR ANY INCREASED DEPOSIT. (C.A.R. FORM RID)**

| Buyer's Initials _____/_____ | Seller's Initials _____/_____ |
|---|---|

**17. DISPUTE RESOLUTION:**

**A. MEDIATION:** Buyer and Seller agree to mediate any dispute or claim arising between them out of this Agreement, or any resulting transaction, before resorting to arbitration or court action. Paragraphs 17B(2) and (3) below apply whether or not the Arbitration provision is initialed. Mediation fees, if any, shall be divided equally among the parties involved. If, for any dispute or claim to which this paragraph applies, any party commences an action without first attempting to resolve the matter through mediation, or refuses to mediate after a request has been made, then that party shall not be entitled to recover attorney fees, even if they would otherwise be available to that party in any such action. THIS MEDIATION PROVISION APPLIES WHETHER OR NOT THE ARBITRATION PROVISION IS INITIALED.

**B. ARBITRATION OF DISPUTES: (1) Buyer and Seller agree that any dispute or claim in Law or equity arising between them out of this Agreement or any resulting transaction, which is not settled through mediation, shall be decided by neutral, binding arbitration, including and subject to paragraphs 17B(2) and (3) below. The arbitrator shall be a retired judge or justice, or an attorney with at least 5 years of residential real estate Law experience, unless the parties mutually agree to a different arbitrator, who shall render an award in accordance with substantive California Law. The parties shall have the right to discovery in accordance with California Code of Civil Procedure §1283.05. In all other respects, the arbitration shall be conducted in accordance with Title 9 of Part III of the California Code of Civil Procedure. Judgment upon the award of the arbitrator(s) may be entered into any court having jurisdiction. Interpretation of this agreement to arbitrate shall be governed by the Federal Arbitration Act.**
**(2) EXCLUSIONS FROM MEDIATION AND ARBITRATION: The following matters are excluded from mediation and arbitration: (i) a judicial or non-judicial foreclosure or other action or proceeding to enforce a deed of trust, mortgage or installment land sale contract as defined in California Civil Code §2985; (ii) an unlawful detainer action; (iii) the filing or enforcement of a mechanic's lien; and (iv) any matter that is within the jurisdiction of a probate, small claims or bankruptcy court. The filing of a court action to enable the recording of a notice of pending action, for order of attachment, receivership, injunction, or other provisional remedies, shall not constitute a waiver of the mediation and arbitration provisions.**
**(3) BROKERS: Buyer and Seller agree to mediate and arbitrate disputes or claims involving either or both Brokers, consistent with 17A and B, provided either or both Brokers shall have agreed to such mediation or arbitration prior to, or within a reasonable time after, the dispute or claim is presented to Brokers. Any election by either or both Brokers to participate in mediation or arbitration shall not result in Brokers being deemed parties to the Agreement.**
**"NOTICE: BY INITIALING IN THE SPACE BELOW YOU ARE AGREEING TO HAVE ANY DISPUTE ARISING OUT OF THE MATTERS INCLUDED IN THE 'ARBITRATION OF DISPUTES' PROVISION DECIDED BY NEUTRAL ARBITRATION AS PROVIDED BY CALIFORNIA LAW AND YOU ARE GIVING UP ANY RIGHTS YOU MIGHT POSSESS TO HAVE THE DISPUTE LITIGATED IN A COURT OR JURY TRIAL. BY INITIALING IN THE SPACE BELOW YOU ARE GIVING UP YOUR JUDICIAL RIGHTS TO DISCOVERY AND APPEAL, UNLESS THOSE RIGHTS ARE SPECIFICALLY INCLUDED IN THE 'ARBITRATION OF DISPUTES' PROVISION. IF YOU REFUSE TO SUBMIT TO ARBITRATION AFTER AGREEING TO THIS PROVISION, YOU MAY BE COMPELLED TO ARBITRATE UNDER THE AUTHORITY OF THE CALIFORNIA CODE OF CIVIL PROCEDURE. YOUR AGREEMENT TO THIS ARBITRATION PROVISION IS VOLUNTARY."**
**"WE HAVE READ AND UNDERSTAND THE FOREGOING AND AGREE TO SUBMIT DISPUTES ARISING OUT OF THE MATTERS INCLUDED IN THE 'ARBITRATION OF DISPUTES' PROVISION TO NEUTRAL ARBITRATION."**

| Buyer's Initials _____/_____ | Seller's Initials _____/_____ |
|---|---|

Copyright © 1991-2004, CALIFORNIA ASSOCIATION OF REALTORS®, INC.
**RPA-CA REVISED 10/02 (PAGE 5 OF 8)**

Buyer's Initials (_____)(_____)
Seller's Initials (_____)(_____)

Reviewed by _____ Date _____

EQUAL HOUSING OPPORTUNITY

Reprinted with permission, CALIFORNIA ASSOCIATION OF REALTORS. Endorsement not implied.

## California Residential Purchase Agreement

Property Address: _____ Date: _____

**27. AGENCY:**

    **A. DISCLOSURE:** Buyer and Seller each acknowledge prior receipt of C.A.R. Form AD "Disclosure Regarding Real Estate Agency Relationships."

    **B. POTENTIALLY COMPETING BUYERS AND SELLERS:** Buyer and Seller each acknowledge receipt of a disclosure of the possibility of multiple representation by the Broker representing that principal. This disclosure may be part of a listing agreement, buyer-broker agreement or separate document (C.A.R. Form DA). Buyer understands that Broker representing Buyer may also represent other potential buyers, who may consider, make offers on or ultimately acquire the Property. Seller understands that Broker representing Seller may also represent other sellers with competing properties of interest to this Buyer.

    **C. CONFIRMATION:** The following agency relationships are hereby confirmed for this transaction:
    Listing Agent _____ (Print Firm Name) is the agent of (check one): ☐ the Seller exclusively; or ☐ both the Buyer and Seller.
    Selling Agent _____ (Print Firm Name) (if not same as Listing Agent) is the agent of (check one): ☐ the Buyer exclusively; or ☐ the Seller exclusively; or ☐ both the Buyer and Seller. Real Estate Brokers are not parties to the Agreement between Buyer and Seller.

**28. JOINT ESCROW INSTRUCTIONS TO ESCROW HOLDER:**

    **A. The following paragraphs, or applicable portions thereof, of this Agreement constitute the joint escrow instructions of Buyer and Seller to Escrow Holder,** which Escrow Holder is to use along with any related counter offers and addenda, and any additional mutual instructions to close the escrow: 1, 2, 4, 12, 13B, 14E, 18, 19, 24, 25B and 25D, 26, 28, 29, 32A, 33 and paragraph D of the section titled Real Estate Brokers on page 8. If a Copy of the separate compensation agreement(s) provided for in paragraph 29 or 32A, or paragraph D of the section titled Real Estate Brokers on page 8 is deposited with Escrow Holder by Broker, Escrow Holder shall accept such agreement(s) and pay out from Buyer's or Seller's funds, or both, as applicable, the Broker's compensation provided for in such agreement(s). The terms and conditions of this Agreement not set forth in the specified paragraphs are additional matters for the information of Escrow Holder, but about which Escrow Holder need not be concerned. Buyer and Seller will receive Escrow Holder's general provisions directly from Escrow Holder and will execute such provisions upon Escrow Holder's request. To the extent the general provisions are inconsistent or conflict with this Agreement, the general provisions will control as to the duties and obligations of Escrow Holder only. Buyer and Seller will execute additional instructions, documents and forms provided by Escrow Holder that are reasonably necessary to close the escrow.

    **B.** A Copy of this Agreement shall be delivered to Escrow Holder within **3** business days after Acceptance (or ☐ _____). Buyer and Seller authorize Escrow Holder to accept and rely on Copies and Signatures as defined in this Agreement as originals, to open escrow and for other purposes of escrow. The validity of this Agreement as between Buyer and Seller is not affected by whether or when Escrow Holder Signs this Agreement.

    **C.** Brokers are a party to the escrow for the sole purpose of compensation pursuant to paragraphs 29, 32A and paragraph D of the section titled Real Estate Brokers on page 8. Buyer and Seller irrevocably assign to Brokers compensation specified in paragraphs 29 and 32A, respectively, and irrevocably instruct Escrow Holder to disburse those funds to Brokers at Close Of Escrow or pursuant to any other mutually executed cancellation agreement. Compensation instructions can be amended or revoked only with the written consent of Brokers. Escrow Holder shall immediately notify Brokers: **(I)** if Buyer's initial or any additional deposit is not made pursuant to this Agreement, or is not good at time of deposit with Escrow Holder; or **(II)** if Buyer and Seller instruct Escrow Holder to cancel escrow.

    **D.** A Copy of any amendment that affects any paragraph of this Agreement for which Escrow Holder is responsible shall be delivered to Escrow Holder within **2** business days after mutual execution of the amendment.

**29. BROKER COMPENSATION FROM BUYER:** If applicable, upon Close Of Escrow, **Buyer** agrees to pay compensation to Broker as specified in a separate written agreement between Buyer and Broker.

**30. TERMS AND CONDITIONS OF OFFER:**

This is an offer to purchase the Property on the above terms and conditions. All paragraphs with spaces for initials by Buyer and Seller are incorporated in this Agreement only if initialed by all parties. If at least one but not all parties initial, a counter offer is required until agreement is reached. Seller has the right to continue to offer the Property for sale and to accept any other offer at any time prior to notification of Acceptance. Buyer has read and acknowledges receipt of a Copy of the offer and agrees to the above confirmation of agency relationships. If this offer is accepted and Buyer subsequently defaults, Buyer may be responsible for payment of Brokers' compensation. This Agreement and any supplement, addendum or modification, including any Copy, may be Signed in two or more counterparts, all of which shall constitute one and the same writing.

Buyer's Initials (_____)(_____)
Seller's Initials (_____)(_____)

Copyright © 1991-2004, CALIFORNIA ASSOCIATION OF REALTORS®, INC.
**RPA-CA REVISED 10/02 (PAGE 7 OF 8)**

Reviewed by _____ Date _____

EQUAL HOUSING OPPORTUNITY

Reprinted with permission, CALIFORNIA ASSOCIATION OF REALTORS. Endorsement not implied.

# Appendices

California Residential Purchase Agreement

Property Address: _____ Date: _____

**27. AGENCY:**
    **A. DISCLOSURE:** Buyer and Seller each acknowledge prior receipt of C.A.R. Form AD "Disclosure Regarding Real Estate Agency Relationships."
    **B. POTENTIALLY COMPETING BUYERS AND SELLERS:** Buyer and Seller each acknowledge receipt of a disclosure of the possibility of multiple representation by the Broker representing that principal. This disclosure may be part of a listing agreement, buyer-broker agreement or separate document (C.A.R. Form DA). Buyer understands that Broker representing Buyer may also represent other potential buyers, who may consider, make offers on or ultimately acquire the Property. Seller understands that Broker representing Seller may also represent other sellers with competing properties of interest to this Buyer.
    **C. CONFIRMATION:** The following agency relationships are hereby confirmed for this transaction:
    Listing Agent _____ (Print Firm Name) is the agent
    of (check one):☐ the Seller exclusively; or ☐ both the Buyer and Seller.
    Selling Agent _____(Print Firm Name) (if not same
    as Listing Agent) is the agent of (check one): ☐ the Buyer exclusively; or ☐ the Seller exclusively; or ☐ both the Buyer and Seller. Real Estate Brokers are not parties to the Agreement between Buyer and Seller.

**28. JOINT ESCROW INSTRUCTIONS TO ESCROW HOLDER:**
    **A. The following paragraphs, or applicable portions thereof, of this Agreement constitute the joint escrow instructions of Buyer and Seller to Escrow Holder,** which Escrow Holder is to use along with any related counter offers and addenda, and any additional mutual instructions to close the escrow: 1, 2, 4, 12, 13B, 14E, 18, 19, 24, 25B and 25D, 26, 28, 29, 32A, 33 and paragraph D of the section titled Real Estate Brokers on page 8. If a Copy of the separate compensation agreement(s) provided for in paragraph 29 or 32A, or paragraph D of the section titled Real Estate Brokers on page 8 is deposited with Escrow Holder by Broker, Escrow Holder shall accept such agreement(s) and pay out from Buyer's or Seller's funds, or both, as applicable, the Broker's compensation provided for in such agreement(s). The terms and conditions of this Agreement not set forth in the specified paragraphs are additional matters for the information of Escrow Holder, but about which Escrow Holder need not be concerned. Buyer and Seller will receive Escrow Holder's general provisions directly from Escrow Holder and will execute such provisions upon Escrow Holder's request. To the extent the general provisions are inconsistent or conflict with this Agreement, the general provisions will control as to the duties and obligations of Escrow Holder only. Buyer and Seller will execute additional instructions, documents and forms provided by Escrow Holder that are reasonably necessary to close the escrow.
    **B.** A Copy of this Agreement shall be delivered to Escrow Holder within **3** business days after Acceptance (or ☐ _____). Buyer and Seller authorize Escrow Holder to accept and rely on Copies and Signatures as defined in this Agreement as originals, to open escrow and for other purposes of escrow. The validity of this Agreement as between Buyer and Seller is not affected by whether or when Escrow Holder Signs this Agreement.
    **C.** Brokers are a party to the escrow for the sole purpose of compensation pursuant to paragraphs 29, 32A and paragraph D of the section titled Real Estate Brokers on page 8. Buyer and Seller irrevocably assign to Brokers compensation specified in paragraphs 29 and 32A, respectively, and irrevocably instruct Escrow Holder to disburse those funds to Brokers at Close Of Escrow or pursuant to any other mutually executed cancellation agreement. Compensation instructions can be amended or revoked only with the written consent of Brokers. Escrow Holder shall immediately notify Brokers: **(i)** if Buyer's initial or any additional deposit is not made pursuant to this Agreement, or is not good at time of deposit with Escrow Holder; or **(ii)** if Buyer and Seller instruct Escrow Holder to cancel escrow.
    **D.** A Copy of any amendment that affects any paragraph of this Agreement for which Escrow Holder is responsible shall be delivered to Escrow Holder within **2** business days after mutual execution of the amendment.

**29. BROKER COMPENSATION FROM BUYER:** If applicable, upon Close Of Escrow, **Buyer** agrees to pay compensation to Broker as specified in a separate written agreement between Buyer and Broker.

**30. TERMS AND CONDITIONS OF OFFER:**
    This is an offer to purchase the Property on the above terms and conditions. All paragraphs with spaces for initials by Buyer and Seller are incorporated in this Agreement only if initialed by all parties. If at least one but not all parties initial, a counter offer is required until agreement is reached. Seller has the right to continue to offer the Property for sale and to accept any other offer at any time prior to notification of Acceptance. Buyer has read and acknowledges receipt of a Copy of the offer and agrees to the above confirmation of agency relationships. If this offer is accepted and Buyer subsequently defaults, Buyer may be responsible for payment of Brokers' compensation. This Agreement and any supplement, addendum or modification, including any Copy, may be Signed in two or more counterparts, all of which shall constitute one and the same writing.

Buyer's Initials (_____)(_____)
Seller's Initials (_____)(_____)

Reviewed by _____ Date _____

Copyright © 1991-2004, CALIFORNIA ASSOCIATION OF REALTORS®, INC.
**RPA-CA REVISED 10/02 (PAGE 7 OF 8)**

Reprinted with permission, CALIFORNIA ASSOCIATION OF REALTORS. Endorsement not implied.

## California Residential Purchase Agreement

Property Address: _____ Date: _____

**31. EXPIRATION OF OFFER:** This offer shall be deemed revoked and the deposit shall be returned unless the offer is Signed by Seller and a Copy of the Signed offer is personally received by Buyer, or by _____, who is authorized to receive it by 5:00 PM on the third Day after this offer is signed by Buyer (or, if checked, ☐ by _____ (date), at _____ AM/PM).

Date _____ Date _____

BUYER _____ BUYER _____

_____ _____
**(Print name)** **(Print name)**

_____
**(Address)**

**32. BROKER COMPENSATION FROM SELLER:**
   **A.** Upon Close Of Escrow, **Seller** agrees to pay compensation to Broker as specified in a separate written agreement between Seller and Broker.
   **B.** If escrow does not close, compensation is payable as specified in that separate written agreement.
**33. ACCEPTANCE OF OFFER:** Seller warrants that Seller is the owner of the Property, or has the authority to execute this Agreement. Seller accepts the above offer, agrees to sell the Property on the above terms and conditions, and agrees to the above confirmation of agency relationships. Seller has read and acknowledges receipt of a Copy of this Agreement, and authorizes Broker to deliver a Signed Copy to Buyer.
   ☐ (If checked) **SUBJECT TO ATTACHED COUNTER OFFER, DATED** _____.

Date _____ Date _____

SELLER _____ SELLER _____

_____ _____
**(Print name)** **(Print name)**

_____
**(Address)**

(___/___) **CONFIRMATION OF ACCEPTANCE:** A Copy of Signed Acceptance was personally received by Buyer or Buyer's authorized
(Initials) agent on (date) _____ at _____ AM/PM. **A binding Agreement is created when a Copy of Signed Acceptance is personally received by Buyer or Buyer's authorized agent whether or not confirmed in this document. Completion of this confirmation is not legally required in order to create a binding Agreement; it is solely intended to evidence the date that Confirmation of Acceptance has occurred.**

**REAL ESTATE BROKERS:**
**A. Real Estate Brokers are not parties to the Agreement between Buyer and Seller.**
**B. Agency relationships are confirmed as stated in paragraph 27.**
**C.** If specified in paragraph 2A, Agent who submitted the offer for Buyer acknowledges receipt of deposit.
**D. COOPERATING BROKER COMPENSATION:** Listing Broker agrees to pay Cooperating Broker **(Selling Firm)** and Cooperating Broker agrees to accept, out of Listing Broker's proceeds in escrow: **(i)** the amount specified in the MLS, provided Cooperating Broker is a Participant of the MLS in which the Property is offered for sale or a reciprocal MLS; or **(ii)** ☐ (if checked) the amount specified in a separate written agreement (C.A.R. Form CBC) between Listing Broker and Cooperating Broker.

Real Estate Broker (Selling Firm) _____
By _____ Date _____
Address _____ City _____ State _____ Zip _____
Telephone _____ Fax _____ E-mail _____

Real Estate Broker (Listing Firm) _____
By _____ Date _____
Address _____ City _____ State _____ Zip _____
Telephone _____ Fax _____ E-mail _____

**ESCROW HOLDER ACKNOWLEDGMENT:**
Escrow Holder acknowledges receipt of a Copy of this Agreement, (if checked, ☐ a deposit in the amount of $ _____ ), counter offer numbers _____ and _____, and agrees to act as Escrow Holder subject to paragraph 28 of this Agreement, any supplemental escrow instructions and the terms of Escrow Holder's general provisions.

Escrow Holder is advised that the date of Confirmation of Acceptance of the Agreement as between Buyer and Seller is _____

Escrow Holder _____ Escrow # _____
By _____ Date _____
Address _____
Phone/Fax/E-mail _____
Escrow Holder is licensed by the California Department of ☐ Corporations, ☐ Insurance, ☐ Real Estate. License # _____

(___/___) **REJECTION OF OFFER:** No counter offer is being made. This offer was reviewed and rejected by Seller on
(Seller's Initials) _____ (Date)

THIS FORM HAS BEEN APPROVED BY THE CALIFORNIA ASSOCIATION OF REALTORS® (C.A.R.). NO REPRESENTATION IS MADE AS TO THE LEGAL VALIDITY OR ADEQUACY OF ANY PROVISION IN ANY SPECIFIC TRANSACTION. A REAL ESTATE BROKER IS THE PERSON QUALIFIED TO ADVISE ON REAL ESTATE TRANSACTIONS. IF YOU DESIRE LEGAL OR TAX ADVICE, CONSULT AN APPROPRIATE PROFESSIONAL.
This form is available for use by the entire real estate industry. It is not intended to identify the user as a REALTOR®. REALTOR® is a registered collective membership mark which may be used only by members of the NATIONAL ASSOCIATION OF REALTORS® who subscribe to its Code of Ethics.

Published and Distributed by:
REAL ESTATE BUSINESS SERVICES, INC.
a subsidiary of the California Association of REALTORS®
525 South Virgil Avenue, Los Angeles, California 90020

The System for Success®

**RPA-CA REVISED 10/02 (PAGE 8 OF 8)**

Reviewed by _____ Date _____

EQUAL HOUSING OPPORTUNITY

Reprinted with permission, CALIFORNIA ASSOCIATION OF REALTORS. Endorsement not implied.

# GLOSSARY

**ABR:** Accredited Buyer Representative. A designation available to Realtors who have documented their experience representing home buyers, completed coursework, and passed a test.

**Abstract:** Short for *abstract of title*, this is a history of all deeds or other legal documents (such as a *lien*) affecting ownership of the property.

**Adjustment period:** The frequency with which the interest rate changes on an adjustable-rate loan. A one-year ARM, for example, has an annual adjustment period.

**Agent:** Someone who acts on behalf of someone else. A real estate agent is working on behalf of a *broker*, who, in turn, is an agent of the buyer or seller who hired that broker. A buyer cannot assume a real estate agent is representing the buyer's interests unless the buyer has signed an agreement with a broker who agrees to act as the buyer's agent.

**Amortization:** The process of paying off a debt through a series of regularly scheduled payments of *principal* and *interest*.

**Appraisal:** A licensed appraiser's estimate of market value based on recent completed sales of comparable properties and taking into account a home's special features and flaws.

**APR:** Annual Percentage Rate. This single number, stated as a percentage (0 percent to 10 percent, for example) combines pre-paid interest and the monthly rate to indicate the real cost of a loan. Federal law requires that lenders disclose the APR on all loans.

**ARM:** Adjustable-rate mortgage. These loans carry interest rates that will rise and fall with market rates from year to year, or perhaps at shorter intervals, depending on the specifics of the loan.

**ASHI:** The American Society of Home Inspectors and its members.

**Assessment:** An estimate of a property's market value conducted by an assessor (either a government employee or private contractor). Local governments use these assessments in calculating property taxes. The assessment will assign a dollar value to the land and a dollar value to the home or other structures built upon it.

**Balloon:** A single, lump-sum payment required at the end of a loan's term if the schedule of monthly payments has not been great enough to pay off the loan's *principal*. See *negative amortization*.

**Bridge loan:** A loan (often a home-equity loan on your current residence) designed to provide money to make the down payment on a new home before the other one has been sold.

**Broker:** Someone who is licensed by the state to represent buyers and/or sellers in the purchase or sale of real estate. Some states require that all people who offer real estate sales services hold a broker's license; others issue different licenses to brokers and to salespeople (agents). Typically, a licensed real estate agent works under the umbrella of a licensed broker, and it is the broker with whom buyers and sellers have contracts for representation in the sale or purchase of real estate. Often, if an experienced agent has qualified for a broker's license but is still performing the duties of an agent, he or she will be called a broker-associate and still will work under the umbrella of another broker.

**Buy-down:** To lower the interest rate by paying upfront interest, or *points*, at closing. A seller may offer to buy down the interest rate for

359

a buyer by paying for those points, typically 1 percent to 3 percent of the loan amount. See *points*.

**Buyer's broker, buyer's agent**: A real estate salesperson who has agreed to represent the buyer in a transaction. If a buyer has not reached such an agreement the buyer should assume that a salesperson is an agent of the seller.

**Buyer's market**: A market in which there are more sellers than buyers, and therefore buyers have an easier time winning negotiations over price and other terms of the sale.

**Cap**: The maximum interest rate that can be charged on an adjustable-rate mortgage (ARM). ARMs typically have two caps, one limiting how much your interest rate can change at each adjustment period and the other setting a maximum rate over the life of the loan. *Interest-rate caps* limit how much interest the lender may charge. They are preferable to *payment caps*, which limit how much the borrower can be required to pay each month but do not limit the interest rate that is being charged. If there is only an interest-rate cap in place, a lender may boost the interest rate, but hold the monthly payments to the capped amount. When this happens, unpaid interest charges will build up, slowly increasing the borrower's indebtedness and possibly setting up the need for a *balloon payment* at the end of the loan.

**Capital gain**: Profit from a home sale, from the tax collector's point of view. The amount the seller receives from the sale of the home, minus the original cash down payment and the monthly payments toward mortgage principal and the money spent on renovations and remodeling over the years results in the capital gain amount.

**Cash reserve:** The amount of money left in savings or investments after a borrower has closed on a home.

**CCRs:** Codes, Covenants and Restrictions. These are the rules that legally bind the owners of condominiums, co-ops and homeowners associations. They govern things including finances, dues, architectural standards, and lifestyle rules such as prohibitions on decorative banners or parking trucks or boats within the community.

**Closing or close of escrow:** The transfer of property ownership from one party to another. It involves the seller's signing over of the deed to the buyer; the buyer's signing of the loan promissory note and the mortgage document, plus signing assorted disclosure forms, providing proof of a valid homeowners insurance policy, and paying for assorted last-minute closing fees, either through the mortgage loan or in cash at the closing table.

**Closing costs:** Fees payable at closing for expenses associated with a home purchase, including taxes, termite-inspection fees, title insurance, loan origination fees and other expenses.

**Cloud on title:** An outstanding claim on the title to a property that calls ownership into question.

**Comparative Market Analysis:** CMA. An analysis performed by a real estate agent to help determine a likely selling price for a property based on the prices of other properties currently on the market, the prices of those sold within the past year, and the prices on any listings that failed to sell. It is not as rigorous an examination as an appraisal.

**COFI:** The Cost of Funds Index, based on interest rates prevailing in the Federal Home Loan Bank's 11th District, which encompasses Arizona, California and Nevada. Some adjustable-rate mortgages, particularly those with an interest rate that adjusts monthly, are pegged to the COFI index, which tends to rise and fall more slowly than other commonly used indexes. However, more-frequent adjustments mean the overall interest rates remain close to those on ARMs pegged to other indexes.

**Commission:** A fee for real estate brokerage services that is calculated as a percentage of the sales price.

**Comparable:** Recently sold homes that are similar in size, location and amenities. When estimating sales prices or performing official appraisals, real estate agents and appraisers will research the selling prices of comparable properties to back up their price estimates, adjusting those prices for the special features and flaws that are present in one home but not the other.

**Condo:** A condo, short for condominium, is a form of ownership. Most frequently, apartments are owned this way, but the term can refer to townhomes and detached houses. Owners own the inside of their unit, and a share of the common grounds, including the exterior of the building, parking lots, fitness facilities or other features. Condo owners vote among themselves to appoint a condo board, which oversees the business of running the property, including the assessment of mandatory condo fees on owners and, usually, the hiring of a management company to handle day-to-day affairs.

**Condo or co-op fee:** Also called maintenance, this is the monthly payment owed by owners of condo and co-op homes to cover the expenses of maintaining and improving the property and its amenities, such as the services of a doorman or a fitness center.

**Conforming loan:** Mortgage loans that conform to the guidelines established by secondary mortgage market companies Fannie Mae and Freddie Mac. In particular, conforming loans must meet their limits on the size of the loan, which were $359,650 in 2005. The limit is adjusted at the beginning of each year. See *jumbo loan*.

**Contingencies:** Clauses added to a purchase contract that must be satisfied and removed before the deal can be closed. Common contingencies include those requiring a satisfactory home-inspection and an appraisal.

**Conventional loan:** Any mortgage except those that are FHA-insured or VA-guaranteed.

**Co-op:** Short for co-operative, this is a form of ownership in which several people own shares in a corporation that owns, typically, an apartment building. Ownership of shares entitles the owner to reside in one specific unit in that building and to vote on how the co-op will be run. A monthly maintenance fee will be charged to all owners to cover upkeep of common facilities and services.

**Counteroffer:** A seller's response to a buyer's purchase offer that rejects the seller's proposal and proposes, instead, a price and/or terms that are more favorable to the seller.

**Covenants:** See *CCRs*.

**CRS:** Certified Residential Specialist. A designation available to Realtors who have met specific standards for experience and have completed coursework on listing and selling homes.

**Deed:** A legal document that conveys title to a property. See *title*.

**Deed of trust:** See *mortgage*.

**Default:** A buyer's failure to abide by the terms of a loan agreement, mainly by not making the payments due. If the borrower does not soon catch up with the payment schedule, default can go into *foreclosure*.

**Delinquent:** A loan in which the payments are three or more months past-due.

**Deposit:** See *earnest money.*

**Due-on-sale clause:** A provision present in many mortgage contracts that allows the lender to require that the loan be paid off when the original borrower sells the home. It means the new buyer cannot assume the terms of the old loan without the lender's permission.

**Earnest money:** Also called a *deposit,* this is an amount of cash that a buyer offers the seller when presenting an offer to buy a property. Because this cash can be forfeited to the seller if the buyer backs out of the deal for reasons that are not already spelled out as contingencies in the contract (such as the buyer's dissatisfaction with a home-inspection report), it is considered a sign of the buyer's good-faith intent to buy the property. Earnest money checks should be held by a third party (such as a broker's special escrow account) until the transaction is complete.

**Easement:** A legal right, recorded with the deed, for one party to use part of someone else's real estate. A person may have an *easement* to use a neighbor's driveway because that is the only way for him to access the street, or the local utility may have an *easement* to a swath of a homeowner's land which gives it the right to bury and maintain a gas line through the area. An easement may diminish a property's value.

**Equity:** Home equity is the amount of ownership someone has in a property after any loans against it have been paid off. If a home sells for $300,000 and there is a mortgage against it for $100,000, the owner's equity is $200,000.

**Escalation clause:** This addition to a purchase contract says the buyer will increase his or her offer by certain increments (say $5,000 each) over the offers of any legitimate, competing buyer. These are used in *seller's markets* in which there are likely to be many buyers competing for a single property. An escalation clause should have a top dollar amount to limit the buyer's eventual bid.

**Escrow:** The holding of money or documents (such as the deed to a property) by a neutral third party while waiting for the buyer and seller to satisfy all the conditions of a contract. In California, when a purchase offer has been placed on a property and accepted by the seller, the transaction is considered to have *gone into escrow* while the details of title searches, termite inspections and document preparations are handled. When all terms of the contract have been complied with and title changes hands, escrow is closed.

Another common use of the term is when a mortgage company collects property taxes and homeowners' insurance payments and holds them *in escrow* until the payment is due. Earnest-money deposits also should be held in an *escrow account* by a real estate broker or lawyer.

**FHA mortgage:** A low-down payment mortgage program in which mortgage insurance is provided by the federal government. FHA loans are targeted toward buyers of moderately priced homes.

**Fixed-rate mortgage:** A mortgage loan that carries the same interest rate through the life of the loan.

**Foreclosure:** The legal process a lien holder (such as the mortgage lender or tax authority) undertakes when a borrower or owner fails to make required payments. The lender or tax authority will take possession of the property and sell it to provide cash to pay off the loan.

**Good-faith estimate:** Federal law requires that lenders give borrowers a written good-faith estimate of closing costs associated with taking out the loan and purchasing a property.

**GRI:** Graduate, Realtor Institute. A designation available to Realtors who work primarily in residential real estate and who complete coursework on technical aspects and fundamentals of real estate.

**HOA:** Homeowners Association. While this term can apply to condo and co-op associations, it more commonly refers to communities of individually owned town houses and freestanding houses. Owners of these homes are mandatory members of the association, which takes care of community property, which may include road maintenance; streetlights; community swimming pools; tennis courts and parks; landscaping and other amenities. The HOA charges members monthly or annual dues and can place a lien against a member's home for unpaid dues or fees.

**Homeowners' insurance:** An insurance policy that covers the home and its contents for damage or destruction due to fire, lightning, hail, wind storms and burglary. In some high-risk areas, there are limits on coverage for wind storms and hail. Flood insurance and earthquake insurance must be purchased separately.

**Holdback:** Money held back from settlement until certain requirements have been met. For example, buyer and seller may agree to a holdback of some of the sales proceeds due the seller if the property was not in acceptable condition at the time of the pre-closing walk-through.

**Home-equity loan:** See "second mortgage."

**Homestead laws:** Laws in some states that protect a person's home against claims by creditors.

**HUD-1:** The U.S. Department of Housing and Urban Development Settlement Statement, which the government requires to be used at each closing. It details all amounts paid to and from the seller and the buyer.

**Hybrid loan:** A mortgage loan that combines features of fixed-rate loans and adjustable-rate loans. With a 30-year hybrid loan, for example, the interest rate will be fixed for the first 5, 7, or 10 years, after which it converts to an interest rate that adjusts every year for the remaining term of the loan.

**Index:** A specific, regularly published list of interest rates that is used as a basis for setting the new interest rate on adjustable-rate mortgages at each adjustment period. Common indexes are the one-year *Treasury index*; the *COFI*, or Eleventh District Cost of Funds Index, and the *LIBOR*, or London Interbank Offered Rate. See *margin.*

**Interest rate:** Expressed as a percentage, this is the "rent" paid on money borrowed from someone else. It always should be evaluated along with any upfront interest (points) paid at closing. See *points.*

**Interest-only mortgage:** A mortgage loan that gives the home buyer the option of making only interest payments during the early years of the loan, typically the first 10 to 15. While they make only interest payments, the loan balance will not decrease. After that 10- or 15-year period, the loan switches to a new payment schedule that pays off the remaining principal and interest over the remaining 20 or 15 years.

**Joint tenancy with right of survivorship:** A form of holding title used by two or more owners. Each person must have an equal share of ownership.

**Jumbo loan:** Mortgage loans for more than Fannie Mae and Freddie Mac's limit, which was $359,650 in 2005. (It's adjusted at the beginning of each year.) They typically carry higher interest rates than loans under the jumbo threshold, which are called *conforming loans.*

**Junk fees:** Closing costs that are suspected of being superfluous add-ons or that inflate the cost of legitimate closing services. Some fees to question as being junk: "processing fee," "shipping fee," "appraisal review fee," or high fees for photocopying or courier services.

**Kick-out:** A clause added to a contingency in a purchase contract that allows the seller to demand that the buyer remove the contingency (say within 24 or 48 hours) and buy the home if another buyer were to come forward with a competing offer.

**Lease with option to buy:** A rental agreement that credits part of each month's rent toward the eventual down payment on the home.

**Leverage:** The ability to use borrowed money to help turn a small investment into a larger amount of wealth.

**LIBOR:** London Interbank Offered Rate. An index based on the interest rates charged on large loans in Europe. The index is sometimes used as a basis for pegging adjustable-rate mortgages in the U.S.

**Lien:** A creditor's financial claim against the value of a property. Mortgage lenders; homeowners associations and condo/co-op boards; local, state and federal governments; and contractors are among those who can place a lien against your property for unpaid debts, taxes or fees.

**Lifetime cap:** See *Caps.*

**Listing:** A legal agreement by which a homeowner hires a real estate broker to market a property. Brokers consider listings, or the information on homes that they are marketing, to be their property and their inventory.

**Loan-to-value ratio:** LTV. A ratio that lenders use to determine how much equity the borrower has at stake in a mortgage deal. A high LTV is risky for the lender because the odds are greater that a troubled borrower will walk away from his or her obligation to pay off the loan. A $300,000 home bought with a $30,000 (or 10 percent) down payment has an LTV of 90 percent.

**Lock:** When a borrower applies for a mortgage loan, he or she can choose to *lock* in the loan's interest rate at the price that's being charged that day or to allow the rate to *float* with the day-to-day changes in rates until the borrower chooses to lock, or until the loan closes.

**Maintenance fee:** The monthly fee paid by owners of condominiums, co-operatives or homeowners associations to pay for upkeep of commonly owned property, taxes, insurance and special services, such as a doorman or security service. Also called a *condo or co-op fee*.

**Margin:** The markup added to the published interest-rate index to determine the new interest rate to be charged on an adjustable-rate loan at each adjustment period. For example, an ARM's rate might be set at the one-year Treasury index plus a *margin* of 1.5 percentage points. See *index*.

**MLS:** Multiple Listing Service. A system used by participating real estate brokers that allows them to post listings of homes available for sale and promising a split of the sales commission with another broker who comes up with a buyer for that property.

369

**Mortgage**: A document the borrower signs placing a lien against the property giving the lender the right to foreclose, or seize the property, if the borrower fails to pay back the loan. In some places a "deed of trust" is used instead, which allows an easier foreclosure process for the lender.

**Mortgage banker**: A business that originates, sells and services mortgage loans.

**Mortgage broker**: A person who deals with a number of different loan originators and can shop a borrower's loan application around for the best combination of interest rate and terms. The broker will earn a fee for each mortgage he or she originates. While good mortgage brokers will shop hard on behalf of borrowers, there is nothing to require a mortgage broker to represent the interests of the borrower. Some steer borrowers into loans that earn the most profit for the broker.

**Mortgage life insurance**: Life insurance policies payable to the mortgage lender if one or both of the homeowners dies during the term of the policy. Usually you're better off buying an ordinary term life insurance policy that pays the survivor—and not the lender—which allows the survivor to decide whether it's prudent to pay off the loan or to use the insurance proceeds for other purposes.

**Mortgagee, mortgagor**: The *mortgagee* is the lender. The *mortgagor* is the borrower, who agrees to offer his or her property as security for the loan.

**Mortgage-interest deduction**: The deduction from taxable income for interest paid on a mortgage of up to $1 million used to buy, build or significantly rehabilitate a primary residence and one vacation home. Also deductible is interest on an additional $100,000 in home-equity debt (such as a home equity line of credit) used for any purpose. The deduction applies to both state and federal income tax returns.

**Negative amortization:** A loan repayment plan in which the monthly payments are not enough to pay off the borrowed amount by the end of the loan term. If your loan has negative amortization, the amount of money you owe gradually increases and you will have to pay it off in a lump sum, usually by refinancing to a new loan. See *balloon.*

**Origination fee:** A fee charged by lenders for a mortgage, perhaps 1 percent of the loan amount.

**Ownership in severalty:** A form of holding title to a property used when there is a single owner.

**Perc test:** Short for *percolation test.* A test by a qualified contractor to determine if the land has the proper drainage to support the operation of a septic tank and drain field. If the land does not pass the perc test, you may not build a home there.

**Personal property:** Property that is not considered *real estate,* such as furniture, appliances that are not permanently attached to the home and mobile homes that do not have permanent foundations.

**PITI:** Principal, Interest, Taxes, and Insurance. These are the four components of your monthly mortgage payment. Principal pays off part of your original loan balance; Interest is, essentially, the rent you pay on the borrowed money; Taxes cover local property taxes; and Insurance covers your homeowner's policy.

**Pledged-asset mortgages:** These loan programs allow buyers to pledge assets such as stocks, bonds, mutual funds, or certificates of deposit as collateral for the mortgage loan, instead of making a down payment.

**Points:**  Pre-paid interest, due at closing, designed to reduce the interest rate charged on the loan. One point equals 1 percent of the loan amount.  Each point of prepaid interest typically reduces the interest rate by 1/8 percentage point.

**Pre-approval, pre-qualification:**  Pre-approval for a mortgage loan requires that you submit a full loan application, supplying information on your employment, income, debts, bank accounts and other assets and liabilities, and allowing the lender to pull your credit scores. Based on this, the lender will pre-approve you for a loan of a certain size, subject only to a property appraisal once you've found the home. "Pre-qualification" means someone has simply looked at your income and debts to estimate the size of a mortgage you *probably* could obtain. It's not enough to persuade a seller that you're a viable buyer.

**Prepaid interest:**  See *points.*

**Prepayment penalty:**  A provision in the mortgage loan contract that requires the borrower to pay a significant penalty if he or she pays off the loan early. While some borrowers may choose to accept a prepayment penalty in exchange for a discount on the interest rate, these penalties are common among the loans offered to borrowers with poor credit scores—and without any break on the interest rate.

**Prepayment of principal:**  Most mortgage loans allow borrowers to make additional payments toward principal at any time, either as a recurring addition to their monthly payment or as an occasional lump-sum. These prepayments help the borrower pay off the loan early and can result in significant savings on the amount of interest paid over the life of the loan.

**Principal:** The amount of money borrowed.

**Purchase agreement:** Also known as a *contract of sale*. This offer, submitted by the buyers, becomes a binding contract once the sellers sign and accept it.

**Ratified contract:** Your purchase agreement, or contract of sale, once all the contingencies (home inspection, loan qualification, appraisal, etc.) have been satisfied and removed.

**Real property:** Also called *real estate*. Land and the buildings put upon it. See *personal property*.

**Realtor:** A member of the National Association of Realtors, a trade association for real estate brokers, salespeople and rental property managers. Members agree to abide by a code of ethics.

**RESPA:** The Real Estate Settlement Procedures Act. This federal law prohibits unearned kickbacks (such as a free cruise to the real estate agent who refers the most business to a title insurance company each year) among professionals who provide settlement services. It also requires that all fees related to the real estate transaction be detailed on the HUD-1 Closing Statement.

**Second mortgage:** A loan, usually a home equity loan or a home equity line of credit, that is secured by your home. It's called a "second" mortgage, because, if you were to quit paying off the loan, the holder of this loan is second in line, behind the holder of your "first" mortgage (usually the one used to buy the home) in sharing the proceeds from a foreclosure sale.

**Seller's market:** A market in which there are more buyers than homes available for sale. This gives the sellers the advantage in negotiations, resulting at sales at the asking price or higher.

**Special assessment:** A mandatory collection of extra fees by a condo or cooperative board or a homeowners' association to pay a large, unbudgeted bill. Well-managed boards and associations try to avoid the need for special assessments by maintaining a contingency fund and by routinely budgeting for periodic maintenance and rehabilitation.

**Tenancy in common:** A form of holding title available to two or more co-owners who may have unequal shares in the property.

**Tenancy by the entirety:** A form of holding title available only to married couples. It gives each spouse 100 percent ownership.

**Title:** Evidence of ownership of a property. There are specific, legal formats for holding title, including *tenancy in common* and *tenancy by the entirety.*

**Title company:** A company that researches title histories and issues title insurance.

**Title insurance:** An insurance policy issued by title companies after they have searched the history of ownership of a property. Lenders require a policy to cover their financial risk if someone were to come forward claiming ownership; borrowers are wise to pay extra to have the coverage apply to them as well.

**Title search:** An examination of land-ownership records on file with the local government to determine the history of how ownership of that property has changed hands over the years.

**Townhouse, townhome:** A home that is attached to others on one or two sides, formerly known as a *rowhouse*. It may be owned as a condominium or individually.

**Treasury rates:** Indexes of interest rates paid on U.S. government securities. Many adjustable-rate loans are pegged to Treasury indexes that match their adjustment periods. The one-year ARM, for example, would be tied to one-year Treasuries.

**VA mortgage:** A zero down-payment mortgage loan available to active-duty military and veterans. The federal government guarantees that, if the borrower doesn't repay the loan, the lender will recover part of the money it lent, replacing the need for a down payment or mortgage insurance.

# Index

private mortgage insurance (PMI), 31,
   49–52, 53
professional designations, 173
promissory note, 272
property taxes, 14, 33, 34, 35, 121, 201
purchase contract, 223

radon gas, 207–8, 324
ranch style, 141
Razzi's Rules, 294–314
real estate:
   ads, terms used in, 171
   balanced market in, 16
   buyer's market in, 16–17
   glossary, 358–75
   as long-term investment, 15–17, 245
   relocation specialists in, 158–59
   rising prices in, 18–19
   seller's market in, 15–16, 41
   state commissions, 331–37
   state laws about, 164–65
real estate agent, 21, 148, 163–78
   choosing, 166–67
   commissions to, 167–69
   complaints against, 177
   contracting with, 169–70, 176
   credentials of, 172–73
   experience of, 172–73
   fee-for-service, 180
   hallmarks of good agent, 174–76
   online connection with, 174–76
   personal chemistry with, 174
   relocation specialist, 158–59
   representation, 164–65
   severing the arrangement with,
      176–77, 246
   supplementing the work of, 235–36
   tour by, 160–61
   word of mouth, 170
real estate broker, 21
real estate lawyer, 182, 212
real price, 201
Realtors, 172, 325
recasting a mortgage, 75
refinancing, 36, 52, 92
RELO, 158–59

relocation specialists, 158–59
relocation to new town, 157–62
   agent's tour, 160–61
   information sources, 325
   learning about new community,
      159–60
   taxes, 160
rental:
   advantages of, 17–19, 32
   condo or co-op, 124–25
   outside appearance of, 149
   temporary, in relocation, 158
rent-back agreement, 211–12, 223
repair costs, typical, 329–30
retaining walls, 127
retirement accounts, borrowing from,
   46–48
roof, inspection of, 241
Roth IRA, borrowing against, 47–48

same-day decision, 236–37
savings:
   as emergency fund, 18
   safety net of, 44
   where to keep, 57–58
SchoolMatch service, 153
school quality, 151–53
seller's agent, and offer, 201
seller's market, 226–47
   aggressive agent in, 233–36
   being your own inspector, 237–43
   bidding wars in, 41
   changeable, 227–28
   escalation clause in, 232
   investment in, 15–16
   low appraisal in, 243–45
   naked buyer in, 230–33
   offer in, 200–201, 232–33
   overpaying in, 229
   *real* top dollar in, 231–32
   remaining, 229–30
   same-day decision in, 236–37
   signs of, 229
septic system, 127, 209
settlement, 257–58
shopping for mortgage, 77–104